BESTSELLING BOOK SERIES

PC Modding For Dummies®

Cheat Sheet

Things to Remember While Working on Your Computer

Tooling around in a PC case is fun, but you must always keep the following points in mind when y

D0891055

- ✔ **Back up any data you don't want to lose.** Yo contents when you alter your PC's configura

- ✔ **Prepare your work space.** Use a large, clean, flat surface.

- ✔ **Gather the tools you'll need before starting a project.**

- ✔ **Shut down the computer and unplug it from the AC outlet.**

- ✔ **Be static-safe.**

- ✔ **Keep track of the screws, cables, and other hardware you remove.** I like to keep loose screws in those little, black, 35mm film canisters.

- ✔ **Keep any stray circuit boards in antistatic bags.**

- ✔ **Check all cable and wire connections before sealing up the case.**

Antistatic Advice

One of your PC's biggest enemies is electrostatic discharge (ESD). To avoid blowing a piece of equipment, only touch your PC circuit boards by the edges. You may handle expansion cards by the edges and the metal gate. Never touch chips, contact edges, or other components directly. Follow these procedures to be sure you stay static-free:

1. **Before touching your computer's internals, plant your feet.**

2. **Ground yourself by touching something metal (the PC chassis, a workbench leg, a power strip, and so on).**

3. **Keep your feet planted as you touch your PC equipment.**

4. **If you move or shuffle your feet, repeat Steps 1 through 3.**

Also, be sure to use an antistatic bracelet. Put the bracelet on, being sure that it's not inside-out. Clip the other end of the wire to something metal and grounded, like the PC chassis. Wear the antistatic bracelet the whole time you work inside your PC. If you live in a particularly dry area, or you're working in winter where the air can get quite dry, invest in a humidifier for your work area. That will reduce the chance of static discharge.

Parts List

Here is everything you need to create a PC from scratch:

- ✔ A case to match the form factor you've chosen for your motherboard and power supply

- ✔ A power supply to match the form factor you've chosen for your motherboard and case

- ✔ A motherboard of the proper form factor and that supports the CPU you've chosen

- ✔ A CPU that works with your motherboard

- ✔ Memory that works with your motherboard and CPU

- ✔ A graphics card that works with your motherboard's graphics card slot

- ✔ Audio (either on the motherboard, or an add-in sound card)

- ✔ A hard drive (SATA, IDE, or, if you're brave, SCSI)

- ✔ An optical drive (a reader and, if you want, a writer)

- ✔ A floppy drive (optional)

- ✔ Speakers

- ✔ A keyboard

- ✔ A mouse

For Dummies: Bestselling Book Series for Beginners

PC Modding For Dummies®

Case Cutting

Follow these steps to cut a window into your case:

1. **Prepare a work area away from any electronic equipment.**

2. **Shut down and unplug the computer.**

3. **Remove the panel to be cut (or the whole cover, if it's one piece) and take it to your work area.**

4. **Measuring meticulously, draw the design you plan to cut out of the panel.**

   Draw it on the inside of the panel, if possible.

5. **Wear work gloves and safety goggles.**

6. **Using a rotary tool with a cut-off blade, slowly and deliberately cut along your drawn lines.**

   Hold the tool with two hands.

7. **Use gentle pressure — don't force the cut or you'll wear out the wheel.**

8. **When you've made the cut, handle the cut-out metal with care — the edges will be sharp.**

9. **Using sandpaper, or a sanding band on your rotary tool, sand the edge of the cut-out on the panel until it's smooth and free of burrs.**

Painting Procedure

Follow these steps to apply a nice, even paint job to your PC's case:

1. **Pick a painting area that's well-ventilated.**

   Paint outside if you need to.

2. **Shut down and unplug the computer.**

3. **Disassemble the case completely.**

   Move the case panels, front panel, and drive bezels to your painting area *away* from the rest of the PC.

4. **Put on a dust mask and safety glasses.**

5. **Sand the metal case panels until you achieve a nice, smooth surface.**

6. **Sand the plastic parts lightly.**

7. **Clean and dry the sanded surfaces of all dust.**

8. **Spray primer onto the metal surfaces.**

   Use even strokes, overlapping each pass a little bit.

9. **Let the primer cure overnight (or, for quick-drying primer, at least four hours).**

10. **Sand the primer lightly, clean it, and apply a second coat.**

11. **If the primer layer isn't even, sand, clean, and apply a third coat.**

12. **Apply the paint with the same technique, sanding and cleaning the surfaces between each application.**

    Apply at least two coats, three if necessary. Apply paint to the metal and plastic pieces.

13. **Optional but recommended: Apply clear enamel with the same technique.**

    Apply at least two coats, more for a glossier finish.

Wiley, the Wiley Publishing logo, For Dummies, the Dummies Man logo, the For Dummies Bestselling Book Series logo and all related trade dress are trademarks or registered trademarks of John Wiley & Sons, Inc. and/or its affiliates. All other trademarks are property of their respective owners.

Copyright © 2005 Wiley Publishing, Inc.
All rights reserved.

Item 7576-7.

For more information about Wiley Publishing, call 1-800-762-2974.

For Dummies: Bestselling Book Series for Beginners

PC Modding

FOR

DUMMIES®

CENTRAL ARKANSAS LIBRARY SYSTEM
LITTLE ROCK PUBLIC LIBRARY
100 ROCK STREET
LITTLE ROCK, ARKANSAS 72201

PC Modding

FOR

DUMMIES®

by Joel Durham Jr.

WILEY

Wiley Publishing, Inc.

PC Modding For Dummies®

Published by
Wiley Publishing, Inc.
111 River Street
Hoboken, NJ 07030-5774

Copyright © 2005 by Wiley Publishing, Inc., Indianapolis, Indiana

Published by Wiley Publishing, Inc., Indianapolis, Indiana

Published simultaneously in Canada

No part of this publication may be reproduced, stored in a retrieval system or transmitted in any form or by any means, electronic, mechanical, photocopying, recording, scanning or otherwise, except as permitted under Sections 107 or 108 of the 1976 United States Copyright Act, without either the prior written permission of the Publisher, or authorization through payment of the appropriate per-copy fee to the Copyright Clearance Center, 222 Rosewood Drive, Danvers, MA 01923, (978) 750-8400, fax (978) 646-8600. Requests to the Publisher for permission should be addressed to the Legal Department, Wiley Publishing, Inc., 10475 Crosspoint Blvd., Indianapolis, IN 46256, (317) 572-3447, fax (317) 572-4355, e-mail: brand review@wiley.com.

Trademarks: Wiley, the Wiley Publishing logo, For Dummies, the Dummies Man logo, A Reference for the Rest of Us!, The Dummies Way, Dummies Daily, The Fun and Easy Way, Dummies.com, and related trade dress are trademarks or registered trademarks of John Wiley & Sons, Inc. and/or its affiliates in the United States and other countries, and may not be used without written permission. All other trademarks are the property of their respective owners. Wiley Publishing, Inc., is not associated with any product or vendor mentioned in this book.

LIMIT OF LIABILITY/DISCLAIMER OF WARRANTY: THE PUBLISHER AND THE AUTHOR MAKE NO REPRESENTATIONS OR WARRANTIES WITH RESPECT TO THE ACCURACY OR COMPLETENESS OF THE CONTENTS OF THIS WORK AND SPECIFICALLY DISCLAIM ALL WARRANTIES, INCLUDING WITHOUT LIMITATION WARRANTIES OF FITNESS FOR A PARTICULAR PURPOSE. NO WARRANTY MAY BE CREATED OR EXTENDED BY SALES OR PROMOTIONAL MATERIALS. THE ADVICE AND STRATEGIES CONTAINED HEREIN MAY NOT BE SUITABLE FOR EVERY SITUATION. THIS WORK IS SOLD WITH THE UNDERSTANDING THAT THE PUBLISHER IS NOT ENGAGED IN RENDERING LEGAL, ACCOUNTING, OR OTHER PROFESSIONAL SERVICES. IF PROFESSIONAL ASSISTANCE IS REQUIRED, THE SERVICES OF A COMPETENT PROFESSIONAL PERSON SHOULD BE SOUGHT. NEITHER THE PUBLISHER NOR THE AUTHOR SHALL BE LIABLE FOR DAMAGES ARISING HEREFROM. THE FACT THAT AN ORGANIZATION OR WEBSITE IS REFERRED TO IN THIS WORK AS A CITATION AND/OR A POTENTIAL SOURCE OF FURTHER INFORMATION DOES NOT MEAN THAT THE AUTHOR OR THE PUBLISHER ENDORSES THE INFORMATION THE ORGANIZATION OR WEBSITE MAY PROVIDE OR RECOMMENDATIONS IT MAY MAKE. FURTHER, READERS SHOULD BE AWARE THAT INTERNET WEBSITES LISTED IN THIS WORK MAY HAVE CHANGED OR DISAPPEARED BETWEEN WHEN THIS WORK WAS WRITTEN AND WHEN IT IS READ.

For general information on our other products and services, please contact our Customer Care Department within the U.S. at 800-762-2974, outside the U.S. at 317-572-3993, or fax 317-572-4002.

For technical support, please visit www.wiley.com/techsupport.

Wiley also publishes its books in a variety of electronic formats. Some content that appears in print may not be available in electronic books.

Library of Congress Control Number: 2004108182

ISBN: 0-7645-7576-7

Manufactured in the United States of America

10 9 8 7 6 5 4 3 2 1

1O/RU/QR/QV/IN

WILEY

About the Author

Joel Durham, Jr., was born with a serial interface in the back of his neck. He's lived for computers and videogames and computer-related things all his life. When he was 6, he got his Atari 2600 and didn't stop playing until he was 10, when he secured his first Commodore 64, which he modded with a reset button and a turbo chip.

Things haven't changed all that much. He sits surrounded by PC parts — piles of motherboards, optical drives, fans, cases, scanners, joysticks, keyboards, sound cards, mice, driving wheels, and gear of all kinds constantly threaten to fall over and bury him forever in his basement office. There are those who feel that wouldn't be a bad thing. . . .

When he's not cutting a case, building up a server, or benchmarking a new system, he's probably playing games. Some of his all-time favorites include M.U.L.E., Elite, Doom (of course), Duke Nukem 3D, XCOM: UFO Defense, Civilization II, and Planescape: Torment. While writing this book, he played Doom 3, Tribes: Vengeance, Call of Duty, Arena Wars, and Fable. He loves games so much he's written a half-dozen strategy guides for Prima.

Speaking of writing, Joel got his first big break by somehow convincing Matt Firme to hire him as *PC Gamer*'s first Technical Editor. There, he molded and shaped the "Hard Stuff" section of the popular magazine into something vaguely readable. He went on to pursue a career as a freelancer, pausing for a year to serve as Senior Technical Editor of CNET's Gamecenter (before the site's untimely demise). As a freelance tech guy, he's written for *PC Magazine,* ExtremeTech.com, *Computer Gaming World,* GameSpot, GameSpy, Gamer's Depot, *Computer Source* magazine, 1Up.com, EZTech Guides, *Technophile* magazine, *Official Xbox Magazine,* and anyone else who dares pay him for his punchy prose.

Joel lives in Farmington, New York, with his wife and two children. He's recently had the serial interface in his neck replaced with a USB 2.0 adapter.

Dedication

Dedicated to the two best-behaved children a harried tech writer could ever ask for: Andrew (age 6) and Jeanne (age 3). Thank you both for being so good all the time. Daddy loves you!

Author's Acknowledgments

I'd like to thank the following people and companies, who donated time, encouragement, parts, and other invaluable assets without which I couldn't have finished this work:

My wife, Emily, for constant encouragement and for putting up with me as I stressed out over deadline after deadline.

The Moseley Durhams and the Carstens for their infinite support.

My editor, Elizabeth Kuball, for dealing with a ridiculous amount of obstacles, from an almost-broken foot to an actual broken hand and a hernia — and also for the AWESOME note full of kind words.

Tom Heine, my acquisitions editor at Wiley, for taking a chance and hiring me to write this tome.

Loyd Case, my technical editor, for getting my back.

The modders, whose work appears in the color section: Del Belyea, James Anderson, Doom_Prophet, Peter Dickison, Brent A. Crosby, Tailin, Brent Ross, and BrainEater.

AMD, Antec, ASUS, ATI, Corsair, Creative Labs, Crucial, DFI, Mark Friga, FrozenCPU.com, Fujifilm, HP, Intel (especially Chris Bulaon), Jasc, Logitech, Microsoft, MonsterGecko, NVIDIA, Morgan Owen, Philips, Plextor, Saitek, Seagate, Shuttle, Thermaltake, Toshiba, and Turtle Beach.

And everyone else who made this book possible by facilitating my needs in any way. Your help is deeply appreciated.

Publisher's Acknowledgments

We're proud of this book; please send us your comments through our online registration form located at www.dummies.com/register/.

Some of the people who helped bring this book to market include the following:

Acquisitions, Editorial, and Media Development

Project Editor: Elizabeth Kuball

Acquisitions Editor: Tom Heine

Technical Editor: Loyd Case

Editorial Manager: Robyn Siesky

Media Development Supervisor: Richard Graves

Editorial Assistant: Adrienne Porter

Cartoons: Rich Tennant (www.the5thwave.com)

Composition Services

Project Coordinator: Adrienne Martinez

Layout and Graphics: Carl Byers, Andrea Dahl, Lauren Goddard, Denny Hager, Heather Ryan, Jacque Roth

Proofreaders: Joe Niesen, Leean Harney, Jessica Kramer, Carl Pierce, TECHBOOKS Production Services

Indexer: TECHBOOKS Production Services

Publishing and Editorial for Technology Publishing

Richard Swadley, Vice President and Executive Group Publisher

Barry Pruett, Vice President and Publisher, Visual/Web Graphics

Andy Cummings, Vice President and Publisher, Technology Dummies

Mary Bednarek, Executive Acquisitions Director, Technology Dummies

Mary C. Corder, Editorial Director, Technology Dummies

Publishing for Consumer Dummies

Diane Graves Steele, Vice President and Publisher

Joyce Pepple, Acquisitions Director

Composition Services

Gerry Fahey, Vice President of Production Services

Debbie Stailey, Director of Composition Services

Contents at a Glance

Table of Contents

Introduction

Computers are big, complicated calculators. All their chips and circuit boards and resistors and capacitors are designed around one thing: doing math problems. When a computer runs a program, all it's doing is calculating math functions really, really quickly.

However, computers are more than just information-crunching machines. Users aren't pigeonholed into using them only for balancing checkbooks, writing dissertations, looking up phone numbers on the World Wide Web, burning music CDs, managing spreadsheets, and so on.

Computers can also be *fun!* Chances are, if you're perusing this book, you're a computer gamer or, at the very least, an enthusiast. Computers can be more than just data machines — they're bona fide hobbies. As a matter of fact, they're grueling, interesting, frustrating, rewarding, expensive, and ultimately very satisfying hobbies.

Consider this: You probably know someone who works on cars. He'll buy a 1969 Camaro that doesn't run and that's covered with rust, strip it down to its chassis, rebuild the engine and transmission, sandblast or replace the body panels, adorn it with a sparkling new paint job, put huge wheels on it, and take it out to track day at his local racetrack. He'll do this at great expense, and solely for his own gratification.

Well, people (myself included) do the same thing with computers. That's not to say we rebuild engines and put new transmissions in them — but we do the equivalent. We open the case, upgrade the graphics card, slap a huge heat sink on the main processor, cut the case to add blow holes and windows, sand off the boring beige paint and spray it with a more appealing color, add lighting, and take it to a LAN fest to show it off to fellow enthusiasts. This, my friends, is the art of modding.

Modding can be thought of as building a new computer or taking an existing one and turning it into a hot rod. Modders want their PCs to be the fastest, most powerful, most interesting, and generally the coolest PCs that you've ever encountered. Modders are not satisfied with a computer that meets the bare minimum requirements to get stuff done. They want their PCs to ooze adrenaline, steeped in testosterone. They want people to fear meeting their computers in a dark alley.

About This Book

PC Modding For Dummies is a step-by-step procedure for putting together and adding flair to a computer, as well as a reference book for curious souls who want to work on one or two components, or figure out how to do one or two things. It's both a guidebook and a reference. For example, if you just want to see what you can do to upgrade and mod your computer's graphics card, you can flip to Chapter 6 and read up. If all you want to do is cut a window into a computer case, grab your favorite cutting tool and check out Chapter 17. On the other hand, if you're starting from scratch to build the greatest computer the world has ever seen, plow through the book in order and you'll soon have a PC that will give your friends nightmares.

How to Use This Book

How you use this book is up to you; it functions as both a tutorial and as a reference tome. It's designed to be friendly to the novice computer enthusiast — someone who's been exposed to modding and wants to know how it's done, but who isn't advanced enough to machine parts in a tool-and-die shop to add to his computer. I've tried to make it both comprehensive and user-friendly, both knowledgeable and fun to read. I hope you find yourself enjoying this book and discovering all kinds of new tips and tricks in it at the same time.

Conventions Used in This Book

Before you get started, you need to know a few things in order to get the most out of *PC Modding For Dummies.* As you wander through the wonder that is this book, you'll encounter different conventions:

✔ **Bold:** I use **bold** to indicate anything you have to type (for example, "In the text box, type the word **msconfig** and press Enter"). If the surrounding text is already bold (for example, in a numbered list), the word you type will be in regular text (not bold). Either way, it stands out from the text around it so you can clearly tell what you're supposed to type.

✔ **Italic:** I use *italic* when I use a new term that I'm defining nearby (often in parentheses). In the "Where to Go from Here" section later in this Introduction, for example, I italicize the word *overclocking* and define it for you in parentheses.

✔ **Monofont:** I use `monofont` for screen messages (for example, "The program asks `Do you want to proceed?`"). I also use monofont for e-mail addresses and URLs (for example, "Go to `www.dummies.com`").

Foolish Assumptions

You're no dummy. However, if you're interested in this book, you're looking for an introduction to modding a PC. This book is about building and tricking out a supercomputer — or at least the most muscular computer you can afford. It serves as a friendly, handy introduction to modding, to whet your appetite and drive you to put together a machine that can rule the world.

This book is about getting your hands dirty. If screwdrivers make you squeamish, it may be too much for you. You're going to tear open the computer case, drop in electronic components, run cabling, void warranties, cut holes in perfectly good panels, and so on.

How This Book Is Organized

I worked long and hard on the table of contents before the publisher agreed to let me write this book. The fruit of my labors, I believe, is a well-organized piece of prose that's useful both as a step-by-step guide and a reference. It's organized in such a way that it introduces the components of the PC one by one, explains a little about why they're so important, helps you choose the best one for your dream system, and, of course, shows you how to work them into a modded PC. The book is organized into different parts as follows.

Part 1: Introducing the Awesome, High-Octane World of Modding

As you may have guessed, this part serves as an introduction to the practice of modding. It discusses what modding is, why modders tend to demand amazing performance out of their PCs, and helps you create a plan of attack for your modding efforts.

Part II: Building a Modded PC

Here's where I go through the components of the computer, helping you select what's right for you and discussing the modability of the various parts of a PC. I take you in-depth, from the case to the peripherals to the operating system — everything you need to know to create the PC of your dreams.

Part III: Modding for Speed: Tweaking and Overclocking

Who's to say that software can't be modded? Windows XP, the operating system of choice, can be tweaked and fine-tuned to squeeze peak performance out of your PC. So can your components — namely your CPU and graphics card. In this part, I discuss how to push them to limits that the manufacturer doesn't want them to reach and show you how to avoid breaking them in the process.

Part IV: Cooling, Cutting, and Painting

Some people think of modding only as chopping up a case with a rotary tool and throwing in a Plexiglas window. If that's your idea of modding, this is the part for you. It covers chilling out your components by adding extra fans and amazing liquid cooling systems, cutting windows and blowholes into your computer's case, and throwing on an amazing paint job.

Part V: The Part of Tens

If you've read other *For Dummies* books, you've encountered a Part of Tens. It's a fun section about interesting things that have to do with the subject of the book. Here I show ten amazing pre-modded cases, ten insane mods for advanced modders, and ten utterly cool peripherals to garnish your modded PC.

Icons Used in This Book

You'll encounter a number of icons as you work your way through the text. I use them to point out important pieces of information, to add a little extra knowledge to the task at hand, and to generally be helpful. Here's what they mean.

The Tip icon points out fun and interesting things to do. It adds flavor to your work and introduces shortcuts and handy bits of information to make your life easier.

The Remember icon points out pieces of information that are so important I mention them more than once. These are the tidbits you'll want to remember when you're at work.

Now, I know this is a *For Dummies* book, and *For Dummies* books are known for being friendly and avoiding the use of boring, complicated jargon that causes novice computer users' eyes to glaze over. I really try to avoid using such gobbledygook, but sometimes I get carried away with myself. When I delve into geek speak, I warn you with a Technical Stuff icon. This is information that's really cool and fun to know, but it isn't necessary to your understanding of the topic at hand.

Although you don't have to read the Technical Stuff stuff, you should definitely read the information next to the Warning icon. I use Warning icons for a very good reason: to prevent you from doing something that may cause damage to your computer, cause data loss, or cause you to spontaneously combust. Because you should never work on a computer while you're on fire, reading my warnings is important.

Where to Go from Here

If you've made it this far, you're done with the Introduction. You now know everything you need to page through the rest of *PC Modding For Dummies*.

Let's say you just discovered the art of *overclocking* (the process of pushing components past the manufacturer's specifications, discussed in Chapter 15), and you need to chop some holes in the case to add cooling fans. Let it be known that computer components are very much heat-oriented beings. Processors, including the central processing unit (CPU), the graphics processor on the graphics card, and other chips, need constant cooling to keep them from burning themselves out. Overclocking them increases the heat that they generate and, therefore, requires extra cooling to ensure that you don't blow an expensive component.

So where was I? Oh yes, you want to cut some blowholes in the case. Let your fingers do the walking (I know this isn't the Yellow Pages but it *is* a big yellow book) to Chapter 16. It talks about measuring, drawing, and cutting holes appropriate for fans. It also introduces the concepts of positive and negative airflow, an important subject for an air-cooled system.

No matter what cool things you read about in the pages ahead, always consider your budget and your goals. With this book, you can build a new computer from scratch or swap out the parts you're concerned with. You can cut windows into a case and paint it, or just cut a few blowholes and be done with it. When it comes to buying computer components, I have one rule of thumb: Get the best and most advanced gear you can possibly afford. Don't settle for last year's model unless you absolutely have to. If you buy fresh, you actually end up money ahead, because you won't have to upgrade your parts nearly as soon as you would if you bought year-old parts. Modders tend to be enthusiasts, and enthusiasts tend to demand performance. You'll be happier with a machine that can run all the latest games and multimedia applications with all the features turned on, as opposed to a box that barely meets the requirements of current titles.

Happy modding!

Part I

Introducing the Awesome, High-Octane World of Modding

The 5th Wave   By Rich Tennant

"Why am I modding my PC? I pimped my Xbox, my fish tank, and my Water Pik. This was next."

In this part . . .

This part is mainly about getting started. I take you through the tools you need to build and trick out an incredible modded PC, show you the parts you require to put this thing together, and help you come up with a plan of attack to do this thing the right way. When you're finished with this part, you should have a good understanding of what stuff you'll need — you should even have a shopping list ready for parts that you're not moving over from an existing computer. You'll also have an idea as to what order to do things in, so you won't get ahead of yourself.

Chapter 1

Creating a Mod-Worthy PC

· ·

In This Chapter

▶ Studying the modder species

▶ Looking at the parts of your computer

▶ Equipping yourself with the right tools

▶ Finding a place to do the work

▶ Handling your PC parts correctly

· ·

*W*hether you've never ventured to open your computer's case to look at the mysterious circuit boards and cables inside, or you upgrade so frequently you feel more intimate with your PC's innards than you feel with your family (and trust me, I understand — some of my PCs' cases are open on a permanent basis), modding is something totally different from day-to-day PC use and maintenance. Modding requires a different mindset, a more adventurous attitude, an almost reckless desire to bust out the baddest box on your block.

The subject of computer gaming comes up often in these pages. Computer modders tend to be enthusiasts, and enthusiasts tend to be gamers. Running modern 3-D games is by far the most power-intensive activity likely to be pursued outside of Hollywood. If you ask me, computers exist for the sole purpose of playing games — everything else, including banging out these words in my word-processing program, comes second.

One of the best venues, in fact, for showing off your PC modding skills is gaming LAN parties. LAN parties are gatherings of gamers who want to play games with/against each other in a latency-free environment.

Latency, or lag, is the phenomenon that affects computers communicating over networks, including the Internet. It's measured in milliseconds, and a function known as *ping* is used to determine the actual amount of latency. Ping times particularly affect gaming: Low pings, say around 50 milliseconds, result in smooth gameplay, while high pings, over 200 milliseconds, cause play to become choppy and degrade the experience. Figure 1-1 shows a Doom 3 server list with ping times.

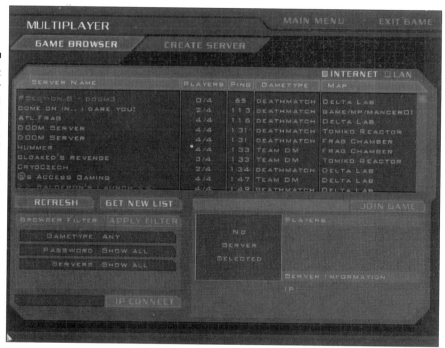

Figure 1-1:
The popular game Doom 3 (from Id Software), like many games with online components, lets you browse through available servers to hunt down the one with the lowest ping.

Understanding Why Modders Build Their Own Systems

It's all about power!

Modding is a hands-on activity. When someone mods a computer, he wants it to be an incredible system that can plow through data with the intensity of Cookie Monster attacking a plate of Oreos. Although you can certainly mod for your own satisfaction, one of the greatest joys of modding is showing off your creation to your fellow PC enthusiasts. Just like guys who drag-race with souped-up muscle cars, modders tend to ask each other the age-old question: "Whatcha got in that thing?"

Chances are, you're not going to want to answer, "I don't know," or indicate ancient parts like "a Celeron 133 and 64MB of RAM." Those drag racers aren't going to say that they've got a stock 4-cylinder, 100-horsepower engine. They're going to brag about having a huge motor, dual exhaust pipes, and those funky hubcaps that spin around.

So instead of ancient hardware, you want to make sure your computer is equipped with the most powerful gadgetry you can afford. This ties into gaming, too: Current games like Half-Life 2 and Doom 3 demand incredibly powerful computers with advanced processors and graphics equipment to get the most out of them.

Modders are control freaks. Instead of buying a system from a manufacturer that may or may not really care about placing the most horsepower into its computers, modders would rather buy the parts that they really want and assemble them into a monster rig. Major computer manufacturers have contracts with certain parts makers that, even if they allow you to customize the computer you buy from them, limit your choice of components. Modders can't handle such restraints. They want what they want and they'd rather do their own dirty work to get it.

That's not to say you absolutely must start from scratch and build a system to mod. You can certainly take an existing system, beef it up, trick it out, and mod the living hell out of it. You may run into problems, though.

Some computer manufacturers build their wares out of proprietary equipment. For example, if you bought a Bob's PC 3000 last year, and you want to upgrade it, you may discover that a standard motherboard won't fit in the case, or you may find out that it uses a graphics processor built into its motherboard and there's no slot to add a new one. You may be able to take what you've got, rip it open, and make it look like a beast, but what are you going to do when it won't run the latest games at a decent frame rate, or when someone asks you what's in it? Modding an old Bob's 3000 would be like putting a 12-inch lift kit on an '82 Chevy Citation. It's possible to do, but would you really *want* to?

Before you buy parts to upgrade a system you bought from a manufacturer, do a thorough check for compatibility in the documentation, at the manufacturer's Web site, or by calling the manufacturer's tech support. You don't want to end up with parts you can't install in your computer or, worse, parts that *seem* like they should work. One very prominent computer manufacturer in the recent past turned out computers with motherboards and power supplies that were designed specifically for each other. People who went to upgrade those computers found out the hard way that the proprietary power supply actually damaged standard motherboards. Don't let this happen to you. Be well-informed before you start your upgrade.

Looking At Your Computer as a Hot Rod

Cars have distinct parts: They have engines that determine how fast they go, they have bodies that show how cool they look, and they can be performance-tuned to max out their potential. Computers are the same way.

The engine and transmission: Your computer's internal parts

I love mucking about inside a computer. I know I said computers exist to play games, but even more than gaming I love to have a screwdriver in hand, a PC on my bench with its cover open, and a pile of components nearby. There's something very rewarding about swapping this out, putting this in, making sure the cables are connected tightly, being sure not to spill my coffee on my motherboard, and so on.

Car freaks like to rip into their vehicle's engine. They like to put in spark plugs, widen the intake, and such. To be honest, I don't know much about cars — I'd rather work on a computer — but I do have friends who are automobile gearheads and, in a way, we're brethren. We like to make stuff go.

The insides of a computer (see Figure 1-2) can be compared to the engine and transmission of a car:

- The size of a car's engine largely determines the power the car has to go fast. Similarly, the computer's central processing unit (CPU) determines how efficiently it deals with all those math problems that make the computer work.

- A car's transmission transfers the power of the engine to the wheels to make it go. A computer's main memory (often called RAM) serves as a depository of data the processor has to work on as well as work that the processor has completed. It transfers the data to and from the working program. Data conduits called *buses* provide pathways along which the various data are transmitted. RAM and buses serve a similar function to the computer as a transmission does to a car. Figure 1-3 shows installed RAM modules.

A car's engine generates power to make the car go, but it's the transmission that spins the wheels. Without a transmission, the car would probably sound spectacular if it had a big, roaring engine and some straight pipes, but it wouldn't go anywhere. The computer's CPU is in a similar situation: It can process math problems with amazing speed and grace, but it needs a little help getting the information to and from the programs that are running.

Later in this book, I babble in depth about CPUs and RAM. Chances are, if you're curious about modding, you're already well-versed in those concepts, but don't worry if you're not — I get to them in Chapter 5.

Figure 1-2:
To me, there isn't a more satisfying way to spend a Sunday afternoon than fiddling with a PC's parts.

Figure 1-3:
Those little modules sticking up from the motherboard house the PC's RAM.

When a program runs, it can send information to the CPU in separate pro-cesses known as *threads*. Some programs are simply one long thread. Some modern CPUs can run multiple threads at the same time in a process known as *multithreading*. Threads are essentially subparts of a program that can run semi-independently but need to communicate with each other to complete program tasks.

Performance tuning: Making the engine (or the PC) purr

Car guys know all sorts of tricks to make cars fun smoother, faster, better. They can spend hours working on timing, air transfer, and other stuff that affects how well the car runs. In fact, you probably take your car to a dealer or repair shop every so often to have a tune-up performed on it. After it's tuned, it probably runs much better and gets better gas mileage than it did before.

Computers can be tuned, too. It's less of a physical task than tuning a car. You don't turn screws and adjust the internal equipment to tune up a computer; instead, you tweak settings in the BIOS and in Windows.

The BIOS (which stands for *basic input/output system*) is the computer's link to the components that are installed. The BIOS is built into the hardware of the system and is the program that enables the computer to start, check to see what devices are installed, and then turn over control of the system to the bootable operating system. Without a BIOS, the computer wouldn't know anything about its gear — it wouldn't be able to find the memory to transfer data; it wouldn't know where the graphics card is, so it wouldn't be able to give you visual cues; it wouldn't know what kind of storage drives are installed. It would just sit there wondering what to do with itself.

You can use the BIOS's setup program to tweak settings for everything from memory timing to what drive to boot off of (usually your computer's main hard drive, but alternately a floppy drive or an optical drive). The BIOS setup program is a powerful tool for tweaking your PC's performance by telling the PC exactly how to use each of its components. Figure 1-4 shows a BIOS setup screen.

Although I get into BIOS tuning in depth later on in this book, I want to say this now: Be careful when you change your PC's BIOS settings. You can degrade performance, overclock components, and generally cause mayhem if you don't know what you're doing. Never make an adjustment if you don't know what it does.

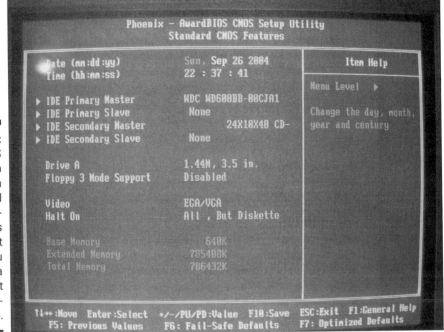

Figure 1-4:
The BIOS
setup
screen of a
typical
mother-
board. It's
here that
you
can get a
little bit
of tweak-
ing done.

Similarly, Windows itself contains a myriad of settings that you can alter, adjust, and tweak to squeeze the utmost performance out of your computer. Windows makes a lot of assumptions about how it expects you to use your computer, and its default settings leave a lot of room for improvement. By tuning the BIOS and Windows, you'll squeeze a lot more performance out of your system.

The body: Your computer's case

When you look at a car, you see its body. That includes the shape of the car (which automakers typically design around aerodynamics), its paint job, and its trim. The body of the car determines how utterly cool it looks at first glance. You're more likely to drop your jaw at the sight of a red Lamborghini than you are at a featureless tan sedan.

Your computer's case is like the car's body. It can be a standard, boring, opaque, beige case, which makes me think of working in a cubicle in a huge faceless company under fluorescent lights with a little phone headset and a sensible desk. Or, your computer could have windows, lights, lit fans, and an awesome paint job, which makes me think of an ultracool dance club with disco balls and flashing lights and designer shots in test tubes and happy party people all around. Where would you rather be: the office or the club?

After you get your computer's guts in gear, you'll probably want to trick it out to look like a work of art. This is the heart of modding: making something that's awesome to behold, something that you'd be proud to show your friends, something your mother would fear at first sight.

Getting the Right Tools for the Job

Building, cutting and painting a computer are largely mechanical tasks. For any mechanical task, you need the right tools for the job.

If you don't have any of the tools I cover in this section, expect to shell out a bare minimum of $100 for the full complement. You can get most of the tools discussed in any hardware store or home-improvement store.

The quality of the tools you purchase is entirely in your power. Typically, the more you spend, the more convenient, powerful, comfortable, and reliable the tools will be. I'm not saying that you have to buy the top-shelf gear in every category; let your budget dictate exactly what you procure.

The building and modding process can be broken down into three major steps: assembling or upgrading the PC, cutting the case, and painting the case. For each task, you need a different set of tools.

Tools for building or upgrading your PC

To work on a PC, you'll rely mostly on two tools:

- A small Phillips head screwdriver (no. 1–size head)
- A medium Phillips head screwdriver (no. 2–size head)

Nearly any task you take on involving swapping out circuit boards, opening and closing the case, adding and removing fans, and securing drives in their bays, you can accomplish with the right size Phillips head. I tend to work with one of those four-in-one screwdrivers that has reversible heads — two sizes of flatheads (that I don't think I've ever used) and two sizes of Phillips heads.

In rare instances, you may need special tools to crack the case and swap out parts. I've encountered some older systems that required star-head screwdrivers (also called Torx heads). To be prepared for the rare instance that I need a specialized head, I purchased a set of tools that contains a screwdriver handle and a host of bits of all shapes and sizes, including star heads, square heads (also called Robertson heads), hex heads (also known as Allen heads), and more. You probably won't need this, but if you discover your case has odd screws, you may want a multibit screwdriver set.

If you have to install a motherboard, in most cases you'll have to position little hex-shaped brass standoffs in the case, into which go the screws that hold the motherboard in position. To loosen and tighten the standoffs, I use an ordinary pair of pliers.

Because you'll be using these tools often, especially the screwdrivers, I suggest purchasing high-quality versions of them. Make sure they're comfortable in your hand and that they're made with casehardened metal so that the blades won't deteriorate over time.

Some computer-geek friends of mine use a cordless screwdriver with a comprehensive bit set to loosen and tighten the screws they encounter while working on a computer. I find that I don't actually need one; the screws are short enough that my wrist doesn't fatigue from manually turning the screws.

In some cases, seeing into the recesses of your computer case can be difficult. You may want to locate a dropped screw, or read the model number of your motherboard printed in between the expansion slots. For such instances, it's optional but nice to have a penlight.

Tools for cutting the case

You're likely to cut the case in two scenarios: when adding a blowhole for a fan, and when chopping a window into the case. This is where it gets expensive: You'll need power tools to accomplish this job. I don't suggest tearing away at your computer case with a pair of tin snips.

Let's start with blowholes. You'll need to measure, square, draw, and cut a hole right through the case. First, you'll want to draw the hole on the case itself. You'll need:

- A tape measure
- A pencil
- A compass (the drawing tool, not the lost-in-the-woods tool)
- A hammer
- An awl or metal punch

You'll measure out and map your hole, mark the center with the punch and the hammer, and draw the hole with the compass.

Don't assume you can draw the hole with the compass without a metal punch. The sharp end of the compass won't stay still on flat metal. Trust me, I've found this out the hard way. Profit from my mistakes!

After you've marked the hole, you'll have to cut it and smooth it. To do so, I suggest using:

- ✔ A drill
- ✔ A hole saw (around the same diameter as the fan blades of your fan)
- ✔ Sandpaper

To ensure you obtain a hole saw of the proper diameter, you'll either need to measure the diameter of the blades of the fan you plan to install, or you can just buy a set of hole saws that contains different sizes. You never know when you'll need to make a hole in something, so it's nice to have a set. Make sure they're designed to cut through metal if your computer case is metal. If it's plastic, just about any hole saw will do.

You'll also need to line up and drill the mounting holes for the fan. For that, you'll need:

- ✔ A square
- ✔ A ⁵⁄₃₂-inch drill bit (or another drill bit that's slightly thinner than your fan screws' threads)

As with the hole saws, I suggest you purchase a set of drill bits rather than just one. They could very well come in handy one day.

Blowholes aren't the only things you'll likely cut into the case. You may also want to add a window. You'll need the pencil, square, sandpaper, and drill mentioned earlier. For measuring rounded corners, you may want a protractor. For cutting the case and the clear plastic sheet of acrylic that will serve as the window, I strongly suggest a rotary tool (such as a Dremel) with an attachment appropriate for cutting metal. You may also use a jigsaw, but they're expensive.

To secure the acrylic in place, I suggest using one of two methods. By far the easiest method is to use strips of Velcro. You can get Velcro strips at any hardware store. To cut them to the correct size, all you need is a pair of scissors.

Alternately, you can secure the acrylic in place with nuts, bolts, and the appropriate-size drill bit for your bolts. The number of nuts and bolts you need depends on the shape of your cut and how you want it to look. Some people go for a gritty, mechanized look with bolts every few inches, while minimalists with square windows only use one in each corner. Ultimately, it's up to you how many you use, but be sure to securely fasten your acrylic to the case panel.

Safety first! When you're cutting metal, little shards will fly everywhere. You'll also encounter sharp edges that will easily cut your fingers. While chopping up your case, be sure to wear a pair of work gloves and safety glasses. I know, I know — you'll be careful. You don't want to spend the money. You're too cool for safety. Guess what: I *insist* that you wear gloves and safety glasses. Sanding jagged edges of aluminum or steel is a terrific way to shred the skin on your fingers, resulting in blood and carnage. And you absolutely do not want a tiny shard of metal to lodge itself in your eye. That would require a trip to the emergency room. Be safe! Wear gloves and safety glasses!

Tools for painting

Why settle for a boring, beige paint job when you can throw on a few coats of a more appealing color? Painting requires time and patience.

To start the painting process, you'll need:

- A sanding block
- Several sheets of wet-dry various-grit sandpaper, from 320 to 600 grit
- Clean rags

If you don't have a well-ventilated area, or if you're unable to do your painting outdoors, you should strongly consider buying a face mask.

You'll need lots of sandpaper because you'll sand in between each coat of primer and paint you apply. Although a sanding block is technically optional, you should strongly consider buying one — they're inexpensive and they give you something to grip while you sand your case.

Of course, you'll need paint. Plan to purchase:

- A can of primer
- Two or three cans of spray paint in the color you desire
- A can of clear coat

Creating the Ideal Work Area

Technically, you can build a computer just about anywhere that you can lay the case on its side. It would be reckless, however, to work on a carpet or on a little wobbly table. To do the work I discuss in this book, you'll need to find a large, well-lit bench where you can lay out all your stuff with room to spare.

Conquering the fear of handling electronic components

If you handle electronic components by the edges and you pay attention to the excellent advice in this chapter about preventing electrostatic discharge (ESD), you really have nothing to worry about when you handle electronic parts, but there are a few things you should know.

You'll notice that when you buy a graphics card, a sound card, a motherboard, or some other amazing piece of PC technology, it comes in a bag that's usually silver, pink, or clear with black designs on it. This is what's known as an *antistatic bag*. It protects components from being accidentally damaged by ESD. You should keep your components in antistatic bags when they're not installed in a PC (see the figure).

You'll notice that expansion cards, including sound cards, graphics cards, network interface cards, modems, and other gear have a metal plate on the back that corresponds to the slots in the back of your computer's case. If you have to walk around with a component that's not in an antistatic bag, hold it by the metal plate.

Also on expansion cards is a little edge that's covered in gold stripes. This is the contact edge, where the card meets the motherboard and through which data are transferred back and forth. Don't handle the card by the edge — the oils in your hands could coat the metal contacts and interfere with the electrical signals, causing all sorts of problems.

That sounds like a lot to be worried about, but it really isn't. The more you handle components, the more you'll get used to it; these tips will quickly become second nature.

Electronic components are hardier than you may think. I'm not suggesting that you do this, but I actually have stacks of circuit boards on my shelves, without antistatic bags, and they all work perfectly fine. Of course, I wouldn't miss most of them if something bad were to happen, and I do keep the ones I care about in antistatic bags to protect them not only from static, but from dust as well.

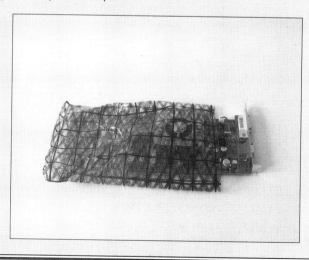

Consider a long table or a bona fide workbench in a workshop or garage. It should be clean and free of oil, grit, and grime, and you should have a few lights around it or even a fluorescent fixture mounted above.

In the course of working on your computer, you'll encounter tons of little bits of hardware: screws, standoffs, *gates* (those little metal panels that fit over the holes behind unused expansion slots), and other odds and ends. I have several small boxes that I use to toss such debris into. For the computer that I'm working on at the moment, I'll use those little black canisters that 35mm film comes in (I know, nobody uses film anymore) to store screws and stuff that I'll need to find later on.

For cutting the case, take precautions to keep a handle on metal shavings. Take care to vacuum them up with a shop vacuum cleaner or a handheld vacuum.

Never, *never* cut a metal case anywhere near your computer's components! Metal shavings are good electrical conductors, and if they land on a motherboard or other circuit board, they can wreak havoc with its current, rendering the board useless! Before you cut your case, get the computer and all its circuitry out of there, far away from where you're cutting.

Finally, work in an area free of carpeting. Carpeting generates static, and static is the enemy.

Getting a Handle on Static Electricity

Electrostatic discharge (ESD) is the computer gearhead's greatest enemy. ESD is what happens when you walk on a carpeted floor and touch a doorknob. That little pop is static electricity, and if you can feel it then it's about three times more powerful than the discharge it would take to blow a component on a circuit board.

You can combat ESD in several ways. First, and most important, handle circuit boards by their edges. Don't touch the chips or the resistors or other electronic components.

Second, before you reach into your computer or pick up a board:

1. **Plant your feet.**

2. **Ground yourself to eliminate any static charge you've built up by touching the metal computer chassis.**

3. **Don't move your feet as you work on your PC.**

4. **If you shuffle your feet, repeat steps 1 through 3 before handling more components.**

If you want to be really safe, go to a computer store and buy an antistatic bracelet (see Figure 1-5). It consists of a strip that wraps around your wrist, which has a metal contact. The contact is attached to a cord. You clamp the other end of the cord to grounded metal, such as the computer chassis or a metal table strut or something else. It'll feel like you're on a leash, but an antistatic bracelet will keep you from accidentally making a costly mistake by rendering an expansion card utterly useless.

Figure 1-5:
If you're worried about static electricity, an antistatic bracelet will keep you grounded and free from static buildup.

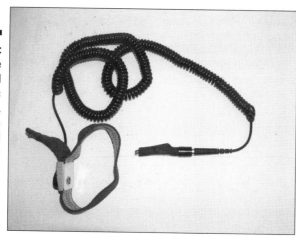

Chapter 2

Creating a Plan of Attack

*Y*ou are a general in the war for creating a perfect PC. A general doesn't charge off into battle, making it up as he goes. Instead, he consults with advisers and creates a battle plan. He flanks his enemies, cuts off their supplies, gathers intelligence from spies, takes control of strategic locations, and makes his enemies pay with their lives.

Modding, thankfully, doesn't involve bloodshed (unless you cut yourself sanding a rough edge because you chose not to wear work gloves). However, it does have some resemblance to battle: Before you build an incredible modded PC, you have to lay down plans to accomplish your goals in a manner that makes sense, that makes it easier, and that keeps you from running into snags and forcing you to backtrack. The goal of this chapter is create a shopping list and go over the order in which to build and mod an incredible PC. The chapter gives you a step-by-step outline of the work you have ahead of you, with all the steps in the right order.

The first thing I go over is creating a list of parts that you'll need to slap together and mod a PC. You might reuse some parts from a PC you already have, and others you'll have to buy new. I'm also going to mention some specialty items that mainly interest modders; I finish up with a section on where you can go to find such things, plus a profile of one specialty shop.

Creating a Parts List

Before you rush off to the computer store, you need to know exactly what you plan to buy. With the number of processors, CPUs, expansion cards, and other components available to you, there are literally thousands of combinations of hardware you could end up with. Grab a pen and a ream of paper; you're going to make a parts list.

I can't possibly describe every single product available for the PC. A book that does so would be 1,000 pages long and be outdated before it went to press. It's hard enough keeping *this* book current throughout its production! Rather than trying to recommend a specific make and model of every part you need, I'm going to go over each component your PC requires and leave the research of choosing which particular brand and product to buy up to you.

There are plenty of reputable sources for reviews and recommendations; some of my favorites include the following:

- ExtremeTech.com (and the relatively new, printed magazine version of *ExtremeTech*)
- *MaximumPC* magazine
- Gamer's Depot (www.gamersdepot.com)
- AnandTech.com
- HardOCP.com
- *PC Modder* magazine
- Computer Gaming World magazine

A great site to find deals on components is Pricewatch.com; you choose a component, and it lists online retailers sorted by the price they charge for the item in question.

The case

Of course, you'll need something to contain all your components. (See Chapter 3 for a full discussion of the case.)

Modders consider the case a canvas for their art: Case cutting is the core action of modding. The beauty of being a modder is that you don't have to spend a ridiculous amount of money on a really cool case; you're going to *make* your case cool. You can go for the cheapo beige tower. Just make sure there are ample fan mounts for cooling; there should be at least one mount for a 120mm fan. Of course, you can always cut in your *own* fan mounts. . . .

The case will come with hardware like screws and drive rails for securing expansion cards and storage devices. Pay attention to the number of bays it offers; tiny mini-ATX and mini-ITX cases only have room for a couple of drives, while mid-tower and full-tower ATX cases can store drives galore.

The case may come with a power supply. Be wary: Power supplies included with cases aren't always the best quality. They're often underpowered (you may get a 300W power supply with a mid-tower case), and off-brand power supplies sometimes don't provide stable current.

The power supply

If you're putting together a modern PC, you'll want a power supply capable of at least 400W of total power. Modern Pentium 4 and Athlon 64 processors need lots of juice to perform correctly. (Check out Chapter 4 for a thorough look at power supplies.)

Be sure to get the right power supply for the computer you're building. In most cases, an ATX12V power supply is sufficient; it comes with every connector your PC will need, including a four-pin supplemental motherboard connector for CPU juice. If you're going cutting edge, building a PCI Express–based system, you'll need an ATX12V 2.0 power supply; the new form factor has a larger motherboard connector and a special connector for PCI Express X16 graphics cards.

The motherboard

The computer's motherboard is communications central for the PC's many components. Everything — the expansion cards, the CPU, the memory, the expansion drives — connects to the motherboard and relies on its efficiency to perform at its peak. See Chapter 5 for a discussion of the motherboard.

Bargain hunters can get a name-brand motherboard for less than $75, but that's a challenge. A full-featured board with a recent chipset and lots of extras will cost more.

If you plan on overclocking, be wary of motherboards with too many extras. That additional IDE RAID chip may give you more storage options, but it may not run well if you overclock the system.

You'll have to take your CPU of choice into account when you choose a motherboard; the two parts need to be compatible with each other. Reputable motherboard manufacturers (companies like ASUS, Abit, Shuttle, DFI, and many others) offer a lot of information about each model on their Web sites, including the CPUs with which the motherboard in question is compatible.

The CPU

You can spend as much as $1,000 or as little as $100 on a modern processor, depending on the fatness of your wallet and your desire for power. Although the latest, fastest, most advanced processors are expensive, CPUs' prices get cut as newer models come out. Thus, an AMD Athlon 64 3500+ is considerably cheaper than an AMD Athlon 4000+. (See Chapter 5 for everything you need to know about CPUs.)

Make sure your CPU and your motherboard will talk to each other. The motherboard chipset must support the CPU to be compatible, and the motherboard itself needs to be physically compatible with the processor.

Know your CPU sockets. Some processors — most notably Intel's Pentium 4 Extreme Edition CPUs — are available in two different socket configurations. The EE CPUs come in two forms: LGA775 and mPGA478. They are *not* interchangeable; a 775-pin CPU will not fit in a 478-pin socket.

The CPU, if you buy it in a kit, will come with a stock cooler (a heat sink with a fan attached). You may choose to upgrade the cooler to a more extreme air cooler or even a water or electronic cooler.

The memory

Your motherboard will support certain types of memory modules. You'll need compatible memory — and as much of it as you can afford, up to about 1GB (beyond that, there's little performance gain unless you do things like render 3-D movies, edit scads of video, or manipulate massive photographs). Consider 512MB a minimum for Windows XP and modern applications and games. (Check out Chapter 5 for memory recommendations.)

The most important thing to do when deciding what kind of memory to buy is to know what your motherboard supports. If your motherboard only supports DDR2 memory (as some Intel motherboards do), and you come home with PC3200 DDR memory, you'll have to make another trip to the store.

The graphics card

If you're a gamer, this is your most important component. If you're a 3-D CAD user this is also a key component. If you're into video, like DVD movies and TV shows you download from Suprnova.com, this component isn't as dire as it is for gamers and 3-D artists. (Check out Chapter 6 for a talk about graphics cards.)

Your motherboard will either house an AGP slot or a PCI Express X16 slot (or, in rare cases, both) for a graphics card. Be sure to get the proper type.

Graphics cards range from cost-effective consumer models priced at $100, which are pretty weak in terms of game performance and 3-D rendering, to $500 gaming cards, to $1,000 professional cards for graphics artists. Consider your needs, read the reviews, and make an informed purchase.

The sound card

If you're really strapped for cash and you're not an audiophile, you may be able to get away with the kinda-weak-ish audio integrated onto your motherboard. If you're a hardcore gamer or you crave the cleanest sound around, you'll want a PCI add-in sound card. (Check out Chapter 7 for more.)

Sound cards come barebones, with merely a card and drivers; they come with bundled games and audio programs like MP3 burning software; they come with support for four, five, six, and seven speakers plus a subwoofer; they come with consoles that mount in drive bays and contain digital inputs and outputs; they come with FireWire ports and optical connectors; and so on. You can spend from $25 for a model that won't be much better than integrated motherboard sound to almost $200 for a super-deluxe monster card and console.

The hard drive

Most motherboards support one type of hard drive: IDE (of the ultra-DMA variety). Many also support serial-ATA (SATA). You can also purchase an add-in card to support SCSI hard drives. The hard drive serves as the storage bay for all your software, your data files, your digital photographs, your music files, your word-processing documents, your e-mail, your spreadsheets, and virtually everything you download, install, or create on your PC. (For more about hard drives, see Chapter 8.)

Hard drives fail. That's a simple fact. Even the best brands are prone to crashes, to mechanical failure, and to data loss. *Back up your important files to removable media,* be it writeable CDs or DVDs, zip drives, external hard drives — heck, even floppies. Backing up is not an option — it's an absolute must.

Go with whatever type of hard drive your motherboard supports, and spend more money on volume than performance. If your system has enough memory, the difference between pokey and super-speedy hard drives won't impact performance of applications and games all that much. For instance, if your motherboard only supports IDE drives, get an ultra-DMA/100 or ultra-ATA/133 drive with as much volume as you can afford; don't worry about buying a SATA adapter. All those files take up a lot of space, and you'll be amazed at how quickly you can fill even huge hard drives to capacity.

The optical drive

You'll need at least one optical drive. *Optical drives* are drives that use lasers, rather than magnetic heads, to read and write data. They include CD-ROM drives, CD-R burners, DVD-ROM drives, combination DVD-ROM/CD-R drives, DVD writers, and multi-format drives. (See Chapter 9 for more on optical drives.)

The best path to choose when delving into optical drives is to buy a single drive that does everything. You can get drives that write to every DVD format, that write CDs, and that read virtually any DVD and CD known to man.

The floppy drive?

Do you need a floppy drive? The answer is: Sometimes. They're outdated, indeed — they only hold a tiny bit of data (1.44MB, which seemed huge when they first came in that capacity). Alternatives, like LS-120 "SuperDisk" drives that read and write both floppy disks and LS-120 120MB disks, are available, but they haven't really caught on.

You may run into the need for a floppy drive if you plan to install Windows on a SATA or SCSI hard drive that requires special drivers during the Windows installation, or when you're *flashing* (updating) the motherboard's BIOS. I have about four or five working computers at any given time and I currently have two floppy drives, which I toss into systems as I need them. Some of my systems have *never* needed a floppy drive, but I wouldn't want to be without them, because they do come in handy at times. I'd suggest getting one; you can secure a generic floppy drive for less than $20.

Network stuff

Most motherboards have a 10/100 Mbps network interface built in, but yours may not — or, it may not suit your needs if your network is wireless. (See Chapter 10 for a discussion of networking.)

If you're setting up a home network, I strongly recommend going wireless with a Wi-Fi 802.11b or 802.11g network. You can secure it almost as tightly as a wired network, and you don't have to run cables all over the house to achieve connectivity. Access points and gateways make sharing files, folders, printers, and an Internet connection incredibly easy. Although some motherboards come with Wi-Fi wireless hardware, most don't; you'll probably need an add-in card or, at the least, a USB adapter.

The monitor

You can spend hundreds or over a thousand dollars on a monitor, depending on several factors: whether you're content with a bulky CRT monitor or you must have a flat-panel LCD monitor; the screen size; the sharpness; and other performance issues. (Check out Chapter 11 for information on monitors.)

Input devices

At the very minimum, you'll need a keyboard and mouse. You may also want specialized input devices, like game controllers or drawing tablets. (See Chapter 11 for more on input devices.)

Keyboards range from generic, 104-key featureless models to beefed-up media controllers that not only have the traditional keys, but also buttons for things like e-mail, Web surfing, and media playing. Similarly, mice come in models from stripped-down two-button devices to wireless, multi-buttoned animals closer to the size of rats than mice. Be prepared to spend anywhere from $30 to $150 on basic input devices depending on the features you crave.

Speakers

You can divide people into two categories: those who demand the best, cleanest, and most powerful audio, and those who don't really notice a difference between a clock radio and a THX-certified sound system. I'm the former: I need the best in audio at all costs. My wife, on the other hand, falls into the latter category; as long as she can, say, understand the dialog in a TV show, it doesn't have to sound really *good*. (Check out Chapter 11 for more about speakers.)

People like me can spend more than $400 on 5.1-channel multimedia speaker systems with powerful subwoofers that rattle the windows. People like my wife can get away with dropping $35 on two-speaker systems without subwoofers. you need, how powerful you want them, and how clean they have to sound to satisfy your ears.

Case fans and fan grills

Most modern cases come with fans, but you may want lit fans or more-powerful fans. Plus, if you plan on cutting blowholes into your system, you'll need fans — and fan grills — to fill the holes. Airflow is important in a PC, especially a modded PC that may be overclocked and performance-tuned. (Check out Chapter 16 for cooling basics.)

Window material

You can get Plexiglas, or something equivalent to it, from any hardware store, or you can get premeasured window kits from specialty shops. After you cut a window into your case, you'll need clear or colored plastic to cover the opening. (See Chapter 17 for window modding.)

Fasteners for the case window

You'll need to secure the window into place. You can do so with molding, screws, bolts, Velcro, or anything you can think of that will cause a window to rest over an opening.

Lights

Cutting a case is fun, but you'll want to be able to see into it when you're done. For that, you'll need cool lighting to scare away the shadows lurking in your case. There are all kinds of lighting options for computer cases, from neon tubes to lit fans and power supplies. (See Chapter 18 for lighting ideas.)

Anything else you think is cool

Go nuts! It's your case! In this book, I cover building, cooling, window cutting, and lighting a case, but that's not the end of modding. There are all kinds of accessories you can add to your case, and all manner of cool things you can do to it to make it totally unique. Think things like rounded cables, do-it-yourself water-cooling, UV reactive parts, LED status readouts, and more.

Figuring Out the Order in which to Build and Mod

Now that you know what you need to build and mod a super computer, you need a plan to actually build and mod said computer. In Chapter 1, I fill you in on the tools and materials you'll need — have them all ready and within easy reach when you're ready to assault the task of creating the ultimate modded system.

I suggest building, tuning, and testing the system before cutting, overclocking, and cooling it. Deciding where to cut the window and where to put blowholes is easier if you know where everything is situated in your system.

Here's the order I suggest you tackle this project (details of each step are in the appropriate chapters of the book):

1. **Buy what you need.**

   Have everything ready to go before you start building.

2. **Install the power supply into the case.**

3. **Carefully install the memory and the CPU into the motherboard.**

4. **With the motherboard near the case, connect the front panel connectors to the appropriate pins on the motherboard.**

5. **Connect the cables to the motherboard, including power and drive cables.**

6. **Install the motherboard into the case.**

7. **Install expansion cards, including the graphics card, the sound card, the network card, and so on.**

8. **Install the drives into the case, including the hard drive, the optical drive, and the floppy drive, connecting power and data cables as needed.**

9. **Power up the computer and make sure it reaches its power-on self-test (POST) screen.**

10. **Install Windows XP, and all updates and device drivers.**

11. **Performance-tune the system.**

    You may want to do this in conjunction with overclocking and cooling.

12. **Cool the system — add blowholes, fans, after-market CPU, graphics and hard drive coolers, and so on.**

    You may want to do this in conjunction with overclocking and performance tuning.

13. **Overclock the system if you want.**

14. **Cut the window into the system.**

15. **Light the system.**

16. **Paint the case.**

Buying Pre-Modded Parts and Modding Kits

The beauty of modding is that you don't have to do everything yourself anymore. Years ago, modding was very much a do-it-yourself industry: If you wanted a lit fan, you had to install LEDs on it and figure out a way to power them. You couldn't buy cases with windows already installed. If you wanted a fan control unit, you had to buy your own switches and knobs from Radio Shack and figure out how to wire the circuits yourself. If you wanted to water-cool your processor, you had to buy your own hoses, pump, reservoir, and other stuff, and cobble together a solution of your own. If you wanted rounded data cables, you bought your own sleeves and rounded those gray ribbons on your own.

Of course, you can still do everything yourself if you want to — but you no longer have to. You can purchase pre-lit fans that you simply mount and plug in for a cool, illuminating effect. You can buy pre-modded cases if you don't want to do your own cutting. You can buy self-contained water-cooling kits. You can get power supplies that light up, you can get lighting accessories with Molex connectors for PC power supplies, and you can get rounded data cables that glow when UV light hits them. The computer industry has embraced modders and their ambitions, bringing modding to the masses. One question remains:

When you're in the market for a generic case, a keyboard, a hard drive, or a monitor, you can wander over to your favorite computer store or navigate to NewEgg.com or Buy.com and find exactly what you're looking for. But where do you go when you want stuff like glowing fans and cool fan grills, UV LED case lighting, water-cooling kits, and window kits?

The Web is full of specialty modding shops. Sites like The Cooler Guys (www.coolerguys.com), Crazy PC (www.crazypc.com), and Xoxide.com (www.xoxide.com), and many others, offer all manner of modding gear. For a look inside one such shop, the awesome FrozenCPU.com, check out the nearby sidebar, "Where do you get this stuff?".

Where do you get this stuff?

Located in the Turk Hill Office Park in the little Erie Canal town of Fairport, New York, FrozenCPU. com has grown from a tiny Web site based on one man's overclocking and modding hobby into a massive, $5 million a year powerhouse. It caters to modders, offering a massive catalog of cases, coolers, lights, power supplies (see the figure), fans — heck, it's even got illuminated mouse pads.

In 1999, Mark Friga got into the hobby of performance-tuning and overclocking PCs. "Trying to make them cooler, so they run a little faster," he puts it. Overclocking was still a black art back then, embraced only by the most hardcore performance junkie. Manufacturers didn't condone it, and lots of mainstream computer press recommended against doing it. But Friga turned it into a little business.

"We were putting fans in the sides of computers out of my friend's garage," recalls Friga. "We were buying hole saws at Home Depot and blowing right through them, and installing big 120mm fans." He put up a little shop on the Web, "selling, like, fans with finger guards and screws and a drill template. I was working as a desktop support administrator at a local hospital here, and I started my Web store while I was working there." He never expected the success that FrozenCPU. com has enjoyed; he just wanted to offer gear to hobbyists, things like after-market CPU coolers and fans.

That's all that the market bore back then. "This mod stuff wasn't really around," says Friga. "There was no lighting, window kits, fan controllers. Water-cooling was definitely around, but it was so far removed from what everyday people were willing to do." Now Friga thinks that mainstream computers are not far from coming with stock water coolers.

(continued)

(continued)

FrozenCPU is also responsible for innovations, according to Friga. It was the first shop to market now-popular modular power supplies (with which you only install the cabling you need). Now they're mass-market items. "Manufacturers will see that we're making so much money and doing such a high volume on products that we've invented, they actually steal our idea and start manufacturing it way cheaper overseas."

In its voluptuous growth, FrozenCPU.com has outlasted dozens of specialty mod shops and even purchased the massive PCMods.com when it went out of business. Today, FrozenCPU.com mods its own cases (see the figure), creates its own wiring (see the figure), and houses a massive warehouse *full* of gear.

FrozenCPU.com is only one example of a modding specialty shop, but it's a good one. Few such sites have enjoyed the success of FrozenCPU.com, which Friga attributes to constant innovation.

Part II
Building a
Modded PC

The 5th Wave   By Rich Tennant

"So I guess you forgot to tell me to strip out the components before drilling for blowholes."

In this part . . .

*W*hether you're starting with a working computer or an empty case, this part will walk you through the rigors of making sure each part of the PC is right for your rig, that it's compatible, and that it's powerful enough for modern computing. I discuss the power supply, the CPU, the motherboard, the drives, and more — all in depth, with brand recommendations and instructions concerning how to install the part into your modded system. When you're through with this part, you should have an assembled and working PC.

Chapter 3

Choosing a Case and Securing Components

- -

In This Chapter

▶ Understanding the case's role in computing

▶ Knowing your form factors

▶ Picking a modable case

▶ Mounting your PC's components

- -

*U*ntil recently, the case was an overlooked part in computing. All a computer case did was be a home for the more important parts like the motherboard and the expansion cards. It was often tucked away under the desk or table and virtually ignored. Nobody did anything fancy with the case. Why bother? It serves a simple function, like a sock drawer holds your socks. Who'd gussy up a sock drawer?

Eventually, someone got a really cool idea: Let's make the case fancy! Let's make it something to really look at! How about getting rid of the boring beige boxy look and slapping on a new, glossy paint job? Why not cut a window into it to show off the expensive components inside? Some companies make groovy-looking motherboards and graphics cards, colored red and gray and blue instead of circuit-board green, and what's the point if you can't see them? Why not add lighting to the inside of the case with cool blue cathodes?

And thus, modding was born.

Your choice of a case is an important decision. Although you can mod just about any case, making an informed decision can greatly affect the ease of which your project will go. It also affects the type of components that will fit in your case — remember, the case's primary role is to provide a warm, comfortable home for your computer's components.

After you've chosen a case, you need to know what to do with it. There's a place in your case for each of your PC's internal parts. You have to know how to properly install them.

Securing Your PC's Parts: The Case's Role in Computing

First and foremost, your case is the anchor for your computer's internal components. Big or small, heavy or light, steel or aluminum, it's the fortress of your PC's circuitry.

Here's what a standard tower case is like: The chassis inside the case's panels is usually made of metal, and it's a handy place to ground yourself to eliminate static buildup. The panels that enclose the chassis are, in most cases, metal, but cases with plastic panels do exist. The front panel — which houses the power button, the hard drive, and power LEDs, as well as the front bezels of various storage drives — is almost always plastic.

For this book, I concentrate on ATX tower cases. They're the most common type of cases and they're by far the easiest to mod. Other types of computer cases exist, including small cube-style cases that don't have a lot of room for expansion, and even flat server cases designed to be mounted in racks in server rooms. I won't be discussing how to mod those.

 Ideally, your case should be roomy enough for you to work on your components within. Being able to reach the connectors for data cables and the memory modules without having to strain or sprain your fingers is nice.

Knowing Your Form Factors: Matching Your Case to Your PC's Components

Computer components — including cases, motherboards, and power supplies — are designed to work with each other. For ease of use, they're made to be easily swappable, to fit each other physically, and to properly power the computer components. They do this by conforming to various *form factors*. A form factor is a set of guidelines that tells the manufacturers of computer parts how to ensure interoperability with other parts. A case built under the guidelines of a certain form factor will be able to house both a motherboard and a power supply of the same form factor. As long as the form factors are matched up, everything goes together just fine.

There have been and still are a number of form factors in the computer world. For years, the most common form factor was called AT, so named after IBM's original PC-AT. AT cases and motherboards were characterized by having the I/O ports on expansion cards. I/O ports include serial ports, often used for mice and modems; parallel ports, also called printer ports; and floppy and hard drive connectors. AT motherboards had an old-style keyboard connector — it was big and round, with five pins.

The AT form factor was, in recent years, eclipsed by the form factor I concentrate on in this book, which is called ATX. The latest version of ATX form factors is ATX 2.2. It has many advantages over AT, including the following:

- ✔ **PS/2 keyboard and mouse connectors:** These connectors are the ones used by recent, non-USB keyboards and mice, although USB is gradually overshadowing them. PS/2 connectors are small and contain six pins.

- ✔ **I/O ports on board:** *On board* means on the motherboard. ATX boards have a riser on the back next to the expansion slots, which corresponds to a gap in the back of an ATX case. The riser houses serial, parallel, keyboard, mouse, USB, and other connectors. Internally, the floppy- and hard-drive ports and the controller that drives them are also on board.

- ✔ **A more finger-friendly layout:** ATX boards are arranged more conveniently, with the CPU and, often, the RAM, easier to reach and work on.

- ✔ **Easier to reach drive bays:** Most ATX cases have a hard-drive bay that actually comes out of the case, for ease of securing and swapping hard drives.

Check out the diagram in Figure 3-1 for the layout of an ATX board.

The very latest ATX boards have new power connectors to accommodate PCI Express, a new type of expansion slot. Don't worry — I cover PCI Express in Chapter 5.

ATX has a little brother in the form of microATX, a form factor designed to accommodate less-expensive computers by reducing the size of the motherboard and the case. You'll often encounter microATX cases and boards in sub-$1,000 name-brand computers. MicroATX is a subset of the ATX standard. MicroATX boards can fit into ATX cases, but ATX boards cannot fit into compact cases designed only for ATX motherboards.

In Chapter 5, I cover how the form factors affect motherboards, including the differences between ATX 2.1 and ATX 2.2. For your case, all you need to worry about is that it's an ATX case. It will accommodate all versions of ATX motherboards and power supplies.

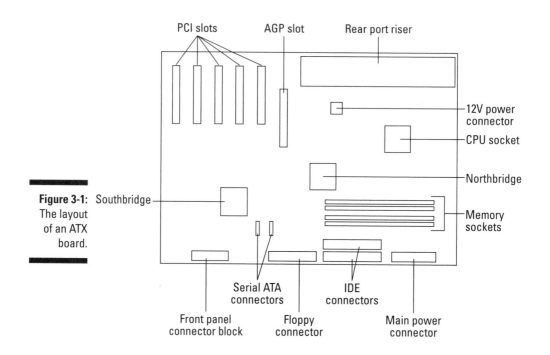

Figure 3-1:
The layout
of an ATX
board.

PCI slots   AGP slot   Rear port riser

12V power connector

CPU socket

Northbridge

Southbridge

Memory sockets

Serial ATA connectors

IDE connectors

Front panel connector block   Floppy connector   Main power connector

Picking a Modable Case

When you're shopping for an ATX computer case, you may discover lots of pre-modded cases with windows already cut into them. Buy one if you like, but if you want to partake in the full modding experience, you probably should look for a case without a window.

Similarly, having pretty, glossy paint jobs has become fashionable for case designers. This book covers case painting, but if you'd like to take a shortcut, buy a case with a paint job that pleases you.

For convenience, look for a computer with panels that come off separately. You'll only be cutting a window in the side of the case that reveals the components within, so you won't need to take the other side off except to mount some storage devices. That said, buying a case with a cover that wraps around from one side, over the top and down the other side is okay; such U-shaped case covers are also very amenable to cutting.

Steel case covers are easier to cut than aluminum. Aluminum cases are coming into fashion because they're easier to cool, but, in Chapter 16, I cover cooling that applies to any kind of case. With enough blowholes and fans, a steel case can be made just as cool as an aluminum case.

For your first modding job, you may want to go with an inexpensive, beige, flat case that you wouldn't feel terribly bad about if something were to go awry.

Mounting Your PC's Components

Cases have provisions to mount everything you need to toss into your computer. The motherboard, the expansion slots, and the storage devices all have their own special places within the computer's case.

When you buy a new case, it comes with a handful of hardware used for securing the various devices. It includes a number of screws, drive rails if the case requires them, brass standoffs that support the motherboard, and sometimes keys if the case has a locking door on the front panel. The rear gaps for expansion cards (shown in Figure 3-2) are usually covered with metal plates called *gates* that either clip into place or are secured with screws. The front panel is usually covered by false bevel covers to cover up the external drive bays that aren't in use, and sometimes they're backed up by removable metal plates (see Figures 3-3 and 3-4).

In the following sections, I show you what goes where.

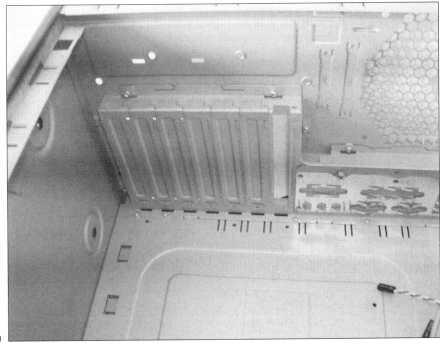

Figure 3-2:
The rear of the case has several slots to house the back plates of expansion cards. In the absence of expansion cards, they can be covered with metal gates.

Figure 3-3:
The front of
the case
contains
several
dummy
bezels to
cover
unused
drive bays.

Figure 3-4:
Sometimes,
the front
bezels are
backed by
metal plates.
You can pop
this armor
out of the
chassis by
twisting until
it gives way.

Mounting the motherboard

When you pop the cover off of a tower case and turn it on its side, the most prominent feature is a big metal plate, part of the chassis, with holes scattered about it hither and yon. Behind the plate are the slots for expansion cards and a square area for the I/O riser (see Figure 3-5).

To mount the motherboard in the case, you have to line up the board with the holes in the case. For each case hole that corresponds with a motherboard hole, screw in one of the brass motherboard standoffs that came with the case's spare hardware. Tighten them into place with a pair of pliers. Make sure they're very tight, but don't strip the holes (see Figure 3-6).

Most motherboards come with a bezel for the gap in the case where the rear I/O risers fit into place. You should pop this bezel into place before you insert the motherboard into the case (see Figure 3-7).

Then you can drop the motherboard into place, line up the holes in the motherboard with the standoffs, insert a screw in each hole, and tighten it snugly. It should look like what you see in Figure 3-8.

Figure 3-5:
The motherboard mounts to the big, flat metal plate in the chassis.

Figure 3-6:
Screw in standoffs wherever the motherboard holes line up with holes in the mounting place.

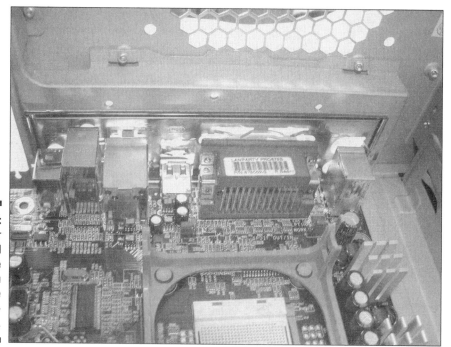

Figure 3-7:
Pop the rear I/O bezel into place before you insert the motherboard.

Figure 3-8:
A properly
inserted
mother-
board.

Don't force the motherboard into place. You may have to gently wrangle it a little to get the I/O ports to fit through the bezel, but avoid using too much pressure. If you bend the board, you can damage the electrical conduits that carry data to and fro. A poor connection can result in all sorts of headaches, from Windows errors to system hangs, failure to boot, or a completely unresponsive board.

Installing drive bays and your storage devices

Every computer case has a wide array of mounts for the storage devices a computer needs to operate. You'll probably want to mount at least three: a hard drive, a floppy drive, and a CD or DVD writer or reader (also called an *optical drive*). Any respectable computer case has three primary types of drive bays:

- External, 5¼-inch bays, for optical drives, tape drives, and other drives (see Figure 3-9)
- External 3½-inch bays for floppy drives, Zip drives, LS120 SuperDisk drives, and other small drives (see Figure 3-10)
- Internal 3½-inch bays for hard drives (see Figure 3-11)

Figure 3-9:
Externally
accessible,
5¼-inch
drive bays
tend to be
toward the
top of the
front of the
tower.

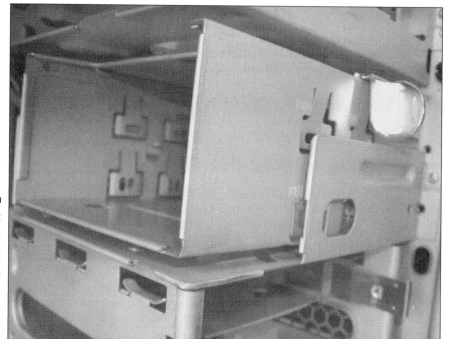

Figure 3-10:
External,
3½-inch
drive bays
are usually
under the
5¼-inch
bays.

Figure 3-11:
Internal,
3½-inch
drive bays
aren't reach-
able from
outside the
computer
case.

External drive bays aren't actually outside the computer. They're called that because they can be manipulated from outside the PC; for example, you can pop CD-ROMs in an optical drive mounted in a 5¼-inch external drive bay. You may also see them referred to as *removable drive bays.*

Although most cases allow you to secure the drives directly to the bay with screws, some cases require you to mount drive rails on the sides of your drives, which then clip into the bays.

Externally accessible drives

To secure a drive into an externally accessible drive bay, such as an optical drive or a floppy drive, your first step is usually to remove a front bezel cover so that the drive can be mounted flush with the front panel of the computer. If necessary, remove the metal plate behind the bezel from the computer chassis.

If your case doesn't use drive rails, simply slide the drive into the bay until the screw holes on the side of the drive line up with the screw holes through the bay. Make sure the drive is flush with the front panel of the computer (as shown in Figure 3-12). Then secure the drive with four screws, two on each side.

Figure 3-12:
A properly
installed
internal
drive will be
flush with
the front
panel of the
computer
case.

If the case uses drive rails, you'll probably have to pop the front panel off the case. Secure the drive rails to the drive however you need to — some come with clips that fit into the drive's screw holes, while others you have to screw to the drive. Then slide the drive into the bay until the rails snap into place.

In most modern cases, the 3½-inch drive bays are actually removable (see Figure 3-13). This makes it easy to install floppy and other small drives, as well as hard drives. The bay mount may be screwed or clipped into place.

You may have to do some experimenting with the placement of the drive in relation to the screw holes to get the external drive's front bezel to be flush with the front panel of the computer. The floppy drive will stick out the front of the removable bay.

Internal drives

Most 3½-inch drive bays come out of the computer (refer to Figure 3-13). Although the floppy drive will protrude from the front of the drive bay to be accessible from the outside of the computer, a hard drive will protrude from the back of the drive bay because it stays inside the computer.

Slide in the hard drive, with the connectors facing into the case so that its screw holes line up with the screw holes in the bay (see Figure 3-14). Secure the drive with four screws, two on each side.

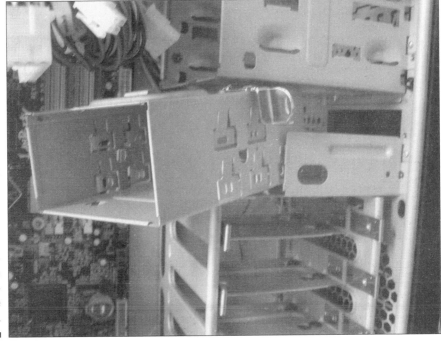

Figure 3-13:
The mount holding the 3½-inch drive bays can often be removed from the case to ease the installation of the drives.

Figure 3-14:
A properly installed hard drive.

Installing expansion cards

After your motherboard is in place, take a look at the row of slots along the back of it that line up with those metal gate covers in the case. Those are the system's expansion slots. They may consist of a bunch of PCI slots and one AGP slot (which are the most prevalent standards) or a slew of PCI Express slots (a new, emerging technology). For now, I'm only going to cover how to slide expansion cards — such as a graphics card, a sound card, a network interface card, a modem, and so on.

First, remove the *gate* (the little, rectangular cover over a gap in the back of the case) that corresponds to the slot into which you plan to install an expansion card. (Some people call gates *slot covers.*) You may have to remove a screw, or the gate may be clipped into place. Sometimes, for clipped-on gates, you need a flathead screwdriver to pop them out.

Next, grasping the card by the edges, line up the gold contacts with the expansion slot, being sure the metal plate on the card corresponds to the opening behind the slot. Press the card firmly into place, making sure the contact edge is seated completely into the expansion slot. Secure the card into place with a screw (see Figure 3-15). Repeat the process for your other expansion cards.

Now you know more about computer cases than most people who took computer-science courses! The next thing you'll do with your case will probably be to chop some holes into it and paint it. Goodbye, boring beige!

Figure 3-15:
A properly installed expansion card.

Chapter 4

The Juice: Choosing a Power Supply

*P*Cs are power-hungry little beasts. They want to rule the world!

But don't worry — that won't happen for years to come. Current PCs aren't power-hungry in *that* way; instead they crave electricity. They eat current for breakfast, voltage for lunch, wattage for dinner — and they've been known to gobble down late-night snacks.

A power supply is one component you definitely shouldn't skimp on. Your system absolutely *needs* reliable, stable power in order for it to offer you a dependable computing experience. Insufficient power supplies can cause problems that many users blame on something else: spontaneous reboots, sudden shutdowns and blackouts, and other chaos. Users often assume that something's wrong with the motherboard or graphics card, but insufficient or uneven power is responsible for all kinds of mayhem.

I won't get into the mathematics of calculating the exact power requirements needed by a system. You can, if you want, take stock of the power requirements of each of your computer's components — the power requirements are listed in their specifications. You can use the equation Volts × Amps = Watts, check the wattage specs for various power supplies, and try to come up with a ballpark guesstimate of your computer's needs — but I'd rather stick with a much simpler rule of thumb: *Go big.*

Why? Because you'll probably be upgrading your system for years to come. New components, especially graphics cards, tend to want more juice than the older ones you'll be replacing. I've encountered the problems I mention earlier (spontaneous reboots, sudden shutdowns and blackouts, and other chaos) when I've swapped out a graphics board, or even a motherboard and processor, without upgrading the power supply. The first time it happened to me, I thought I'd purchased a defective component, but the truth was my system needed more power.

Typically, a power supply is a dull gray box (see Figure 4-1) full of circuitry and a couple of fans — one that sucks air from inside the PC and another that blows air out the rear of the chassis. Later, I go over a couple of easy ways to dress up a power supply unit (PSU) to make it fit a modded system.

A power supply exists to turn the 120-volt, 60-hertz AC electricity that comes out of the outlets in the walls of your house into various voltages of DC current usable by computer equipment. Modern power supplies are *switching devices,* which means they only draw as much AC as needed to supply the computer with enough current to do its thing.

Power supplies kick out several levels of voltage. They include +3.3 volts (V), +5V, +12V, –5V and –12V. The negative voltages are no longer used, but power supplies include them on the off chance that they'll encounter really old hardware that needs them. The various voltages are used to power different components. For instance, the motherboard's chipset uses +3.3V, disk drive controllers use +5V, motors use +12V, and so on. Pentium 4 processors are so power-thirsty that, on motherboards prior to PCI Express (ATX 2.2) motherboards, they require their own separate +12V power connector from the power supply.

Figure 4-1:
A typical
power
supply.

Introducing Power Supply Form Factors

Here we go with form factors again!

A *form factor* is a set of guidelines for computer component builders to ensure that various parts will work with each other. Cases, motherboards, power supplies, and other components all conform to form factors to ensure interoperability.

In modern computing, you'll encounter three power-supply form factors: ATX, ATX12V, and ATX12V 2.01. They all conform to ATX computer cases, so physically mounting them into your chassis won't be a problem. The differences concern their included connectors and how they distribute power.

Plain Jane ATX power supplies have been more or less phased out by modern Pentium 4 motherboards, thanks to that extra power connector needed — which, in turn, is supplied by newer ATX12V power supplies.

The form factor of the power supply you need for your system depends largely on your choice of motherboard and processor. If you're going with an AMD Athlon solution or a non–PCI Express Intel setup, you can get away with an ATX12V power supply. For PCI Express–equipped motherboards, you'll need an ATX12V 2.01 power supply.

The chief differences between the two are the following:

- ✔ ATX12V 2.01 features increased +12V output for more power-hungry components.
- ✔ ATX12V power supplies, by design, feature a four-pin (two-by-two) connector for extra voltage needed by Pentium 4 processors. ATX12V 2.01 power supplies often include the same connector for backward compatibility (see Figure 4-2).
- ✔ ATX12V 2.01's main power connector has 24 pins (two rows of 12), as shown in Figure 4-3. ATX12V's main power connector has 20 pins (two rows of ten), as shown in Figure 4-4.
- ✔ ATX12V 2.01 power supplies often have a special, six-pin (two-by-three) power connector for PCI Express graphics cards, as shown in Figure 4-5.

Note that backward compatibility is normally a rule when new technologies become available. For example, most ATX12V 2.01 power supplies have adapters to fit ten-pin main power connectors on non–PCI Express motherboards.

Modding a power supply

Power supplies are about the most boring looking components found inside a computer. All the cool stuff, like the capacitors and other circuitry, is locked inside a drab little box. You can make your PC's power supply much more interesting in a couple of ways:

✔ **You can buy a power supply with lighted fans.** The exterior and often the interior fans of many power supplies, from companies like Antec and PC Power and Cooling, are available with cool blue LED lighting. Cool blue lights add a touch of flare to an otherwise dull component. Lighting that shines into your computer's case can supplement lighting that you actually add to it.

✔ **You can cut a window into a power supply.** It's easy and fun. Check out Chapter 17, which shows you the art of cutting a window into your computer's case. You can follow the same instructions, only on a much smaller scale, to add a window to your computer's power supply.

Warning: Never work inside a power supply that's plugged in. Furthermore, to avoid getting shocked, give the power supply a few minutes of alone time after you unplug it and before you open it up. The capacitors can hold a charge for a few moments, and you don't want to touch them and get shocked.

Figure 4-2: A four-pin 12V connector for powering Pentium 4 processors.

Figure 4-3:
A main
power
connector
on an
ATX12V 2.01
power
supply.

Power supplies also have connectors for powering pre–PCI Express graphics cards and other devices. These include two types of Molex connectors, each of which contain four pins. The larger of the two (see Figure 4-6) powers hard drives, optical drives, and graphics cards like the ATI Radeon X800. The smaller connector (see Figure 4-7) is for graphics cards like the ATI Radeon 9700 and smaller drives, like floppy drives and LS120 SuperDisk drives.

Figure 4-4:
A main
power
connector
on an
ATX12V
power
supply.

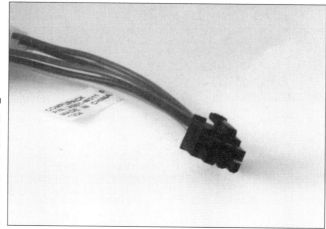

Figure 4-5:
The six-pin connector for a PCI Express graphics card.

Figure 4-6:
A large Molex power connector.

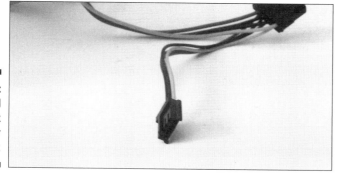

Figure 4-7:
A small Molex power connector.

Choosing a Power Supply

When I'm in the market for a power supply, I go for muscle. For the sake of future upgrades, I want more power than I could possibly need. Currently, the weakest power supply I'll buy is a 450W model.

Breaking down the power

Power supplies are rated in terms of total wattage they supply to the computer. When you go to the computer store or an online merchant to see what's out there, you'll be confronted with power supplies ranging from less than 300W to more than 600W.

The total wattage ratings advertised can be broken up into various wattages for different voltages supplied. For example, the Global Win 520-Watt Super Silent power supply breaks down its power output as shown in Table 4-1.

Table 4-1	Global Win 520-Watt Super Silent Power Supply					
Load	*+3.3V*	*+5V*	*+12V*	*−12V*	*−5V*	*+5VSB*
Max load	26A	52A	28A	1A	0.8A	2.5A
Max watt	260W	260W	336W	12W	4W	12.5W
Peak load	500W	500W	500W	28W	28W	28W

Notice that the peak load for the voltages actually used (+3.3V, +5V, and +12V) totals 500W. The rest, designated for −12V and −5V, is largely unused. The +5VSB indicates power used for monitoring the system when it's turned off; the motherboard still draws a tiny bit of power to monitor for wakeup events, like pressing the front panel power button. Not all power-supply manufacturers make their components' power breakdown so clear. In most cases, the negative voltages are only rated for less than 30W.

Brand matters

I've worked with power supplies from many different companies. Based on my experience, I can hands-down recommend power supplies from Antec, Global Win, and PC Power and Cooling. That's not to say that those are the only brands that supply good, hard working, and generally fun-to-be-around power supplies. Vantec, Nexus, High Power, and others compete for your dollars. Do some online research and look for reviews, such as the comprehensive comparison posted at Tom's Hardware Guide (www6.tomshardware.com/howto/20040122/index.html).

If you discover a power supply of a brand that's not listed and it's priced ridiculously lower than brand-name power supplies of the same wattage, beware. You've stumbled upon a generic model. Don't skimp on power supplies. I've been burned many times trying to save money by buying generic and ending up with unreliable power — I can't possibly recommend that you do the same.

Noisy neighbors

Power supplies have fans. Fans make noise. You may or may not care, but enough people do that a cottage industry has given birth to low-noise power supplies. If noise is a concern to you, look for low-noise alternatives such as Antec's TrueBlue line with Low Noise Technology or Global Win's Super Silent products.

Chapter 5

Assembling the Core Components: The Motherboard, CPU, and Memory

● ●

In This Chapter

▶ Introducing the motherboard, CPU, and memory

▶ Choosing a motherboard

▶ Finding mod-worthy motherboards

▶ Deciding on a CPU

▶ Cooling your system's CPU

▶ Choosing memory that fits your motherboard

▶ Installing a CPU and memory

● ●

I cram all three of a computer's core components into a single chapter for a good reason: You can't select one without affecting your selection of the others. This chapter covers your biggest decision when it comes to assembling or upgrading a mod PC: Which motherboard and CPU will your system be built around, and what kind of memory do they support?

These collections of circuitry form the beating heart of your computer. The motherboard is communication central: All the major components of your PC connect in some way to the motherboard, be it through a CPU socket, a memory socket, an expansion slot, or a data cable affixed to a connector that's driven by a logic controller.

The central processing unit (CPU) is also referred to simply as the *processor.* It's your computer's brain — the place where all the major calculations required by running programs take place. The CPU has many characteristics, from its operating speed (measured in megahertz [MHz] or gigahertz [GHz]) to the size of its onboard *cache* (storage area). For gamers, the CPU is especially important: Although the graphics card's processor crunches most of the 3-D animation that games require, the CPU runs the actual game code and handles things like damage calculations, artificial intelligence, game flow, location data, and other important stuff. The CPU has a direct effect on all-important frame rates, which provide smooth animation and a better gaming experience.

Meanwhile, the main memory (often referred to as the system's RAM, short for *random access memory*) is where the program instructions reside until the CPU fetches them. The CPU is fed calculations that the program requires to be processed from the memory, and it also returns the results to the memory. Memory needs to be fast, accurate, and plentiful. It also serves as backup storage for graphics processors; if a graphics card runs out of its own local memory, graphical information is stored in the main memory.

If you're upgrading rather than building, or if you're just curious, you can find out your PC's CPU frequency and its amount of memory with Windows XP's System Information tool. Choose Start ➪ All Programs ➪ Accessories ➪ System Tools ➪ System Information. A new window, called (surprisingly) System Information, opens (see Figure 5-1). Look at the list on the right side and find the Processor and Total Physical Memory entries. They disclose the processor's operating frequency in megahertz and the total amount of main memory with which the system is outfitted.

Figure 5-1:
Windows XP's System Information window gives you a peek at the components that make up your computer.

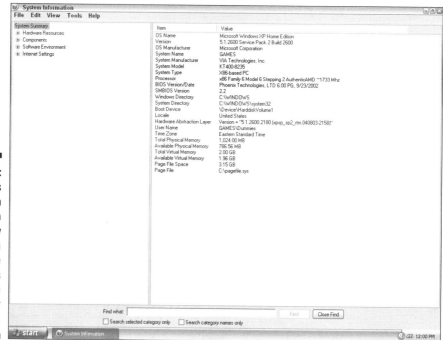

Ouch, that hertz!

You'll encounter a term quite often when I discuss things like CPUs, memory, data buses, graphics cards, and lots of other components. Such things operate at what some people call clock speeds, but the proper term is *frequency.* Frequencies are measured in hertz, megahertz, and gigahertz.

One hertz is one cycle per second. If the turn signal on your car blinks once each second, it's operating at a frequency of 1 hertz (Hz).

Now let's say that, due to some bizarre electrical problem in your vehicle, your turn signal

suddenly starts blinking 1,000 times per second. Now it's blinking at 1 kilohertz — kilohertz (KHz) means "1,000 hertz." One megahertz (MHz) equals 1 million hertz. And, 1,000 megahertz, or 1 billion hertz, equals 1 gigahertz (GHz).

Throughout this book, I refer to things rated in hertz. For example, 400 MHz memory goes through 400,000,000 cycles per second. A cycle is simply one round of duty; for memory, that means transferring data 400,000,000 times each second.

In this chapter, I fill you in on everything you need to know about motherboards, CPUs, and memory.

Choosing a Motherboard

The first thing to know about selecting the perfect motherboard is that you absolutely should not get a cheapie knockoff. Generic motherboards are cheap for a reason; most often, they compromise performance and sometimes even compatibility for the sake of lower cost.

Plan to spend over $100 on a quality, name-brand motherboard. A number of companies make solid motherboards. Some of my favorites include ABIT, ASUS, DFI, Gigabyte, MSI, Soltek, SOYO, and VIA. That's by no means a complete list of major motherboard manufacturers, but I really like working with these companies.

Motherboards are built around several technologies that you need to know about before you can make an informed decision. Most important, motherboards are designed for use with a particular family of CPUs. Possibly the most important feature of a motherboard is its *processor socket,* which contains an array of holes that correspond to the contact pins of a given CPU.

I discuss CPUs in detail later in the chapter, but understand that it's impossible to choose a motherboard without choosing a CPU, and vice versa.

Choose a motherboard based on features that you like and reviews at informative Web sites like www.tomshardware.com, www.extremetech.com, www.anandtech.com, and www.motherboards.org, and in magazines like *MaximumPC.* Your goal is to get a board that has everything you want on it and that's as efficient, fast, and powerful as possible. You'll also find yourself choosing a motherboard based on your choice of processor: a Pentium 4 or an AMD Athlon. Both processor families offer awesome power and excellent stability.

Motherboard features, each of which I explain in the following sections, include the chipset, the expansion slots, the support for technologies like Serial ATA and PCI Express, the form factor, onboard conveniences like audio capability and integrated Ethernet, and more.

Onboard simply means on the motherboard. If a motherboard has an audio processor affixed to it and jacks on the rear riser into which you can plug multimedia speakers, it's said to have audio onboard.

A guided tour of a typical motherboard

Before I fill you in on all the features of a motherboard, I want to show you one. You'll notice that motherboards are practically choked with electronic components, connectors, chips, sockets, slots, heat sinks, jumper blocks, and so on. In the following sections, I give you a tour of a typical motherboard.

When I refer to the *front, left side, back,* or some other area of the motherboard, I'm assuming you're looking at it as it's oriented inside a computer case. The CPU socket would be in the right-rear quadrant, the riser with the external connectors is on the back-right, and the row of PCI slots is along the back-left.

CPU socket

The most prominent feature on the motherboard is the socket into which the CPU is seated (see Figure 5-2). It's a square, plastic seat with a lever that unlocks the array of holes into which the CPU's contact pins fit.

Memory sockets

Toward the front of the CPU socket, you'll see two, three, or four long sockets with clips on either end (see Figure 5-3). These are the memory sockets, also called DIMM sockets (memory modules are called DIMMs, which stands for Dual In-Line Memory Modules). The modules that make up your computer's main memory live in these sockets.

Figure 5-2:
A CPU
socket.

Figure 5-3:
The memory
sockets.

Power connectors

AMD-based motherboards have big, 20-pin connectors for power from the PC's power supply (see Figure 5-4). Traditional Intel-based boards have a similar socket along with a four-pin plug, known as an ATX12V connector, for the extra power Pentium 4 processors require (see Figure 5-5). Note that Intel motherboards with PCI Express capability (with the ATX 2.2 form factor) have a single, 24-pin connector, plus an ATX12V connector. Motherboards supporting the Athlon 64, AMD's flagship CPU, also have ATX12V connectors.

Expansion slots

Over in the left rear of the board, a row of PCI, AGP, and/or PCI Express slots waits patiently for something to do. It's into these slots that you stick your computer's expansion cards, which include things like sound cards, graphics cards, and network interface cards. The motherboard shown in Figure 5-6 has a row of five PC slots for PCI cards, and an AGP slot for graphics cards. The AGP slot is the one situated all the way on the right, slightly forward of the PCI slots.

IDE and floppy drive connectors

The connectors for IDE hard drives, ATAPI optical drives, and other drives, as well as the floppy drive connector, all reside in the front of the motherboard, usually near the memory sockets. IDE connectors (see Figure 5-7) have 40 pins, while floppy drive connectors (see Figure 5-8) have 34 pins.

Figure 5-4:
A 20-pin power connector.

Figure 5-5:
A 4-pin,
ATX12V
power
connector.

Figure 5-6:
The mother-
board's
expansion
slots.

Figure 5-7: A pair of IDE connectors.

Figure 5-8: On this mother-board, the floppy drive connector is way over in the front left portion of the board.

Chipset

The logic that makes up the motherboard's chipset rests in two places:

- ✔ **Near the CPU socket (the north bridge):** Often, the north bridge (see Figure 5-9) is adorned with a heat sink — and sometimes even a fan. Intel also calls the north bridge the memory controller hub (MCH). Note that Athlon 64 systems may not have a north bridge, as the memory controller is built onto the CPU itself.

- ✔ **In the front-left area of the board (the south bridge):** The south bridge (see Figure 5-10) handles all the I/O functions. Intel also refers to the south bridge as the I/O controller hub (ICH).

Serial ATA connectors

Serial ATA is a relatively new technology for high-performance hard drives. It differs from IDE in several ways. (Check out Chapter 8 for a discussion on hard drives.) Most modern motherboards have at least two Serial ATA connectors; they're usually little black nubs with seven electrical contacts (see Figure 5-11).

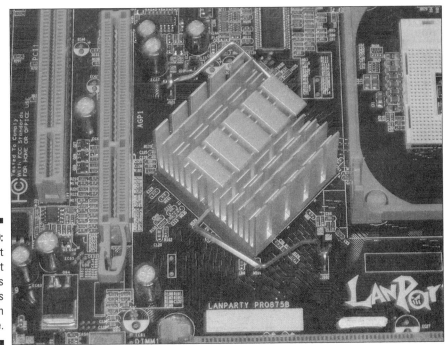

Figure 5-9: Under that big heat sink resides the chipset's north bridge.

Figure 5-10:
This little chip is the chipset's south bridge.

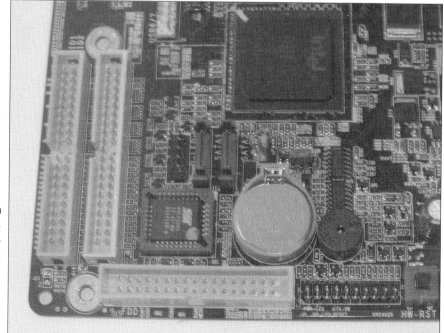

Figure 5-11:
Those tiny black connectors are for Serial ATA hard drives.

BIOS and battery

The BIOS, which is the core piece of logic that tells the computer what to do with its components, resides in a little chip (see Figure 5-12). Nearby, you'll often find a battery that's used to keep information about the BIOS settings. The batteries last for years and years; you'll most likely upgrade your machine long before the battery dies.

RAID

Some motherboards have RAID capability, for use with multiple hard drives. RAID connectors, and their controller chip, are usually found in the front-left area of the motherboard (see Figure 5-13).

Front panel connector pins

A computer case comes with a power button and LED lights on the front panel. Inside the case, you'll find a bunch of little wires with plugs designed for the motherboard's front panel connector (see Figure 5-14). There are usually plugs for the PC speaker, the power LED, the hard drive LED, the power-on button, and the reset button.

Figure 5-12: The BIOS is the little black chip to the left of the silver battery.

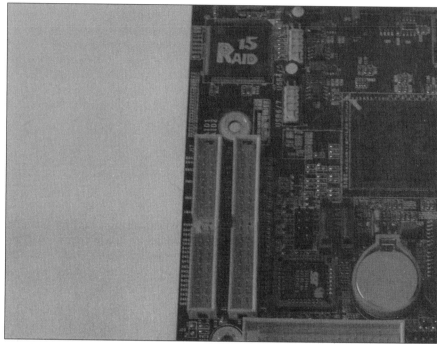

Figure 5-13:
The two 40-pin RAID connectors look exactly like IDE connectors. The nearby chip, situated to the left in this photograph, is the RAID controller.

Figure 5-14:
That row of pins next to the floppy connector drives the front panel lights, the power button, and the reset switch.

Fan connectors

Situated in strategic places around the motherboard you'll find three-pin connectors for fans (see Figure 5-15). One is usually near the CPU socket for the fan on the CPU cooler, and you'll have a couple more that you can use for case fans. Sometimes, the fan connectors actually collect information about the fan itself, such its RPM speed, which it can show you through a system monitoring applet.

Onboard feature logic

On the left rear and center of the motherboard, you may find various chips that drive onboard functionality, like audio and LAN features (see Figure 5-16).

Rear connector riser

The right-rear of the motherboard features a riser with jacks, ports, and connectors that stick out the back of the PC's case (see Figure 5-17). These may include serial and parallel ports, PS/2 keyboard and mouse ports, USB ports, audio jacks, a LAN port, and other connectivity hardware.

Figure 5-15:
A tiny
thee-pin fan
connector.

Figure 5-16:
This chip
near the
back of the
mother-
board is
a LAN
controller.

Figure 5-17:
A rear view
of the riser.

Understanding Motherboard form factors

A *form factor* is a set of guidelines that instruct manufacturers on how to build a part to make it physically, electrically, and otherwise compatible to other parts of the same form factor. Assuming you're buying or using modern components, you'll encounter two motherboard form factors:

- ✔ **ATX 2.1** is the most prevalent form factor. It includes a 20-pin power connector and, on Intel Pentium 4–based motherboards, a 4-pin 12V connector. There are no current ATX 2.1 motherboards that feature PCI Express expansion slots.

- ✔ **ATX 2.2** is designed for PCI Express capability. Such boards are fitted with a 24-pin power connector plus a 4-pin ATX12V connector, and they're usually outfitted with a number of PCI Express expansion slots.

Both are derived from the core ATX form factor, and both will fit an ATX chassis. The differences between the two lie mainly in the types of power connectors they're fitted with and their expansion bus capability.

Demystifying chipsets and buses

Something has to tell a motherboard what to do. That job falls upon the *chipset,* a collection of chips and circuits that define the motherboard's capabilities. A motherboard's chipset determines all kinds of details about the functionality of its host, including which CPUs it supports, whether it supports things like onboard audio, onboard Ethernet (networking connectivity), which types of expansion slots it supports, and much more.

Chipsets consist of two chips: a *north bridge*, which handles things like the interface with the CPU, the memory interface on Intel boards (most current AMD Athlon processors have an integrated memory controller), and the graphics bus interface; and a *south bridge,* which handles interfacing with audio processors, I/O (including keyboard, mouse, USB, LAN, and drive interfacing), the interface with the PCI or PCI Express bus, and more.

A number of semiconductor companies make chipsets, including Intel, VIA, NVIDIA, and SiS. Competition is fierce. Current chipsets include VIA's excellent K8T800 for AMD Athlon processors; Intel's 925X Express, with PCI Express capability, for socket 775 Pentium 4 CPUs; NVIDIA's stalwart Nforce 3 Ultra for Athlon processors; and the SiS 775FX. All these chipsets have rich multimedia capability and excellent performance, and they can be found on a wide variety of motherboards.

As you peruse reviews and product information, you'll find mention of the front-side bus (FSB) on Intel motherboards and HyperTransport technology on AMD hardware. Both indicate the interface between the CPU and the system's memory and other components. The interface must be very fast and efficient, because the CPU and main memory work together constantly. However, my advice is this: Don't worry too much about the FSB. Both Intel and AMD boards have extremely swift interfaces.

The FSB on current Intel motherboards operates at 800 MHz (effective; it's actually 200 MHz with four data transfers per cycle), while HyperTransport technology is reaching frequencies of more than 1,000 MHz. However, the two operate quite differently, making a frequency comparison invalid. Overall, performance benchmarks pitting Athlon 64 processors against Pentium 4 processors in similarly equipped systems show they're pretty much equal.

While we're on the subject of buses, it should be noted that there are actually several buses at work on a given motherboard. Besides the FSB/HyperTransport bus, there are other buses that transfer data to and fro throughout the components on a motherboard. Parallel buses, which transfer lots of data at the same time through a wide tunnel, are measured in *bit width,* which states how many bits can be transferred simultaneously through the bus, and also by frequency (in MHz).

The most prevalent bus has been, for years, the Peripheral Component Interface (PCI) bus. This 32-bit wide, parallel bus operates at 33 MHz, capable of transferring 133MB per second; it was really fast when it replaced the hopelessly dated ISA bus years ago. Lots of components, including PCI expansion cards, hard drives, USB, and FireWire, all send and receive data via the PCI bus, and all that data can cause a bottleneck: Too much data may overload the bus, causing a delay for some of the devices. That translates to a noticeable slowdown in the performance of a given program.

Another prominent connection is the Accelerated Graphics Port (AGP). Current graphics cards are designed to work with the AGP bus. Formerly, graphics cards were PCI devices, but as games needed more and more memory for things like textures, and because graphics cards had limited local memory, a new system had to be developed. AGP has gone through several revisions, from its original 64-bit 66 MHz flavor (known as AGP 1X) all the way to AGP 8X, a 64-bit connection that operates at 266 MHz and transfers more than 2GB per second. AGP connects the graphics card's processor directly with the computer's main memory so it can store texture data there that can't fit in local memory.

Both the PCI bus and the AGP are becoming dated. New components, applications, and games are demanding even more performance. Intel has embraced an evolutionary update to the PCI system called PCI Express. It's a point-to-point serial bus, meaning that, unlike parallel buses, it has narrow (but very fast) tunnels through which data can transfer. Whereas PCI devices all share the same data channel, a PCI Express system contains a separate, four-wire connection for each PCI Express lane — no more bottlenecks. PCI Express comes in several flavors, including X1, X2, X4, X8, and X16. The numbers refer to the number of individual serial connections, or *lanes,* supported. The physical slot for each differs; the higher the designation, the longer the slot.

PCI Express X16 is designed to replace AGP as a graphics card interface. X16 is capable of a whopping 4GB-per-second transfer rate — almost double that of AGP 8X.

Current Intel chipsets and motherboards support PCI Express (see Figure 5-18), and many motherboards contain legacy PCI slots for backward compatibility. As of this writing, there weren't any AMD PCI Express products, although they're in the works.

Figure 5-18:
This motherboard features PCI Express slots.

Understanding the roll of the BIOS

When a PC wakes up — meaning when you or a LAN or USB signal powers it on — it knows nothing about itself. It has no idea whether it has a graphics card, memory, a processor, or anything. It's as confused as a guy with a bad hangover who wakes up on his front lawn.

The BIOS (basic input/output system) takes over to relieve the confusion. The BIOS is the most low-level program in a PC. It's the lifeblood of the mother-board, the hero you can turn to during hard times.

The BIOS contains software that knows exactly what to do with your computer long before Windows boots up. This software is contained on a chip in flash memory, which is a type of read-only memory (ROM) that can be updated with a special program. Updating the BIOS software is referred to as *flashing the BIOS,* so dubbed because the BIOS is stored in rewriteable flash memory.

The BIOS provides the first instructions for the system's CPU to execute. When the processor wakes up, it looks for something to do. It's designed to look in a particular area of system memory where the BIOS drops its instructions.

One of the first things the BIOS tells the CPU to do is execute a Power-On Self-Test (POST). This routine checks the various installed components and makes sure they're responsive. During this time, most computers display a black screen with white lettering that gives you some idea what's going on.

When this POST screen displays, you can hit a key to enter the BIOS setup program. Most BIOSes tell you to hit the Delete key to enter setup. In the setup screen, shown in Figure 5-19, you can make adjustments to your computer's configuration, changing how the system uses its memory, how it views its processor, which drives to attempt to boot off of, and other core behaviors. It's here that you can performance-tweak and overclock your hardware (turn to Chapter 13 for more information).

After it has taken stock of the system, loaded customized data from its setup program, and helped the computer figure out what to do with itself, the BIOS initiates the *bootstrap,* which is the process of finding and loading an operating system. You can tell the BIOS to look for bootable code on a floppy disk, a CD-ROM, or, most often, a hard drive.

Look for a motherboard with a BIOS that offers excellent tweaking features. Boards from DFI, Abit, ASUS, SOYO, and many others let you dynamically tweak memory settings and voltages, CPU and FSB frequencies, and other settings to optimize and overclock your PC's components. Check the specs on the various Web sites of these and other manufacturers, and read reviews before you buy.

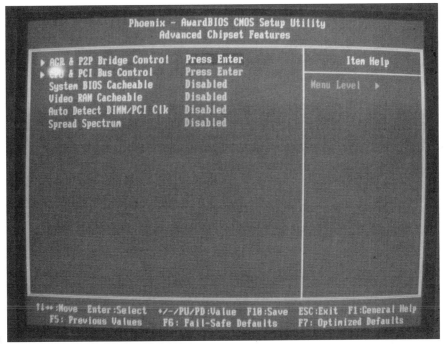

Phoenix - AwardBIOS CMOS Setup Utility
Advanced Chipset Features

▶ AGP & P2P Bridge Control	Press Enter	Item Help
▶ CPU & PCI Bus Control	Press Enter	
System BIOS Cacheable	Disabled	Menu Level ▶
Video RAM Cacheable	Disabled	
Auto Detect DIMM/PCI Clk	Disabled	
Spread Spectrum	Disabled	

↑↓→← :Move Enter :Select +/-/PU/PD :Value F10 :Save ESC :Exit F1 :General Help
F5 : Previous Values   F6 : Fail-Safe Defaults   F7 : Optimized Defaults

Figure 5-19: A BIOS setup screen.

Taking stock of your options

No, I haven't gone off on a tangent about investment portfolios. When you're in the market for a motherboard, you have a lot to consider. Among the things to think about are the various optional features that may interest you. Besides checkpoints like performance, CPU compatibility, and other important factors, you have to figure out if you'd like things like RAID capability, onboard audio, onboard Ethernet, extra USB ports, FireWire, and other stuff.

RAID

RAID stands for *Redundant Array of Inexpensive Disks.* RAID has different levels, which I cover in more depth in Chapter 8. For now, all you need to know is that many motherboards come with three flavors:

- ✔ **RAID 0:** RAID 0 isn't technically RAID because it's not redundant; instead, it uses two hard drives to increase performance.

- ✔ **RAID 1:** RAID 1 mirrors one drive on a second drive, protecting data through redundancy.

- ✔ **RAID 0+1:** RAID 0+1 does both at the same time but requires a minimum of four identical hard drives. That's really more than you need.

Motherboards can contain RAID controllers that support IDE drives, Serial ATA drives, or both. Serial ATA is faster than IDE, resulting in a more pleasant and responsive computing experience. IDE and Serial ATA drives are not compatible with each other.

Onboard goodies

Two components that are typically in the form of PCI expansion cards are also found onboard many motherboards: an Ethernet controller (complete with an RJ-45 jack for a network cable, or even in the form of 802.11*x* Wi-Fi wireless), and an audio chip. Although I'm heavily in favor of onboard network equipment, which usually has more bandwidth than you'll ever use in a home environment, I have yet to be convinced that onboard audio rivals that to be found on expansion cards. All audio isn't alike; some boards only come with an AC'97 codec and rely on the south bridge and the system CPU for audio processing (which can degrade gaming performance). Others have an actual audio processor that typically pales in comparison to stuff from Creative Labs and Hercules.

What the heck is an AC'97 codec? Glad you asked. A codec is a device or program that encodes and decodes a signal. AC'97 is a set of standards developed by Intel to ensure audio interoperability and compatibility. An AC'97 codec on a motherboard is a little chip (see Figure 5-20) that drives audio input and output jacks (see Figure 5-21) and that refers to an audio processor, or to the south bridge to access the CPU, to do the actual audio processing.

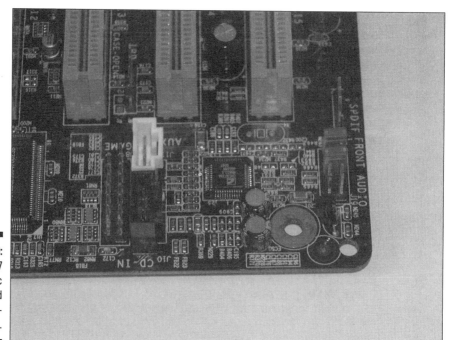

Figure 5-20: A tiny AC'97 codec integrated to a motherboard.

Figure 5-21:
The rear audio jacks on the back panel riser of a mother-board.

USB 2.0

Universal Serial Bus (USB) is an external connectivity bus designed as a high-speed replacement for old serial, parallel, and game ports. All current motherboards have the current version of USB, version 2.0, integrated. You'll find several USB ports on the rear of the motherboard, on the connector riser (see Figure 5-22).

Through the use of external USB hubs, you can connect up to a whopping 128 USB devices to one USB port. These can include game controllers, mice, printers, scanners, external storage devices, and all manner of peripherals. However, USB hubs cost money, so just having a whole bunch of USB ports right on the computer itself is often better. Many motherboards come with not only the USB ports permanently affixed to the riser, but also internal USB headers that you can latch to a metal gate (see Figure 5-23) with the ports on it, and which fits in one of the expansion slot openings on the back of the chassis. Figure 5-24 shows the internal connection for rear gate USB ports.

The more USB ports your computer has to offer, the less likely you are to require a USB hub. For convenience, some computer chassis even have USB ports on the front panel (see Figure 5-25). This eliminates the need to fumble around behind the case to find a free USB port.

Figure 5-22:
USB ports
on a
mother-
board
connector
riser.

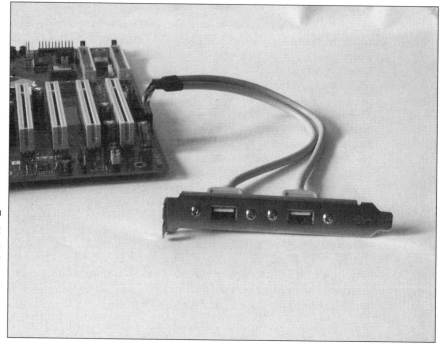

Figure 5-23:
USB ports
on the rear
of the
computer
on a metal
gate.

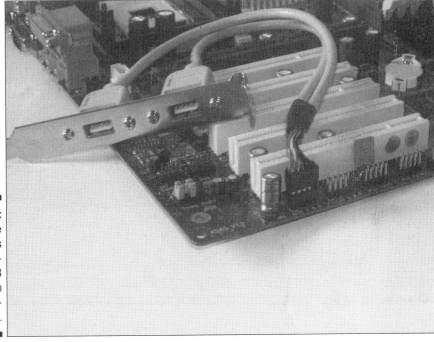

Figure 5-24:
Metal gate
USB ports
are connec-
ted to USB
headers on
the mother-
board.

Figure 5-25:
USB ports
on the front
panel of a
case.

Cool-looking motherboards for modded PCs

The motherboard manufacturers of the world have responded to the idea of PC modding. Many cases come with windows already built in. In Chapter 17, I show you how to cut a window in your own case. Because those windows give a tantalizing look into the inner workings of a PC, motherboard manufacturers have shied away from the drab green color of the traditional circuit board and started making blue, red, silver, and other colored boards. PCI and AGP slots (traditionally white and red, respectively) are giving way to funky colors, too.

Look for a motherboard that will look really cool in a cut and lit case. One of my very favorite product families is the LAN Party line from DFI. The PCI slots, memory sockets, and CPU cooler mount on these amazing boards that are neon colored and sensitive to ultraviolet light, under which they glow!

Most of the pictures of motherboard stuff in this chapter are photographs of the DFI LAN Party Pro875B.

FireWire

IEEE 1392 FireWire is another fast, external bus for connecting high-speed peripherals. It's used chiefly by digital camcorders, external hard drives and optical drives, and other devices that feel the need for speed. Although they rarely appear on motherboard connector risers, some motherboards come with internal headers for FireWire ports. Similar to extra USB ports, the headers are connected to a metal gate, with the actual FireWire connectors, which are affixed to an opening in the rear of the chassis (see Figure 5-26).

If you can't find a motherboard you like that has FireWire ports, don't sweat it. Many sound cards, such as those in the highly recommended Creative Labs SoundBlaster Audigy line, come with FireWire ports built in.

Finding more information about motherboards

I can't tell you which motherboard is perfect for you. I hope the information in this chapter has armed you with enough information to make the decision for yourself. Scores of motherboards are available, and listing detailed information about them would fill about three-quarters of this book. That means you'll have to do a little bit of research on your own to pinpoint the motherboard of your desire.

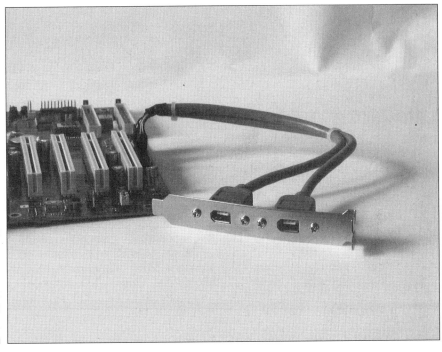

Figure 5-26:
FireWire
ports on the
rear of a PC
on a metal
gate.

You can find out about chipsets and motherboards at various Web sites and in PC oriented magazines. You can also get important specifications directly from motherboard manufacturers' Web sites. To help you out, here's a list of manufacturer Web sites for a number of the most prominent motherboard manufacturers:

- ✔ **Abit:** www.abit-usa.com
- ✔ **AOpen:** www.aopen.com.
- ✔ **ASUS:** www.asus.com
- ✔ **Chaintech:** www.chaintechusa.com
- ✔ **DFI:** www.dfi.com
- ✔ **EPoX:** www.epox.com
- ✔ **Gigabyte:** www.giga-byte.com
- ✔ **Intel:** www.intel.com
- ✔ **MSI:** www.msicomputer.com
- ✔ **Shuttle:** www.shuttle.com

- ✔ **SOYO:** www.soyo.com
- ✔ **Supermicro:** www.supermicro.com
- ✔ **VIA:** www.via.com

Choosing a CPU

There's a war going on. It's a quiet war, fought in laboratories and board-rooms and marketing departments. It's a war for your CPU dollars, a clash of mighty titans bent on getting their technologies into your computer. Their weapons are little, square pieces of amazing technology designed to make computers do remarkable things.

The war is between the massive, monolithic semiconductor powerhouse Intel and scrappy (relatively) little bulldog AMD. Although they're not the only CPU manufacturers on the planet, they're the only two we care about — they make products for the x86 platform that's ruled what were once called IBM-compatible PCs (now simply PCs) for years. These CPUs are designed for the ultraprominent Windows operating systems.

CPUs are the defining parts of computers. When someone asks what kind of computer you have, chances are you'll lead off with the CPU brand and its frequency or marketing rating. Go ahead, ask me! My first response will be, "Which of my computers are you talking about?" Then, after you point one out, I'll say, "It's an Athlon 64 3800+ with 1GB of PC3200 RAM and blah blah blah." Or, if you point at that one over there, I'll reply, "That monster's a Pentium 4 3.2 GHz. . . ."

The father of Moore's law

CPU technology changes constantly. You've probably heard of Moore's law, but in case you haven't, this forward-thinking guy named Gordon Moore predicted, way back in 1965, that complexity of integrated circuits will double every 18 months. To translate that to modern CPUs, that means CPUs in 2007 will have twice as many *transistors* (the little electrical doodads that make a CPU work) as the number they have now. Although making chips with more transistors is

more expensive, the cost drops as new technology for making them becomes available. Furthermore, as the number of transistors grows, it becomes possible to make transistors smaller, so chips don't actually get bigger.

If you'd like to read the fascinating paper in which Moore made his prediction, head over to www.intel.com/research/silicon/mooreslaw.htm.

The CPU industry is in a constant state of flux (see the nearby sidebar, "The father of Moore's law," for more information). No matter which CPU you buy now, a new technology will replace it within a year or so, if not a matter of months. Not only are CPUs changing, but the technologies surrounding them are in constant motion, too. Today's motherboards have updated buses that yesterday's didn't have; there may be a new way of addressing main memory next year; new processors have bigger or different integrated cache; a new pin array makes it impossible to fit a leading edge CPU in last year's motherboard . . . and on and on.

The first thing I'll say about choosing a CPU for your modded PC is this: Get the most utterly recent, bleeding-edge product you can possibly afford. Get one with all the latest stuff that goes really, really fast. The processor is the flagship component of the computer, and although sometimes you can replace it with a faster model on the same motherboard, you don't want to feel the need to upgrade it six months after you build or upgrade your system.

Now let's take a look at the features that processors have to offer, and what truly separates Intel Pentium 4 CPUs from AMD Athlon models. In this chapter, I concentrate on the very latest in processor technology: Intel's Pentium 4 Extreme Edition with Hyper-Threading Technology and AMD's Athlon 64 and 64 FX CPUs.

What's in a CPU?

A CPU is made up of lots and lots of transistors. A *transistor* is a little metal thing that opens or closes an electrical circuit. When a CPU is operating, its transistors are constantly opening and closing, which is how it does all those calculations that programs need in order to operate. Current CPUs are made up not of hundreds, not of thousands, but of tens or hundreds of millions of transistors.

All those transistors serve various functions within the processor. The two we're most concerned with are the processor core and the integrated cache. Figure 5-27 shows a simple block diagram of an Athlon 64 processor.

The processor core is where all the hard work gets done. If the processor was a big, faceless corporation, the core would be the bean counters — the men and women who do all the financial stuff that makes the company go. Instructions from programs, in the form of *threads,* are channeled to the processor core for calculation, after which the results are shuffled off to the system memory where the program can find it.

A thread is a part of a program in need of processing. Today's CPUs support *multithreading,* meaning programs can send more than one thread to the CPU at the same time, which the CPU can calculate in or out of order.

AMD Athlon 64 Processor Diagram

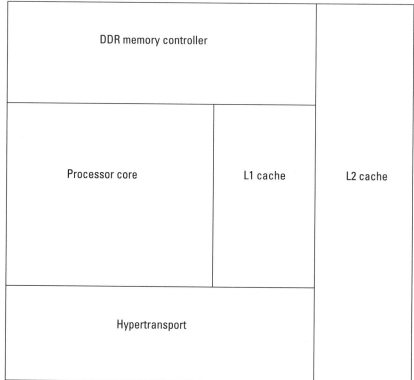

Figure 5-27:
An Athlon 64
block
diagram.

Although working with data in the system's main memory is nice, the CPU has to send its henchmen all the way through the memory bus to the system memory way far away (3 or so inches distant) on the motherboard. Sending data to and from the main memory takes time, and time is the enemy when it comes to processing data efficiently. Wouldn't it be nice if the CPU had its own little memory store right in the chip to work with?

It does! There are several levels of memory called *cache* that sit right there on the CPU. Cache works like this: When the CPU gets data from the main memory to calculate, it figures that the next piece of data it will have to calculate will come right after the first piece of data it has to calculate. Instead of making two trips to the main memory, it takes the next few chunks of data and throws them into cache memory. Then it asks the program what to do next. If the program asks the CPU to work on something already in the cache, it's called a cache hit and the CPU has just saved all the time it would take to shuttle data in from the main memory. The more cache hits the CPU encounters as it putters along, the faster it processes data.

TECHNICAL STUFF

Understanding 32-bit and 64-bit CPUs

Intel and AMD took remarkably different approaches in their handling of the gradual change from 32-bit to 64-bit CPUs. Yet, they're completely compatible with each other at the software-applications level.

With the exception of Athlon 64 CPUs, current processor technology is all 32 bit. Current Windows XP code is written for 32-bit processors. You may have read that the bit width of a CPU determines the width of the chunks of data it can process at the same time. That's not exactly the case. In a move from 32-bit to 64-bit computing, *address fields,* which tell the processor how to find instructions in system memory, would advance from 32 bits to 64 bits. A bit is one binary field — a 0 or a 1. One bit has two possible values. Two bits have four possible values (two bits times two). Higher bit depths increase possible values exponentially.

Because increasing the bit width of the address fields lets processors look for data in scads more memory addresses, the amount of memory that a 64-bit processor can address is substantially higher than 32-bit capability; 32-bit processors can only address 4GB of RAM (and Windows XP's limit is 2GB), while 64-bit processors can theoretically address 16 exabytes (1 exabyte is 1,000 petabytes; 1 petabyte is 1,000 terabytes; 1 terabyte is 1,000 gigabytes). The upcoming 64-bit version of Windows XP will set its memory limit at 16GB with up to 8 terabytes of virtual memory.

Note that the current Athlon 64 generation can "only" address 48 bits of virtual memory — but that's still vastly more address space than a 32-bit processor is capable of.

So why does AMD have 64-bit processors for desktop PCs, while Intel's 64-bit computing solutions are intended only for servers? That's because the two competitors took vastly different strategies in the migration to 64-bit computing.

AMD chose to include a 32-bit compatibility mode, capable of running all software that's written for 32-bit Intel processors, within its 64-bit processors. Because Windows XP is a 32-bit operating system, everything the Athlon 64 processors are running is running in this mode. The reason that it's so much faster than previous AMD processors is because it's a new generation of processor technology — not because it's a 64-bit product. For example, the memory controller — which used to be on the north bridge chip in the motherboard — is now part of the CPU. This substantially decreases the amount of time to get to main memory, improving performance. It won't benefit from its 64-bit nature until it's running 64-bit programs on a 64-bit operating system.

Intel has 64-bit processors available for server environments, called Itanium. But they don't run 32-bit code very well. The company has stuck to offering consumers 32-bit CPUs. It should be noted, however, that for the high-performance workstation market, Intel offers a line of Pentium 4 processors with something called Extended Memory 64 Technology (EM64T), which offers 64-bit memory addressing for applications written for EM64T. The EM64T processors will run the 64-bit edition of Windows XP when that ships in 2005. It's essentially compatible with the 64-bit methodology used by AMD's 64-bit processors. EM64T CPUs will probably eventually be available in consumer PCs in 2005.

The levels of cache are called L1, L2, and, in the case of Pentium 4 Extreme Edition CPUs, L3. The competing processors have different cache configurations. CPUs search L1 cache first, and if the data it's looking for aren't there, it checks the other levels.

AMD Athlon 64 processors have two sets of L1 cache: 64KB for data and 64KB for instructions. For L2 cache, they have a total of 1MB.

Pentium 4 Extreme Edition CPUs have a mere 16KB of L1 cache, 512KB of L2 cache, and a whopping 2MB of L3 cache. The Pentium 4 also has another cache, known as the "trace cache," which stores predecoded instructions that were previously executed.

CPU features

Both AMD and Intel CPUs have a war chest of features, some of which work all the time and others of which are constantly trying to woo the support of application and game developers. They include the following:

- **AMD's HyperTransport technology and integrated memory controller:** I discuss this in the "Demystifying chipsets and buses" section, earlier in this chapter. Basically, it's AMD's technology for communication between the CPU and the rest of the system. Both by both adding an integrated memory controller right on the CPU, and by eliminating other system board buses (by offering a direct link to various components), AMD's Athlon 64 processors greatly increase motherboard data transfer efficiency.

- **AMD's enhanced virus protection for Window XP Service Pack 2:** If you have Window XP Service Pack 2 installed (and you should), your operating system can take advantage of Athlon 64 CPUs' built-in antivirus capabilities. Although it doesn't negate the need for a third-party antivirus program, it provides protection against a very common type of attack called a *buffer overrun attack.*

- **AMD and Intel special instruction sets:** Both AMD and Intel processors not only support the x86 instruction set (which is the operating system's way of knowing exactly what types of calculations a CPU is capable of), but they also have special instructions mostly for multimedia applications. These include MMX, SIMD 1 and 2, Intel's SIMD 3, and AMD's 3DNow!. They allow the processors to crunch data more efficiently, and they include special capabilities for handling multimedia tasks like 3-D graphics.

✔ **Intel's NetBurst architecture:** You may see the term *NetBurst* floating around. NetBurst was the name given to the new CPU architecture Intel introduced with the Pentium 4. The marketing gloss indicated that it made Web surfing that much better — which it did. It was a newer, faster processor. NetBurst architecture is still listed as a feature of the latest Pentium 4 processors.

✔ **Intel's Hyper-Threading Technology (HTT):** Some types of CPUs support multiprocessor technology — on special motherboards, you can mount more than one processor. To get the most out of such setups, both the operating system and the programs running have to specifically support multiprocessing. Intel's Hyper-Threading Technology lets one processor act like two. It actually allows the processor to execute two threads at the same time. It only works in Windows XP and Windows 2000, and it works best with programs designed to use it. Some games (including Medal of Honor: Pacific Assault) were written to take advantage of it.

Matching the CPU to the motherboard

Whether you go with an Athlon 64 FX-53 CPU or a Pentium 4 Extreme Edition 3.4 GHz with HTT, you'll have to ensure that your choice of CPU and motherboard are compatible with each other.

First, they need to physically fit together. There are many flavors of sockets for both the Intel and AMD platforms. AMD currently supports two socket formats: Socket 939 is for their high-end and mainstream CPUs, while socket 754 is for the more budget-conscious systems. Meanwhile, Intel recently switched from Socket mPGA478 to Socket LGA775, while processors for both sockets are still on the market.

I recommend going with the latest socket array (Socket 775 for Intel or Socket 939 for AMD). On the off chance that you decide to upgrade your processor sometime down the line and the new CPUs actually don't require new motherboards (slim chance of that happening, but just in case . . .), you'll be more likely to achieve compatibility.

In addition, the motherboard has to support the CPU in question. Motherboard manufacturers make their products' compatibilities clear on their Web sites, so refer to the list of manufacturers' sites in the "Finding more information about motherboards" section, earlier in this chapter.

Looking at my recommendations

The fastest processors on the planet at the time of this writing are the Athlon 64 FX-53 and the Pentium 4 Extreme Edition 3.4 GHz. The Athlon 64 3800+ doesn't lag very far behind — it, too, is an excellent choice of processor.

If you can't afford one of these, consider a Pentium 4 3.2 or 3.0 GHz with HT support, or an Athlon 64 with a lower designation, such as 3400+.

Spend as much money on a processor as you can possibly afford. You'll actually save money, because you won't need to upgrade as soon.

You should buy a processor in a kit. The kit will include the CPU and a stock cooler. You can upgrade the cooler later if you want to overclock the CPU or just mod the system with an incredible CPU cooler.

Installing a CPU

Popping in a CPU is a simple matter that you can tackle in just a few minutes. Simply follow these steps (being sure to use the static safeguards from Chapter 1):

1. **Locate the CPU socket on your motherboard.**

2. **Look at the socket and at the pins on the bottom of your CPU.**

    Notice the odd corner.

3. **Lift the release lever on the side of the socket.**

4. **Line up the odd corners and drop the CPU into place.**

    You may have to press *very gently* to get it to drop in.

The socket is called a ZIF socket, which stands for Zero Insertion Force. If you have to press any harder than the pressure generated by a gentle breeze, something's wrong. The processor should drop right into place if you have it lined up properly and the socket opened completely. **Do not press hard.** You might bend the pins of the CPU, instantly transforming it into a very expensive paperweight.

If the pins on a CPU do become bent, you can straighten entire rows at a time with a thin piece of hard plastic, like a credit card.

5. **With the CPU in place, lower the socket lever to its locked position (see Figure 5-28).**

Figure 5-28:
A properly
seated CPU.

Now that you've got the processor in place, you need to affix a CPU cooler to it. Look at the bottom of the cooler that came with the CPU. You'll either see bare metal or a thin layer of thermal tape covered by a slip of plastic. If the cooler doesn't have thermal tape, you'll need a small amount of thermal compound, such as Arctic Silver 5.

Super-chilling your CPU

The stock cooler that comes in a CPU kit is sufficient for cooling the CPU — under normal operating circumstances. Modders' need for ultimate speed, however, inspires them to overclock their components to squeeze every ounce of power out of them. If you decide to overclock your CPU, you'll need a better cooler.

I go into cooling in its own separate chapter later on, but CPU cooling is an important mod.

Look for extreme coolers from companies like Thermaltake (www.thermaltake.com) or Arctic Cooling (www.arctic-cooling.com). Make sure you get the right one for your CPU's socket. You'll see features like copper cores (copper is an excellent thermal conductor for drawing heat away from your CPU), high-speed fans, silent fans, and more.

To install the cooler, consult the instructions that came in the CPU kit. There are too many different kinds of stock coolers and mounts to cover here.

You need a layer of thermal transfer between the CPU and the cooler. If the cooler didn't come with thermal tape, spread a thin layer of thermal compound on the top of the CPU before you install the cooler.

Choosing Memory

The third member of the core component trio is the memory. By now you have an idea of what it's for: It's where programs and data are stored pending, or just after, calculation.

The amount and types of memory greatly affect the performance of your system. Faster memory technology allows for more efficient data manipulation. Memory is notorious for being a trouble area in computing. For a while, memory technologies weren't growing as fast as CPU and system bus tech, causing a bottleneck. Groovy new stuff like dual-channel DDR memory and DDR2 have partially alleviated the problem, but memory is still slow enough that CPUs spend time waiting. That's why the L1 and L2 caches still exist on modern CPUs.

Your choice of memory will boil down to what type of RAM your motherboard supports. AMD and Intel are nearly equal when it comes to memory support. Your second decision will be: How much do I need? Windows limits your maximum amount of memory to 2GB, but you don't need that much. For current applications and games, 1GB is plenty.

DDR memory is referred to in two ways: its PC designation and its effective frequency. You'll see the memory called PC<*something*>, such as PC3200 or PC2100. PC2100 memory is also called DDR266 (because it runs at 266 effective MHz). PC2700 is also called DDR333, and PC3200 is called DDR400.

Understanding current memory technologies

Memory comes in sticklike modules called DIMMs (see Figure 5-29).

DIMMs are very susceptible to static discharge so be careful when you handle them.

Figure 5-29:
A pair of
DIMMs.

Memory, like other components, is rated in terms of frequency. Current memory runs at frequencies of 200 MHz or more, and that rating is effectively doubled by technology used in DDR memory.

Today's motherboards support a type of memory called DDR SDRAM. DDR stands for *double data rate,* and SDRAM stands for *synchronous dynamic random access memory.* Don't worry so much about what SDRAM means — for our purposes, it just means memory.

DDR is the more interesting of the two acronyms. Double data rate means that memory is able to transfer data twice for each of its clock cycles. This effectively doubles its usefulness compared to single data rate RAM. All current motherboard and CPU combinations support DDR memory.

Newer DDR2 memory is similar to DDR except it's capable of reaching much higher clock frequencies. Intel has embraced DDR2 and some Pentium 4 boards support DDR2 memory as fast as 533 effective MHz. AMD, for now, is sticking to plain old DDR.

Another technology enhancement is called dual-channel technology. This isn't a type of memory, but rather a motherboard capability. Dual-channel technology only works if memory modules are installed in like pairs rather than in a single module. Dual-channel technology effectively doubles the memory's bandwidth by making it possible to send two streams of data to and from the memory simultaneously. Only certain motherboards support dual-channel technology.

Whether or not your motherboard is dual-channel capable, I recommend purchasing pairs of memory rather than single modules. For instance, if you want 1GB of memory for your system, buy two 512MB modules. I do this because, on the off chance that something catastrophic happens to one of my memory modules, I can remove the defective module and still be able to use the computer.

Before you buy memory, check out your motherboard manual to find out how much memory it supports, which types it supports, and its supported configurations. Motherboards support different combinations of memory in the various DIMM sockets, so make sure you use a supported configuration. If possible, avoid DIMM modules that have chips on both sides of the module circuit board.

Installing memory

Memory is just as easy to install as a CPU. Simply follow these steps:

1. **Look at your memory module and then look at the socket.**

   Notice the notch on the module and the bump in the socket.

2. **Locate and open the clips on either side of the target socket.**

3. **Line up the notch on the DIMM with the bump in the socket.**

4. **Slide the DIMM between the socket clips so that it's perpendicular to the motherboard.**

5. **When you encounter resistance, press down with uniform pressure along the top edge of the module.**

   The DIMM will snap into place and the clips should close by themselves.

6. **Make sure the memory is seated firmly and completely, as shown in Figure 5-30.**

Memory recommendations

There are plenty of manufacturers of computer memory, and most of them offer quality parts. Two that I've had the best luck with in terms of physical quality and performance are Crucial and Corsair. You see modules from one or the other of them pictured in most of the photos that feature memory in this book. Both offer generous warranties, terrific service, and the best memory money can buy. High-quality memory is especially important if you plan on overclocking your PC.

That's not to say that other companies don't boast quality. Mushkin and Viking, in particular, are well recommended by many of my colleagues.

Figure 5-30:
A properly
seated
DIMM.

Avoid generic memory, however. If it's not a brand you've heard of, or if you notice modules priced amazingly cheap compared to name-brand memory, chances are it's of inferior quality. I've had cheap memory go belly up on me within a year after purchase. Beware — if a price on memory seems too good to be true, it probably is.

Chapter 6

Adding Eye-Popping Visuals: The Graphics Card

In This Chapter

▶ Picking out a graphics card

▶ Looking at 3-D graphics features

▶ Introducing AGP and PCI Express

▶ APIs, GPUs, and graphics cards

▶ Importing and exporting video

▶ Installing the graphics card

*B*elieve it or not, your system won't even boot without a graphics card. That makes sense, because a computer's supposed to be interactive, and you can't interact with it if it can't show you what's going on. If you don't believe me, turn off your monitor in the middle of a harrowing game of Unreal Tournament 2004. You'll hear yourself get blown away by some lucky combatant who stumbled upon a blind enemy.

No, your computer is useless without a graphics card, but the graphics card is so much more than just a window into your computer's soul. Its graphics processing unit (GPU) is solely responsible for crunching the mad calculations that make up 3-D graphics used in games. And games, after all, are the reason computers exist.

Your choice of graphics card also affects other display factors, such as the ability to pipe graphics to a television; multiple-display support; and importing and exporting video from camcorders, VCRs, and other video equipment.

Just as two major players dominate the CPU industry, two graphics chip makers are constantly vying for superiority — not to mention your money. They are ATI and NVIDIA. Both make excellent products. Both are worthy of your money-lovin'. Both make parts that hit a wide variety of price points, from a lofty $500 or more down to sub-$100. Competition is a good thing!

In this chapter, I tear into the world of graphics cards and tell you exactly what you need to know to get the best one for your situation.

What Is a Graphics Card?

Graphics cards are circuit boards with various bits of amazing electronics on them. The board itself has two elements you'll be interested in (in most cases, they're covered with a big cooler — like CPUs, GPUs run hot):

- ✔ The graphics processing unit (GPU), the chip located centrally on the board.

- ✔ The other large chips on the card, which make up the graphics card's memory bank.

Figure 6-1 shows a diagram of a graphics card.

The metal gate that fits in the back of the CPU's chassis (shown in Figure 6-2) contains the graphics card's external ports. You're likely to see three major types of ports:

- ✔ A 15-pin VGA port for connecting the graphics card to traditional display devices

- ✔ A little, round TV-out port for displaying graphics on a television

- ✔ A white DVI port, which is designed to interface with digital displays like some current LCD monitors

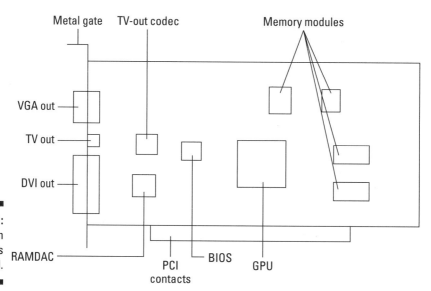

Diagram of a typical VGA graphics card

Figure 6-1:
A diagram of a graphics card.

In many cases, graphics cards come with a DVI-to-VGA adapter so you can use two VGA displays at the same time.

Figure 6-2:
The rear gate of a video card with external connectors.

Some graphics cards feature Video-In/Video-Out (VIVO) ports for importing and exporting video. Some even go far beyond that: ATI's All-In-Wonder series of graphics cards are designed around video editing and digital video recorder (DVR) functions.

The graphics market, in all its forms, is comprised of a number of companies making all kinds of gadgetry, but the bulk of the action has boiled down to competition between two major players. If you're even thinking of adding a new graphics card to your machine, you'll want to go with a part based on technology from ATI or NVIDIA.

ATI and NVIDIA make graphics processors and chipsets. Both companies then sell this technology to other companies that produce the actual card you buy. ATI also makes cards of its own to sell to you, whereas NVIDIA does not; it relies on card manufacturers to sell its GPU technology to the public.

To ensure compatibility between Windows, 3-D games, and graphics chips, chip manufacturers and software developers conform to application programming interfaces (APIs). An API is a set of rules and specifications that guide software developers and hardware makers to create compatible products. The two 3-D graphics APIs are Microsoft's Direct3D (part of the DirectX suite of multimedia APIs for Windows) and OpenGL. The latest version of DirectX is 9.0c, while OpenGL is hovering at version 1.5.

ATI and NVIDIA GPUs are made to accelerate code that comes through those APIs. That way, they don't have to worry about building in compatibility for individual programs and operating systems. Similarly, game writers build their graphics engines around one or both of these APIs and, therefore, don't have to worry about building in compatibility for every individual GPU on the market.

Besides ensuring compatibility, graphics APIs also define a range of features that board manufacturers can support and that game developers can take advantage of. Features include such things as bump mapping, pixel shading, and dynamic lighting.

Try to buy a graphics card with a GPU that supports the latest version of DirectX. Not all GPUs on the market support all the features in DirectX 9, and games are in development that will make full use of those features. A GPU that can't handle the new features either has to render them in software, greatly degrading the game's frame rate, or, if possible, turn them off, which leaves you out of seeing the latest in gaming technology. Most games can detect the graphics card type and will run using older methods of rendering. The visuals you get probably won't look as good as they may with a high-end card.

Understanding How Your Graphics Card Affects Your Gaming

Graphics cards are designed to display what your computer is doing on a monitor, but they do so much more than that. The strength of a GPU can be judged with the most purity by playing games. GPUs are full of features designed around displaying 3-D graphics, and there's no better source of 3-D graphics than a good computer game.

The fluidity of game animation can be quantified in what is known as the game's *frame rate*. Game animation is just like any other form of animation (like Disney movies and flipbooks): It's made up of still images flashed in rapid succession, creating the illusion of motion.

Gauging your graphics card's performance

If you're a gamer, you've got a vested interest in the performance of your graphics card. While the CPU, motherboard, and memory are important factors in game performance, perhaps no part other than the graphics card truly affects how high you can crank the visuals and still expect a smooth gaming experience.

You can gauge the performance of a graphics card in two ways:

- ✔ Simple observation
- ✔ Benchmarking

Simple observation

The most obvious way to gauge your graphics card's performance is through simple observation. If a game is ticking along at a good frame rate, the animation will be smooth and pleasing and the game will respond accurately to input from a mouse, keyboard, or game controller.

Signs that a graphics card is having trouble animating a title include choppy animation that, instead of giving you the illusion of motion, jumps from one frame to the next. This is often accompanied by poor responsiveness to controls. You'll probably notice more problems when lots of objects and character models are on the screen at the same time; the more the GPU has to process, the slower the results.

Benchmarking

You can also gauge performance by testing a 3-D card's muscle through the process known as *benchmarking*. Most benchmarks put a GPU through its paces by making it display a prerecorded snippet of 3-D animation, usually called a *demo*. The benchmark routine keeps track of the *frame rate* at which the demo is displayed. Frame rate is simply how many 3-D still images, or frames, the card displays in one second. The higher the frame rate, the smoother the animation, but there's a law of diminishing returns: Although you can easily tell the difference between frame rates at the low end (say, between 10 frames per second [fps] and 20 fps), when frame rates reach 60 fps it's hard to discern a difference between frame rates higher than that (say, between 70 fps and 90 fps).

There are two types of benchmarks:

- ✔ **Synthetic benchmarks:** These aren't actual games, but they display gamelike environments to gauge frame rate.
- ✔ **Real-world benchmarks:** These are integrated into some 3-D games.

Most real-world benchmarks only gauge frame rate, while synthetic benchmarks measure all kinds of stuff, like how many polygons and textures the GPU can process at the same time and how well it handles advanced processing features like lighting and shading effects.

Comparing benchmarks with your friends is fun. A great time to run benchmarks is before upgrading the graphics card, and then after. You'll have quantifiable results of your labor.

Synthetic benchmarks

The most popular synthetic benchmark is called 3DMark05 and you can download it from www.futuremark.com. 3DMark05 uses environments inspired by actual games to test the GPU's muscle (see Figure 6-3). It also packs visual quality tests, 3-D feature tests, 3-D sound tests, a CPU benchmark, and much more. Its results are broken down into many categories. It'll spit out a score, in 3D Marks, of your system's performance. You can dig deeper than that, though, to check out the frame rates at which the game environments were animated, to check how the card did with 3-D feature tests, and so on.

Real-world benchmarks

Real games can also be used for benchmarking, too. Doom 3, Halo, Far Cry, Quake III Arena, and a host of others contain built-in benchmark capability for running a gameplay demo and gauging its average frame rate. Each game has its own protocols for benchmarking a system. I don't have the space to cover every game that can be used for benchmarking, but in this section, I cover a couple of those titles.

Figure 6-3:
A 3DMark05
game envi-
ronment.

For accurate results, you'll have to turn off a feature called Flip on VSYNC, or just VSYNC for short. VSYNC stands for vertical synchronization, and it tells games not to generate frames of animation faster than your monitor's refresh rate. If your system is capable of running a game faster than your monitor's refresh rate, any frame rates beyond that will get cut off. For example, if your monitor's refresh rate is 75 Hz, you can't run a benchmark faster than 75 fps, even if your system was capable of running it at 90 fps. Turn off VSYNC both within games' graphical options pages, and in your graphics card's driver options utility (explained in the "Messing with Your Graphics Card's Features" section, later in this chapter).

Doom 3 is really easy to use as a benchmark. Just follow these steps:

1. **Start the game.**

2. **Go into the system menu and set the game up with the visual options you want.**

3. **Exit to the main menu and press Ctrl+Alt+` (that's next to the 1 on the keyboard).**

    This brings down the Doom 3 command line console, as shown in Figure 6-4.

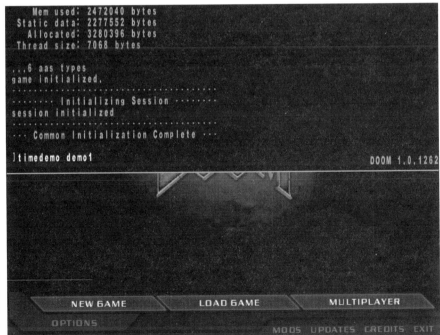

Mem used: 2472040 bytes
Static data: 2277552 bytes
Allocated: 3280396 bytes
Thread size: 7068 bytes

...6 aas types
game initialized.
....
.... Initializing Session ....
session initialized
....
... Common Initialization Complete ...

]timedemo demo1   DOOM 1.0.1262

Figure 6-4:
The Doom 3
console.

4. Type in the words timedemo demo1 **and press Enter.**

Doom 3 executes a demo and, when it's finished, it displays a box telling you the frame rate at which your computer managed to run the demo (see Figure 6-5).

Benchmarking Halo is equally simple. Just follow these steps:

1. Launch the game.

2. Set the graphics options to the configuration you want to test.

3. Exit the game.

4. Choose Start ⇨ Run, and click Browse.

5. Navigate to C:\Program Files\Microsoft Games\Halo **(or whatever directory you installed the game into) and click Halo.exe.**

6. Click OK.

The path to the game executable will appear in the Open field.

7. Place the cursor at the end of the path, outside the quotation marks, and type -timedemo.

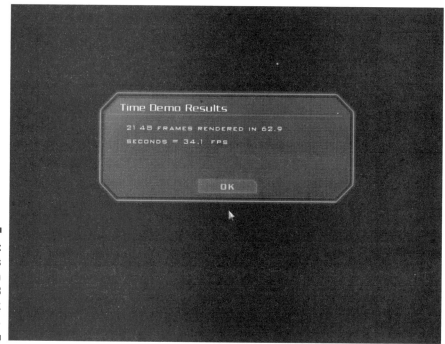

Figure 6-5:
The results
from a
Doom 3
benchmark
test.

8. Click OK.

Halo loads and executes a demo (see Figure 6-6). When it's done, the game will exit. You'll find the results in a file called timedemo.txt in the Halo directory; navigate to it with Windows Explorer.

Many more games lend themselves to benchmarking systems. Check out hardware review sites to see what games reviewers are using, and then search the Web for instructions to benchmark your own system with them.

Tweaking your games: Frame rate versus image quality

3-D games are almost always *scalable.* They let you tweak their animation settings to speed up frame rates or to increase image quality. Unfortunately, increasing one degrades the other. Playing games requires a constant balance of power: You want the game to look its best, but at the same time you want your GPU to animate it smoothly.

Figure 6-6:
A shot of
the Halo
benchmark.

Doom 3, for example, has several options you can tweak in its system menu (refer to Figure 6-7). It's a good representative sample of a game's scaling capability. Let's look at some of the options you can tweak in Doom 3:

- **Screen size:** This is the display resolution. Higher settings result in crisper-looking scenes at the cost of frame rates.

- **Video quality:** You can let Doom 3 scan your hardware and set this option to what it feels is a good level, or you can set it yourself. It has four settings: Low, Medium, High, and Ultra. The settings affect the crispness of the textures in the game and the quality of the light maps (lighting applied to textures).

- **High-quality special effects:** This setting can be set to Yes or No. It affects various effects like halos around light sources and other little tidbits. Turning it on results in more-realistic image quality, while turning it off results in higher frame rates.

- **Enable shadows:** This, too, is a binary setting that can be turned on or off. Turning it on will cause objects in the game to cast realistic shadows at the cost of frame rates.

- **Enable specular:** Set to yes, this setting causes shiny objects in the game to take on a reflective-looking surface, increasing realism at the cost of frame rates.

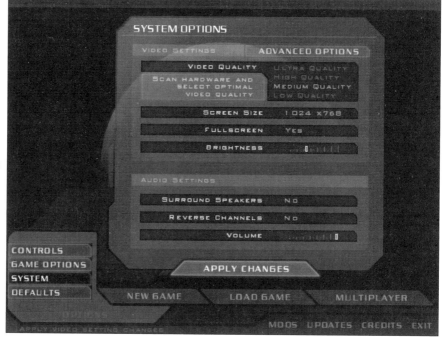

Figure 6-7:
This page in Doom 3's system menu shows various image-quality tweaks.

✔ **Enable bump maps:** *Bump maps* are extra textures that can be applied to polygons to give them a 3-D appearance, with depth and more realistic lighting. Turning on this setting results in cooler textures but degrades frame rates.

✔ **Antialiasing:** I'll explain what this is under "Graphical features" in this chapter. You can set it to different levels: 2X, 4X, and higher. The higher the setting, the crisper the visuals look, but it levels a serious hit on performance.

Finding the sweet spot between image quality and playable frame rates takes a good deal of experimentation. More-powerful GPUs allow you to turn on and ramp up more image detail settings while still getting away with smooth animation, while weaker GPUs require you to make visual sacrifices to achieve decent frame rates.

The Graphics Card as Media Center

Take a break from gaming for a while and check out what else graphics cards can do. Two competing lines of graphics products, ATI's All-In-Wonder brand (shown in Figure 6-8) and NVIDIA's Personal Cinema (shown in Figure 6-9), allow you to transform the PC into a viable part of your home theater.

Figure 6-8:
An ATI All-In-Wonder product.

ATI Technologies

Figure 6-9:
An NVIDIA
Personal
Cinema
product.

Using one of these versatile products (personally, I recommend the All-In-Wonder line), you can pipe your television signal right through your computer. You can enable your computer to act like a TiVO, recording, pausing, rewinding, and fast-forwarding live TV. You can view interactive TV guides and schedule the taping of shows while you're away. They both come with remote controls, so you don't have to worry about sitting at a table with a mouse to control these functions. Using dual-display technology, you can keep your TV on while using the computer for other things.

Moreover, these products are also targeted at people who want to edit video. Both come with video-in and video-out connectors, and they also include software video editing suites. With them, you can import video from your camcorder, cut out the boring parts, add a soundtrack, add titles, add transition effects, and burn the results to a writeable DVD or pipe it out to your VCR and record it on a videotape.

The only downside regarding these PC theater products is that, in order to watch TV and record shows unattended, the computer must stay on all the time. Being able to turn the PC off when you're not around would be nice. Thankfully, computers don't use too much electricity, so you won't see a massive increase in your utility bill if you buy an All-In-Wonder.

Decoding Graphics Card Features

Both ATI and NVIDIA build their GPUs to support as many API features and other tricks as possible. They give their support for such features glossy names that sound really tough and appealing. Although the two companies are at each other's throats, constantly vying for superiority, their products are actually quite similar from a functional point of view.

Physical features

A number of graphics card features have very little to do with API support. Some define the capabilities of the card, while others are nice little extras that you may or may not use:

- ✔ **The memory interface:** Rated in bit width — modern graphics cards range from 64-bit memory interfaces to 256-bit — this determines how much data can travel back and forth from the GPU to the local memory concurrently. A wider memory interface yields better performance.

- ✔ **The amount of memory:** In 3-D game acceleration, textures tend to take up huge amounts of memory. Being able to store them in memory right on the graphics card (local memory) is always best, because if the GPU has to address the PC's main memory for textures, it'll result in a bit of lag. Get as much onboard memory as possible.

- ✔ **APG 8X and PCI Express X16 (see Figure 6-10):** These two data buses are designed to give a graphics card direct access to the PC's main memory to store texture data that it can't fit in local memory. Get whichever your motherboard is designed to handle. PCI Express X16 features a faster pipeline than AGP 8X, but at this point there's little difference in game performance between the two.

- ✔ **NVIDIA's SLI Multi GPU technology:** SLI stands for *Scalable Link Interface.* NVIDIA GeForce 6800 cards have the ability to work in pairs, as long as they're both mounted in PCI X16 slots on the same motherboard. By linking two GeForce 6800–based cards together, you can achieve a huge boost in 3-D performance. It comes at a price, however: GeForce 6800 cards are expensive, not to mention the fact that you'll have to find a motherboard with two PCI Express X16 slots.

- ✔ **TV-out:** Most graphics cards have a circular port on the back for S-video and/or composite video TV-out. With it, you can pump your Windows desktop, applications, and games to a television. Why buy an Xbox to play games on TV when you can do it with your far superior PC?

- ✔ **Multi-display technology:** NVIDIA calls it Nview, and ATI calls it Hydravision. Nearly all graphics cards can support two displays at once. This can include any combination that the card is physically capable of, including two VGA monitors, a VGA and a DVI monitor, a VGA device and a TV, and many other combinations. With multidisplay technology, you can mirror the two displays, you can stretch the Windows desktop across the two, you can show one application on one display while showing something else on the other, you can watch a DVD movie on your TV while crunching a spreadsheet on a VGA monitor, and much more.

Figure 6-10:
An AGP 8X graphics card (above) and a PCI Express X16 card (below). Notice the difference in the location of the gold contacts.

Graphical features

ATI and NVIDIA both support a number of graphical features, some defined in DirectX and others that are just handy to have:

- ✔ **Video acceleration:** Both ATI and NVIDIA have built-in support for various types of video files (like MPEG files) and for DVD video or HDTV.

- ✔ **Antialiasing:** This technology removes the jagged look (see Figure 6-11) from the edges of pixels and textures. Antialiasing uses samples of the textures surrounding jagged edges to smooth them out (see Figure 6-12). The more samples used, the better and sharper the antialiasing comes out — at the expense of frames per second. NVIDIA calls its antialiasing technology Intellisample, and ATI calls its Smoothvision.

Figure 6-11:
This screen-shot isn't antialiased.

Figure 6-12:
This screen-
shot is
antialiased.
See a
difference?

Also part of the Intellisample and Smoothvision features is something called *anisotropic filtering.* As textures move farther away from your point of view, they diminish in detail in a process called *MIP mapping.* Anisotropic filtering makes the transitions smooth and keeps objects in the distance sharp. Turning up this setting hurts performance, however.

✔ **Programmable pixel shaders:** These are used to make uber-realistic lighting effects. The GPUs allow developers to write their own lighting and shading routines, and the shadows are processed per pixel. A *pixel* is the smallest chunk that makes up a texture — basically, it's a dot. Old shading techniques either used light maps or per-polygon shading, which looked unnatural. Per-pixel shading is far more realistic. ATI calls its programmable pixel shader technology Smartshader, while NVIDIA calls it CineFX.

Without getting supertechnical and delving into the mysterious voodoo that is the 3-D graphics pipeline (discussing that would add another 50 pages to this chapter), let me just say that both graphics cards support all previous features that were once heavily touted, like texture mapping, MIP mapping, bump mapping, trilinear filtering, perspective correction, and so on. If you don't know what those are, don't worry. You don't need to.

Similarly, there's a lot going on behind the scenes on any given graphics card. Cards are rated by how fast they can apply textures (called *fill rate*), how many textures they can apply during each pass, how many rendering pipelines and geometry engines they contain, and all kinds of other technical gobbledygook. The bottom line is real-world frame rate performance: All those technologies are great, but you're more concerned with how well graphics cards can animate 3-D games. Eyes on the prize!

Messing with Your Graphics Card's Features

Just as you can fiddle around with the graphics settings in most 3-D games, you can override certain functionality by adjusting settings right in the graphics card's driver control applet. To navigate to the display setting page:

1. **Right-click in an area of the desktop away from any icons.**

2. **Select Properties.**

3. **Select the Settings tab.**

4. **Click the Advanced button.**

   The ATI and NVIDIA control applets look a bit different (see Figures 6-13 and 6-14).

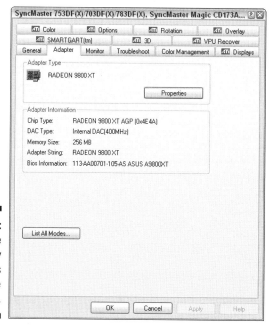

Figure 6-13:
A tab in the ATI display settings page collection.

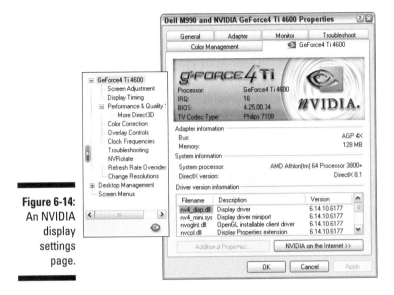

Figure 6-14:
An NVIDIA
display
settings
page.

Using ATI's driver control applet as an example, I'll take you through what settings you can tweak. The driver option applet has many tabs. The tab we're concerned with is called 3D. Select the 3D tab (see Figure 6-15).

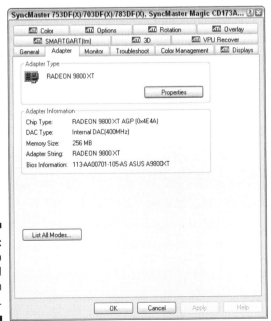

Figure 6-15:
The 3D tab
of the ATI
driver option
applet.

Core and memory clock frequencies

Just as CPUs and main PC memory are rated in clock frequencies, so are graphics cards core chipsets and local memory. The numbers aren't widely advertised, but they often make up the difference between cards of the same family. For example, ATI's Radeon X800 Pro and X800 XT are very similar cards. Besides some architectural differences, one of the key differences is that the X800 XT's core chipset and memory clocks run at 500 MHz, while the X800 Pro's core and memory clocks hum along at 475 MHz and 450 MHz respectively.

Overclocking a graphics card is very easy. It's usually just a simple matter of moving graphical sliders in a software application window!

I get into the ins and outs of overclocking in Chapter 15.

The operating frequencies of a graphics card's core and memory directly affect gaming performance. The faster the frequencies, the faster the frame rates. However, faster frequencies often result in higher priced hardware, and graphics cards are expensive components.

Note that, like motherboards, current graphics cards use DDR memory. DDR stands for *double data rate,* and it means that the memory transfers data twice each clock cycle — doubling its performance over single data rate memory.

At the top of the window, you can choose to tweak the settings of Direct3D or OpenGL. A simple slider lets you choose quality versus performance; if you use it, it will tweak the various options for you. You can also tweak them yourself by selecting the Use Custom Settings check box and clicking the Custom button. You'll see a window like the one shown in Figure 6-16.

At the top of the window, you can either leave antialiasing and anisotropic filtering set to Application Preference (meaning the game or 3-D application settings will determine whether to use these features) or force them to be used at the levels you desire.

Farther down, you'll see two image-quality settings, Texture Preference and Mipmap Detail Level. You can tweak them for speed or quality. The Texture Preference option makes in-game textures sharper, while the Mipmap Detail Level affects how crisply distant textures are drawn.

Next is Wait for Vertical Sync, which I explain in a Tip a little while ago. Finally, ATI cards have an option called Trueform, which makes terrain and character, and other 3-D models more realistic looking.

NVIDIA's ForceWare (which is what NVIDIA calls its drivers) control panel offers comparable options.

TIP

Mod down the noise

In most cases, the GPU cooler that comes with your graphics card will help your board survive the rigors of overclocking. However, many such coolers are loud. Third-party GPU coolers are available, like the Arctic Cooling VGA Silencer (`www.arctic-cooling.com/en/products/vga_silencer/`). This cool cooler lets you adjust it for maximum silence or maximum cool.

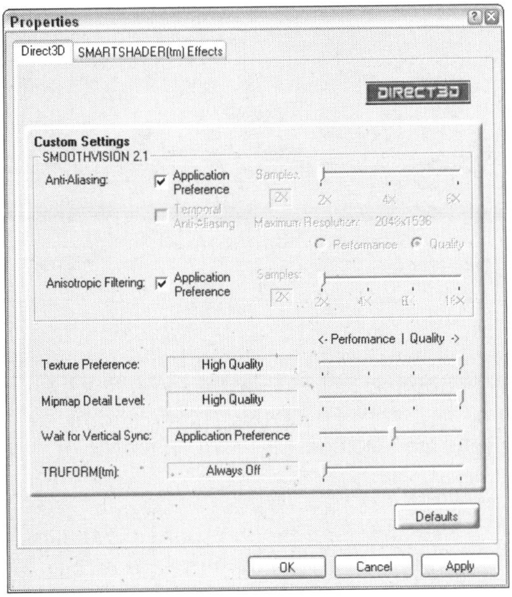

Figure 6-16:
Customizing ATI's driver settings.

Choosing a Graphics Card

Before you decide just which graphics card to buy, you need to know a ton of information. The industry is full of jargon and glossy terms invented by PR departments for various features. And features — there are a ton of them!

Pick a GPU, decide on the features you really want, and then shop for a board by price. Various GPUs are available for a wide array of prices, with the most expensive aimed at performance-hungry PC enthusiasts and gamers. In general, more money means more muscle. More-expensive graphics cards will display game animation more smoothly and support more 3-D features, making games both more playable and realistic looking. A GPU is shown in Figure 6-17.

Figure 6-17:
A graphics
card GPU.

In choosing a graphics card, you have a lot of stuff to consider. Of primary importance is its 3-D animation muscle. Virtually all graphics cards do an excellent job with mundane 2-D stuff, like displaying Windows screens and applications, but 3-D performance separates strong, muscular GPUs from wimpy poseurs.

You need a graphics card to match your motherboard's graphics bus, whether it's AGP or PCI Express. You should pick a graphics card with as much local memory as you can afford — current cards come with 128MB and even 256MB of memory. And these are just a few considerations you'll have to bear in mind when you make your choice.

Rounding up the GPUs

Here's a look at a cross-section of the current crop of graphics GPUs available at the time of this writing. I don't list price points because they change so rapidly, but you can check price comparison sites, like Pricewatch (www. pricewatch.com), and online shops like the gamer's favorite Newegg.com (www.newegg.com). Search by the name of the GPU in question.

I break the data up into three tables. Table 6-1 represents the latest, most cutting-edge, and most expensive GPUs. Get one of these and you won't have to upgrade for a long time. If your wallet can't take the heat, check out the midrange GPUs listed in Table 6-2. They're still powerful, but they may bog down a little on newer games with advanced graphics engines like Doom 3 and Half-Life 2.

If you're an enthusiast, I don't recommend going with one of the mainstream GPUs in Table 6-3, but if you don't care too much about 3-D graphics they're worth considering. They can handle most games with the detail levels turned down, but I wouldn't try running current titles with 4X antialiasing and 16X anisotropic filtering. The poor card would crawl out of your system and beg for mercy.

All these cards are DirectX 9–compliant, have dual display support, and feature TV-out and DVI connectors.

Table 6-1	Cutting-Edge GPUs			
GPU	*Amount of Memory*	*Memory Interface*	*Core Clock Frequency*	*Memory Clock Frequency**
ATI Radeon X800 Pro	256MB	256-bit	475 MHz	900 MHz
ATI Radeon X800 XT	256MB	256-bit	500 MHz	1,000 MHz
NVIDIA GeForce 6800 GT	256MB	256-bit	350 MHz	1,000 MHz
NVIDIA GeForce 6800 Ultra	256MB	256-bit	400 MHz	1,100 MHz

Effective DDR frequency

Table 6-2	Midrange GPUs			
GPU	*Amount of Memory*	*Memory Interface*	*Core Clock Frequency*	*Memory Clock Frequency**
ATI Radeon 9800	256MB	256-bit	325 MHz	580 MHz
ATI Radeon 9800 XT	256MB	256-bit	412 MHz	730 MHz
ATI X700 series	256MB	128-bit	425	430

(continued)

Table 6-2 (continued)

GPU	Amount of Memory	Memory Interface	Core Clock Frequency	Memory Clock Frequency*
NVIDIA GeForce 6800	128MB	256-bit	325 MHz	1,000 MHz
NVIDIA GeForce FX 5900	256MB	256-bit	400 MHz	850 MHz
NVIDIA GeForce FX 5950 Ultra	256MB	256-bit	475 MHz	950 MHz

*Effective DDR frequency

Table 6-3 — **Mainstream GPUs**

GPU	Amount of Memory	Memory Interface	Core Clock Frequency	Memory Clock Frequency*
ATI Radeon 9600	128MB	128-bit	325 MHz	400 MHz
ATI Radeon 9600 XT	128MB	128-bit	500 MHz	600 MHz
NVIDIA GeForce FX 5700	128MB	128-bit	425 MHz	900 MHz

*Effective DDR memory

Which GPU is for you?

Ultimately, the decision of which GPU to get is up to you. I've worked extensively with both ATI and NVIDIA products, and both companies offer excellent performance, stellar driver support, tons of power, and terrific image quality. The two companies' constant attempts to one-up each other results in new features that you may or may not care about.

Read reviews on enthusiast sites around the Web. Some of my favorites are the following:

- ✔ Gamer's Depot (www.gamers-depot.com)
- ✔ Tom's Hardware Guide (www.tomshardware.com)

✔ AnandTech (www.anandtech.com)

✔ Hot Hardware (www.hothardware.com)

Check out magazines like *Computer Gaming World, PC Gamer,* and *MaximumPC.* Watch game news sites like Blues News (www.bluesnews.com) for announcements of new reviews around the Web. Most reviews feature comparative benchmarks as well as analysis of feature sets.

Figure out how much money you have to spend and research the prices of current GPUs. Then compare prices of final market graphics cards featuring the GPU of your choice. You're safe buying just about any brand because the GPU makers are fairly stringent regarding their specifications. One board based on a particular GPU will perform almost identically with another board based on the same GPU. The biggest difference from one graphics card to the next is the color of the circuit board and the GPU and RAM cooler.

There are dozens of board manufacturers, way too many to go over here, but I can tell you some of my favorites:

✔ ATI (as the source of its own GPUs, it makes excellent graphics cards; www.ati.com)

✔ Crucial (a company know for its memory products; www.crucial.com)

✔ ASUS (www.asus.com)

✔ PNY (www.pny.com)

✔ Elsa (www.elsa.com)

✔ MSI (www.msicomputer.com)

✔ Leadtek (www.leadtek.com)

Chapter 7

Giving Your PC a Voice of Its Own: The Sound Card

· ·

· ·

*Y*our computer has a lot to say! Imagine having your mouth taped shut when you step up to the podium to do a reading at a wedding. The way you'd feel right then is how your computer feels without a good sound card. A PC's internal speaker (often referred to as a *squeaker*) can spit out measly beeps and boops, but for realistic, enveloping sound, you need the right gear.

Your computer's sound card determines the quality of all the audio it reproduces, and that's especially true in games. As I discuss in this chapter, a number of standards are used in games to make the in-game sounds enveloping and realistic. Your choice of a sound card determines the standards with which your PC is compatible.

Furthermore, your choice of sound card directly affects your selection of speaker systems with which to fit your rig. Sound cards support four, five, or even seven *satellite speakers* (the little speakers that you place on your desk, as opposed to the bass-oriented subwoofer, which usually gets placed on the floor). Most office-type environments call for a simple pair of satellites, while a monster modded gaming rig should have front and rear speakers for enough noise to shake your house off its foundation.

Meeting the Contenders

By far, the most popular sound cards in the world are the Creative Labs SoundBlaster products. SoundBlaster has been around since the PC was a novelty and the term *modding* had no meaning. To this day, SoundBlaster cards offer more features and support more 3-D standards than any other sound card. Creative Labs likes to pack its products with goodies galore. If there were room in a computer for a kitchen sink, the SoundBlaster line would come with one. Figure 7-1 shows a typical sound card.

Figure 7-1:
The Turtle Beach Catalina resembles most other sound cards. It may look boring, but it sounds terrific.

In the following sections, I let you know what all this stuff means so you'll be well armed with a battery of information when you're ready to select a sound card.

In this book, I tend to leave the final decision of which product to buy up to you — I just try to arm you with the information necessary to make an informed decision. However, I'm going to break from that philosophy here: I heartily recommend Creative Labs SoundBlaster Audigy 2 internal sound cards. They come in various price points, and they're all capable of the best PC audio and the most supported APIs. Games use EAX Advanced HD, and the Audigy line has the only cards that support it. That's not to say other cards are poor contenders. For example, the Turtle Beach cards have the best wave table support (see "MIDI/wave table support" later in this chapter for more info), so if you're more into writing your own MIDI compositions than gaming, check out the Santa Cruz.

Feature Soup: Understanding the Jargon

At some point, you're going to walk into a computer store or navigate your browser to a shopping site and price out a sound card. At that time, you'll be bombarded with feature lists and specification sheets that tell you stuff like the sound card's sample rate, its API (short for *application program interface*) support, and its reaction to kryptonite. All you care about is getting the absolute best sound card worthy of a high-powered, modded system. I can help.

Speaker compatibility: How many do you want?

When you see something that refers to sound card speaker compatibility, or speaker system specs, they include numbers like 5.1, 6.1, or 7.1. The number *before* the period indicates the number of satellite speakers; the .1 means a subwoofer for the low, or bass, tones. Thus, a sound card capable of driving 5.1 speakers would be ready for a speaker system with five little (or big) speakers, and one subwoofer.

Pardon me? You're only using two speakers? How very 20th century of you! When you see a movie in the theater, you're surrounded by speakers built into the walls all around you. When you listen to jams in your car, there are usually speakers built into the dash, the doors, and the rear panel. When you play a DVD in your home theater system, it's designed to take advantage of 5.1 systems. Similarly, computer audio has burst forth into the realm of the third dimension. The market is flooded with solid, high-quality sound cards that support four, five, and seven satellite speakers to envelop you in sound from all sides.

If you use your computer for gaming or watching movies, you owe it to yourself to check out the amazing experience of audio coming from all around you. Although there are 3-D audio tricks that can make noises sound like they're coming from all around you through a pair of speakers, they're imperfect. Multiple speakers rule for positional audio.

A note about motherboard audio

Most PC motherboards have some sort of onboard audio, either in the form of a mere codec (requiring the CPU to do the audio calculations) or in the form of audio processors. The current crop of sound cards tends to perform better and create more pleasing audio than anything I've heard from onboard audio. I suggest you turn it off in the BIOS and go with a sound card.

Nearly all of today's sound cards support lots of speakers. Generally speaking, the more speakers with which your rig is equipped, the more convincing the surround-sound effects.

Don't worry if the sound card you're eyeing supports more speakers than you actually own or plan to buy; you can tweak the settings of the sound card to use any number of speakers. For instance, if you own a four-satellite speaker system, you can still use a sound card that supports seven satellites; you simply tell it how many speakers you're using through its control application, and it takes care of the rest.

Here's how to tweak the speaker settings through the Windows XP multimedia properties sheet:

1. **Choose Start➪Control Panel.**

2. **Click Sound, Speech, and Audio Devices.**

3. **Click Change the Sound Scheme.**

   The Sounds and Audio Devices Properties window appears.

4. **Select the Volume tab.**

5. **Under Speaker Settings, click the Advanced button.**

   The Advanced Audio Properties window appears.

6. **In the Speaker Setup drop-down list, select the option that describes your setup (see Figure 7-2).**

7. **Click OK and close the Control Panel.**

Figure 7-2:
Visit this
little applet
to tell
Windows
your
speaker
config-
uration.

External "sound cards"

What do you do if you have a laptop computer with undeniably crappy audio? You can't open the case and install a new sound card — oh, you can try, but you'll void the warranty searching for nonexistent PCI slots. You can, however, "mod" its audio with an external sound card.

A small number of sound cards exist *outside* the computer case, connected to the PC by a USB cable. They do everything a sound card does — they accelerate audio, they have connectors for speakers, they do 3-D signal processing, and so on. These external "sound cards" are encased in attractive consoles, sometimes with little rubber feet. Creative Labs SoundBlaster Audigy 2 NX and Philips Aurilium are two examples of external sound devices.

Application program interface: Choosing the right one

Application program interfaces (APIs) are designed to make it easier for everybody who designs stuff for, or uses, a computer. An API is basically a translator: It tells your computer how to use its devices, including its sound card. Everybody benefits when APIs work properly:

✔ Multimedia programmers don't have to build support into their products for every possible sound card on the market. They program to an API, which will ensure compatibility with compliant hardware.

✔ Hardware developers benefit because, by building parts compliant with various APIs, the features of their products will automatically be supported by compliant computer programs.

✔ You benefit by not having to make sure that a piece of hardware is compatible with games and programs, or that a software program you buy is compatible with your hardware. As long as they're compliant with the same APIs, you're all set.

The Philips Aurilium is a rebel "sound card." Instead of doing its magic in the confines of the computer case, it prefers the fresh air outside the PC and talks to the computer via a USB cable.

The most prominent APIs pertaining to sound cards are Microsoft's DirectX Audio (which includes DirectSound and DirectSound3D), and several versions of Creative Labs EAX. When you shop for a sound card, check which APIs it's designed for. When you buy a multimedia software program, check its API support.

When seeking the perfect sound card, you'll want to look for one with the broadest API support. If you decide to go with a card other than a Creative Labs SoundBlaster, make sure it supports as many APIs as possible.

The two APIs that dominate the 3-D gaming world are Microsoft DirectSound3D, which is part of DirectX 9's DirectX Audio component, and Creative Labs EAX, the latest version of which is called EAX 4.0 Advanced HD. Although only Creative Labs SoundBlaster cards support EAX 4.0 Advanced HD, nearly all sound cards support DirectSound3D and EAX 2.0 — and nearly all games use these APIs to create 3-D sounds.

Employing their own magic to enhance DirectSound3D, Sensaura and QSound have become popular additions to some sound cards' software suites. Creative Labs doesn't support these APIs, opting instead for its own EAX libraries. However, many top contenders do support them.

Games don't often make it known which audio APIs they support. That makes deciding exactly which sound card is perfect for your situation difficult. Don't despair, however; no matter which sound card you decide upon, it will support DirectX, so you'll get at least *some* of the aural glory the game developers intended you to experience. EAX 4.0 Advanced HD is popular among game developers, which might make you feel pigeonholed to purchase a Creative Labs SoundBlaster audio card.

3-D audio: You can't go wrong

If you're a gamer, and you're enveloped in a 3-D first-person shooter, you want to be able to tell when somebody's sneaking up behind you. Without 3-D audio, the sound would seem to come from your speakers right in front of you, the person sneaking up would get the drop on you, you'd get frustrated, and you'd quit playing in disgust. Okay, maybe not, but you get the idea.

All sound cards are capable of 3-D audio through two speakers or a headset, so you don't have to worry about which one to choose to ensure a three-dimensional experience.

One advantage of this technology is the conundrum of playing loud games after your family has gone to bed; you'll need a headset to get the most out of your titles without waking up the baby (or your parents).

3-D audio through two speakers or a headset is like a Philly cheese steak without onions: It's good, but it could be so much better. That said, if you only have two speakers, sound cards can bust out with somewhat convincing 3-D audio. To do this, they employ tricks, using technology called HRTFs and reverb:

- ✔ **Head-related transfer function (HRTF):** This is a type of math processing used to create sound to fool your ears about the sound's direction. Using HRTFs, sound cards can reproduce 3-D audio through two speakers or a headset. The story goes like this: You have only two ears, and yet you can pinpoint the location of sounds all around you, above you, and below you. Therefore, two audio sources (a pair of speakers or a headset) *should* be able to make sounds that seem to come from anywhere around you. By toying with the timing of signals — say, making a noise arrive in one ear a few milliseconds before reproducing the noise for your other ear, they can produce fairly convincing 3-D audio.

- ✔ **Reverb:** When something makes a sound, it bounces off nearby structures — walls, ceilings, rocks, and so on. The initial sound reaches your ears directly, and a split second or two later, the reverberated sounds that bounce off of stuff also reach your ear. The difference in timing creates a 3-D audio effect.

Using multiple speakers, HRTFs and reverb engines, sound cards can envelop you in a snug blanket of aural bliss. But wait, there's more! Spearheaded by

Creative Labs in the first incarnation of EAX, *environmental audio* is a nifty technology used to make game sounds match the environments in which they originate.

Imagine being alone in a gigantic gymnasium with a hardwood floor and brick walls. You bounce a basketball and charge across the court in your favorite high-top sneakers. The noises that you make should sound different than similar noises on a paved basketball court. Basketball bounces and sneaker squeaks should take on a hollow, echoing effect in the gym, because the sound waves bounce all over the place in that big empty hall. Outside, the sound should be more direct and snappier, without much echo.

Environmental audio effects are created when the sound card applies algorithms to audio code. An *algorithm,* in this context, is a mathematical calculation applied to program code to create a certain effect. Through the use of algorithms, the sound card causes the audio to take on new and convincing properties. That virtual basketball will sound hollow in the gym and more direct outside. Noise sounds accurate in stone caves, concert halls, sewer pipes, and even under water. Environmental audio is all about bringing realism to 3-D gaming environments.

Maximum sample rate and bit depth: Getting the best sound

CDs sound pretty good. The audio CD specification was engineered to provide awesome, clear, high-fidelity sound with digital accuracy and clarity. But believe it or not, sound card technology has surpassed CD quality. Welcome to the world of live, concert-hall quality: Sound cards can make it sound like you're in the same room with the orchestra.

An audio source's *sample rate* refers to how many times per second the sound recording is translated into a digital medium. CD quality is 44.1 KHz (meaning it's sampled 44,100 times every second). If the sample rate is too low, the sampling of the analog source into a digital medium can lose high-frequency sounds. To understand bit depth, remember that a bit is one tiny chunk of information. The bit depth of a digital audio signal indicates how many bits are used to describe the samples. CD audio is sampled at 16 bits, meaning that 16 chunks of data are used to describe each of the 44,100 samples each second. Higher bit depths result in more-faithful digital representation of the audio source.

Basically, all that means is that higher sample rates and bit depths make for better-quality sound. Today's sound cards are able to reproduce sounds at

24 bits and 96 KHz. That's exponentially better than CD quality of 16-bit/44.1 KHz audio.

Does that mean a new sound card capable of 24-bit/96 KHz will make everything sound better? Unfortunately, that's not the case. The CDs you play in your computer were engineered at 16-bit/44.1 KHz, so that's how they're reproduced. However, the door is open for game companies and other producers of audio sources to record at higher sample rates and bit depths, and as they do, you'll be ready to experience the full effect — if your PC has a modern sound card.

Features-o-rama: More stuff to think about

So, you think APIs, 3-D sound, and bit depth/sample rate are enough to consider when choosing a sound card? Although those features are important, keep in mind that sound card manufacturers are competing in a cutthroat battle for your dollars. They tend to add even more features that go above and beyond actual audio. Get a load of the stuff they have to offer.

FireWire

IEEE 1394 FireWire is a standard for transferring data to and from a computer. FireWire ports are external, like USB ports, and they represent a super-high-speed way to pump bits into and out of a PC. They're most commonly used for digital video, swapping movies to and from digital camcorders.

Why Creative Labs decided to marry FireWire with audio cards is beyond me, but it did — and it caught on. Hercules began including FireWire ports with its sound cards shortly after Creative Labs did. Because most modern motherboards have their own FireWire controllers built in, a FireWire-equipped sound card is sort of overkill. But for older systems that don't have their own onboard FireWire, the ports on the sound cards can be handy. Figure 7-3 shows a FireWire port.

Digital audio outputs

If you use your computer to watch movies — and many people do, as some graphics cards can send signals to ordinary television sets — you probably want the best sound possible. If you tie your computer into a high-end home theater system, you'll want a pure, digital stream of audio coming from your sound card right through to your speakers.

S/PDIF is a digital channel for audio signals. Most sound cards have some sort of S/PDIF outputs to pump pure signals to speaker or stereo systems with S/PDIF inputs. Coaxial and optical outputs are popular among sound card manufacturers. Figure 7-4 shows digital outputs.

Figure 7-3: The FireWire port on this Sound Blaster Audigy ZS is handy for hooking up FireWire devices, like digital camcorders and external hard drives.

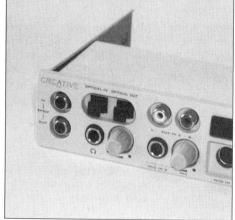

Figure 7-4: You can use these digital outputs to plug your sound card directly into a speaker system or AV receiver equipped with the proper inputs.

Acoustic effects

Some sound cards allow you to add environmental effects to nongaming applications, such as CD playback and general Windows noises. You can make your music sound like you're in a concert hall or a canyon, if that appeals to you. Some sound cards also offer stereo widening effects to make sounds seem to come from a richer, fuller source, rather than directly from the speakers. Creative Labs is known for including an acoustic effect interface with its SoundBlaster sound cards.

MIDI/wave table support

MIDI stands for *Musical Instrument Digital Interface.* It's possible to connect MIDI instruments like keyboards and guitars to a PC to record music. *Wave table synthesizers,* which are banks of presampled sounds, are used to make the MIDI music sound authentic. There are hundreds of wave table sounds, including different types of guitars, pianos, organs, drums and percussion instruments, and so on.

A technology that's fallen by the wayside for games, MIDI is still popular among aspiring musicians. MIDI used to be used heavily in games as background music, but most titles that have come out in the past few years employ digital music. All sound cards support MIDI and usually have a 15-pin MIDI in/out port (also used as a game port for pre-USB gaming peripherals).

Installing Your Sound Card

Now that you've chosen the best sound card ever based on APIs and features, it's time to install it. You'll need a Phillips head screwdriver.

Installing a sound card is one of the simplest PC upgrading procedures. It's *really* easy if you're installing an external unit (you plug it into a USB port and load up the drivers), but popping in an internal card isn't very daunting. It will test your screw-turning skills, your pushing prowess, and your essential plugging-stuff-in talents:

1. **Power down your PC and unplug it.**
2. **Place the PC on a nice, clean surface and open the case.**
3. **Look for a free PCI expansion slot.**

   Such slots are usually white.

4. **Remove the screw holding the *gate cover* (the little slab of removable metal) in place.**
5. **Remove the gate cover and set it aside.**
6. **Holding your sound card by the edges, slide it into place with the metal cover facing the slot on the back of the PC.**

   7. **If your sound card has an internal console, plug the appropriate end of its cable into the card connector and the other into the appropriate port on the bezel.**

   To do so, plug the sound card end of the cable into the sound card receptacle, and then pop the drive bay's bezel out of the PC's front cover and, if necessary, remove the metal guard. Pull the sound card cable through the front of the computer (see Figure 7-5).

   Note: If your sound card didn't come with a console, skip to Step 10.

   8. **If your computer case uses rails for its 5-inch drives, install the rails on the console.**

   Make sure to get the orientation correct, and slide the console into the drive bay until the rails snap it into place.

   9. **If your case doesn't require rails, slide the console into the drive bay until its bezel is flush with the other drive bay bezels.**

   Use four screws, which should be included, to secure it in place (see Figure 7-6).

   10. **Close the PC's case.**

Figure 7-5: If your sound card came with an internal drive bay console, run the cable right through the front of the PC to make it easier to connect it to the console.

Figure 7-6:
When you're done, the console should be flush with the front of the PC.

11. **Plug in your speakers.**

    Most sound cards and speaker systems have color-coded connectors; the wire and jack for the front pair might be green, the rear pair might be black, and so on. If you're unsure of what to plug in where, consult the sound card's instruction manual. (Yes, I know how annoying it is to have to read a manual, but believe me, it can be helpful.)

12. **Plug in your PC and turn it on.**

    When you boot up the PC, Windows will tell you that it found a new device and ask for a driver disk.

13. **Most sound card manufacturers will instruct you to ignore the Windows device installation process and simply run the CD that came with the sound card.**

    It will automatically install drivers and other applets.

14. **Follow the instructions that came with the sound card and everything will work out okay.**

    You'll probably have to reboot after you run the installation program, and after Windows loads back up it might go through a long detection routine. This is normal. By the end of its hardware detection antics, your sound card should be up and running.

Chapter 8

Providing Storage: Your Computer's Hard Drive

*T*he central processing unit (CPU) does the thinking. Main system memory is a trendy hangout for programs that are running and the data they need. But your computer holds scads more bits and bytes than can fit in random access memory (RAM). What about all the stuff you're not using?

The hard drive provides mass storage for programs, data files, the operating system, and virtually everything that makes your computer useful to you. It's the storage depot for data of all sorts.

Think of yourself as a bean counter in a big company. You have a cozy little office (but no window) and a desk with drawers, and across the room is a gigantic file cabinet. You are the processor, working on crunching numbers. The stuff you have on your desk can be thought of as data that are in the CPU's built-in cache. The desk drawer, which is within easy reach, is the system's main memory. That big file cabinet, stuffed with folders full of paperwork that you may or may not occasionally need, is the hard drive.

Of course, getting the stuff out of the file cabinet takes longer than getting the stuff out of your desk drawer. That trip across the room is equivalent to the CPU having to fetch data that are on the hard drive. That's why hard drive manufacturers are constantly researching and developing faster drives and faster *buses* (data conduits) to transfer data between the hard drive and RAM.

Hard drives differ from RAM in another way. Rather than store data on transistors in logic chips, hard drive store data magnetically on spinning platters within their structure. Read/write heads maneuver about the drive to find or store data. If you hear chattering from within your computer, it's probably the drive heads' stepper motor.

That's right: Hard drives are magnetic devices. Therefore, they're susceptible to damage from magnets. Most hard drives are relatively well shielded from stray magnetic fields, but you should *never* allow a magnet to get near your hard drive. Don't stick magnets to your computer's case.

In this chapter, I fill you in on all the jargon surrounding hard drive specifications, and help you choose the drive that's right for you. I don't stop there, though: I end the chapter after helping you install it (don't worry — it's about as easy as it gets).

Choosing a Hard Drive

There's a lot to know about hard drives. There are drive specifications like seek time and transfer rate, there are various buses that your motherboard may or may not support, there are spindle rates, and more.

Don't worry — although a hard drive's capabilities have some effect on game and application performance, the differences are barely perceptible. Game and application programmers are fully aware of the latency caused by fetching data from the hard drive, so they create their software to make judicious use of the RAM and, often, to visit the hard drive in the background while the application's doing other things.

Demystifying hard drive specs

When you pick up a hard drive at the computer store, its package will assault you with a bunch of numbers. These are the hard drive's specifications, which determine how quickly and efficiently the drive operates. The specs include all the information in the following sections.

Don't sweat the specs too much. Although they have an effect on drive performance, often the differences aren't detectable to a human being. We're talking a few milliseconds here or there.

Capacity

Capacity is how much space the hard drive has to store your data. High-capacity drives generally cost more than low-capacity drives.

When is a gigabyte not really a gigabyte? When it's a hard drive gigabyte. You may notice that your drive capacity, as reported by your system, may not match up with the manufacturer's specs. Some of that is the difference between formatted and unformatted capacity — formatting chews up a little data for the organizational overhead. However, there's a more fundamental reason. Memory is organized so that 1 megabyte is 2^{20} (that's 1,048,576) bytes. That's how computers report file sizes, too. But hard drive makers treat 1 megabyte as 1,000,000 bytes — which is less than the normal PC megabyte.

When buying a hard drive, go large. You may think you'll never completely fill, say, a 100GB hard drive, but you very well may. Games are getting bigger and bigger, office software gets more bloated with each release, Windows XP service packs require a good chunk of storage, and so on. If you can afford a 200GB drive, get one. It'll be that much longer before you run out of space and have to add a second drive.

Rotation speed

Rotation speed is how fast the platters spin inside the hard drive. Higher rotation speeds allow hard drives to locate data faster. You'll see rotation speeds of 5,400 rotations per minute (rpm), 7,200 rpm, 10,000 rpm, and, on high-performance, server-oriented drives, 15,000 rpm.

Seek time

Seek time is how fast a hard drive can locate data requested by the computer. It's measured in milliseconds (ms). Common seek times range from 9 ms on consumer-level drives to under 4 ms on high-performance monsters.

Buffer

A hard drive's *buffer* works like a CPU's cache. When a hard drive fetches data requested by the computer, it can also fetch the next few chunks of data in anticipation of the next request. It stores this extra data in a logic circuit — the buffer. Grabbing data from the buffer is faster than grabbing it from the hard drive platters. Buffers typically come in 2MB and 8MB. A larger buffer may marginally improve performance.

Understanding the interface

Another very important aspect of a hard drive is its *interface,* which determines just how quickly and efficiently it can shuttle data to and from the rest of the computer. There are three major interfaces: the rapidly aging IDE (also called PATA); the new, speedy Serial ATA (SATA); and the expensive but really fast SCSI.

The old: IDE technology

IDE stands for *Integrated Drive Electronics*. An updated version of IDE, called EIDE (Enhanced IDE) is actually the most prevalent form of IDE technology. IDE is also called PATA (short for *Parallel Advanced Technology Attachment*).

No matter what you call it, IDE (see Figure 8-1) is dying a slow and painful death. The interface has been pushed to its very limits, and the people who design such things can't make it go any faster.

Figure 8-1:
This is an
IDE hard
drive.

The fastest current IDE drives are called Ultra-ATA/133. Basically, that means that the maximum speed that they can transfer data is 133 megabytes per second (MBps).

The maximum transfer rate is also called the *burst rate;* it's rare that a drive can ever transfer at its theoretical maximum transfer rate, but when it does, it's called *bursting.* For a drive to burst, all conditions must be perfect. The data bus must be free of other passengers, all the components involved have to be ready for the data transfer, the planets must be aligned just right, the gods must smile upon you — well, you get the idea.

IDE technology is a *parallel* technology, meaning it transfers a whole bunch of bits at the same time. IDE drives are connected to the motherboard with 40-pin plugs, and Ultra-ATA cables actually have 80 wires.

Each IDE channel (most motherboards have two) can support two drives. To do this, one drive must be set as a slave, while the other must be set as the master. You make these settings using jumpers on the rear of the drive (shown in Figure 8-2); there's usually a jumper map on the drive's specifica-tion sticker. Note that, although IDE hard drives can share IDE channels with optical drives, it's not recommended; each type of device should have its own channel. Single drives must also be set properly — sometimes, the jumper setting for master doubles as single, and in other cases single drives require a different jumper setting.

If your hard drive doesn't have a map of the jumper settings on it, consult the documentation that came with the drive. If you don't have it, head to the drive manufacturer's Web site. Nearly all drive manufacturers keep reference documentation for their products — old and new.

Figure 8-2:
The jumper block on an IDE hard drive.

My advice to you: If your motherboard supports a newer technology like SATA, avoid IDE drives — even if you find one at a great price. Even if your motherboard doesn't have SATA capability, consider getting a SATA PCI card. IDE's time has come and gone.

The new: SATA technology

SATA stands for *Serial Advanced Technology Attachment.* It's a drop-in replace-ment for IDE and supports the entire set of ATA instructions. That means your computer supports SATA without any special monkeying around. SATA drives (shown in Figure 8-3) are cost-equivalent to IDE drives; they're not an expensive addition to a PC. Nearly all recent motherboards have SATA capability.

SATA cables are seven pins wide. This makes them much thinner than 40-pin IDE connectors and affords better airflow through the PC. SATA cables can be longer than IDE cables; IDE cables are limited to about 45 centimeters, while a SATA cable can be up to a meter long.

Figure 8-3:
This is a
SATA hard
drive.

SATA drive power connectors differ from the standard four-pin Molex connectors that inhabit PC power supplies. SATA drives come with adapters for their 15-pin power sockets.

Unlike IDE drives, SATA drives don't share channels with other drives. SATA is a point-to-point technology, and each drive gets its own cable. Therefore, you don't have to worry about which drive is a master and which is a slave.

The chief advantage of SATA is that it bursts faster than IDE; SATA has a burst rate of 150 MBps, and that's only the beginning. SATA 2.0 will burst at 300 MBps, and a 600 MBps specification is in the works!

I heartily recommend a SATA drive in any self-respecting computer.

The overkill: SCSI technology

The flavors of SCSI (short for *Small Computer System Interface,* and pronounced *skuh*-zee, like the way your bathtub looks when you haven't cleaned it in a while) are as numerous as ice cream flavors at Baskin Robbins. Through the years, there have been tons of SCSI technologies — 8-bit SCSI-1, 8-bit Fast SCSI, 16-bit Wide SCSI, lots of Ultra-SCSIs, and the most recent and most muscular Ultra320 SCSI. To complicate matters, there is a whole host of SCSI connectors, some of which fit some SCSI devices and others of which fit others.

SCSI is a daisy-chain technology. On a SCSI bus, you connect one device to an adapter card — which is necessary because few motherboards support SCSI directly — and then you chain that device to the next one, and so on. SCSI devices can exist inside and outside the computer: There are all manner of SCSI devices, from scanners to hard drives to optical drives to external storage, and so on. Current SCSI can support 15 devices.

TECHNICAL STUFF

An introduction to RAID

Many consumer-level motherboards are equipped with RAID controllers. RAID stands for *Redundant Array of Inexpensive Disks*. There are many levels of RAID with various capabilities, but the most common levels are called level 0, level 1, and level 0+1.

RAID requires more than one hard drive. RAID 0 and RAID 1 both require a minimum of two drives, while RAID 0+1 requires at least four.

RAID 0 isn't technically RAID at all, because there's no redundancy. It spans data across the two drives (in a technique called *striping*), and the drives appear to your computer to be one big volume; for instance, if you have two 80GB hard drives, the computer will see it as one 160GB drive. By writing to two disks at once, RAID 0 can increase drive performance.

RAID 1 takes two drives and writes exactly the same information to each one. This is called *mirroring*. You don't get to use the full capacity of both drives combined; because the data is mirrored, you only get the benefit of the capacity of one drive. In other words, if you have those two 80GB drives in a RAID 1 configuration, your computer will see one 80GB drive. Mirroring is for fault tolerance; if one drive goes bad and the other doesn't, you don't lose any data.

RAID 0+1 does both: It stripes and mirrors. It stripes across two drives, and mirrors the data to the other two. Thus, if you had four 80GB hard drives, your computer would see one 160GB drive.

Higher levels of RAID are mainly used in servers and rarely appear on consumer motherboards.

RAID is available for IDE, SATA, and SCSI. Not all motherboards have RAID capability. To implement RAID, you'll have to connect the drives to the RAID channels, and, when starting the computer, you must enter the RAID controller's BIOS and tell it what to do with the drives attached to your system.

I use RAID 1 in my main computer with all my important data on it (like this chapter I'm writing), but I don't use RAID in my gaming machines. The performance increase, in my opinion, isn't worth procuring a second (or third and fourth) drive.

Each device needs its own ID to avoid conflict. Furthermore, each end of the SCSI chain has to be terminated. If you screw any of that up, say hello to a nasty troubleshooting headache.

Although SCSI does offer performance beyond that of even SATA (Ultra320 SCSI burst at 320 MBps), the adapter card required, as well as drives and other devices, are expensive. In gaming benchmark tests, there is only a negligible difference between a system equipped with an Ultra320 SCSI hard drive and a SATA drive.

TIP

Hardcore enthusiasts insist that SCSI is the only way to go for sheer performance, but in my opinion, SCSI is for servers. If you outfit a desktop machine with a SCSI hard drive, you're paying more for prestige than performance.

The importance of backing up: The truth about hard drive failure

There's a well-known statistic about hard drives. They are extremely precise devices, running at high speeds, generating a lot of heat, and the heads have to be perfectly aligned to a thousandth of an inch. Therefore, given enough time:

Hard drives have a 100 percent failure rate.

The longer you run a hard drive, the closer it comes to dying. I'm not trying to scare you: I have drives that have been running for more than eight years that don't show any signs of mechanical failure. However, if I run them indefinitely, they *will* fail.

That's why it is *imperative* to back up everything on your hard drive that you care the most about to some sort of removable media — be it a tape, an optical disc, a SuperDisk, a zip disc, heck, even floppies. You don't have to back up program files; if your drive crashes, you can always reinstall them. However, data files that you create, such as Quicken accounts, Microsoft Excel spreadsheets, Microsoft Word documents, game saves, your Outlook e-mail messages, and virtually anything else you can't live without, *must* be backed up.

You can back up stuff manually by dragging and dropping files from the hard drive to removable media, or you can automate backups with Windows XP's backup program or a third-party backup program like Backup MyPC.

Windows XP Home Edition doesn't automatically install the Windows backup utility. To install it:

1. **Insert the Windows XP CD in your drive.**

2. **Right-click the Start menu, and choose Explore.**

   Windows Explorer opens.

3. **Navigate to *<optical drive letter>*\VALUE ADD\MSFT\NTBACKUP.**

4. **Double-click the Ntbackup.msi file.**

   This launches an installation wizard for the Windows backup program.

With the Windows backup program, you can select what to back up and when to back it up. My backups are automated to a tape drive; they run every day at 1 a.m. *Remember:* If you set your computer to back up in the middle of the night, you have to leave it on while you sleep — your computer's smart, but it can't turn itself on.

Take 'em or leave 'em: My recommendations

Many manufacturers — including Maxtor, Western Digital, and Seagate — make hard drives. I've used all three makers, and a bunch of others, for years and on dozens of systems.

Only for the insane: Modding a hard drive

Hard drives are precision instruments, sealed tight to prevent exposure to dust and other hazards of the atmosphere. You *can* mod a hard drive, but modding a hard drive is only for advanced modders.

A popular mod is to remove the top cover and replace it with Plexiglas or acrylic. This is an advanced mod not to be undertaken lightly.

Warning: You should *never* open a drive that you would miss if it were to be rendered unusable. Dust on the platters can cause all sorts of problems.

An excellent guide, written by a true master, to add a window and even to light a hard drive, is available at www.gideontech.com/content/articles/206/1.

Performance-wise, there's only a negligible difference between equivalent drives. In terms of performance, I can recommend virtually any high-capacity SATA hard drive.

I have never, however, had a Seagate drive crash due to a hardware failure. I can confidently recommend the Seagate Barracuda series of SATA drives. That's not to say that the other manufacturers don't make excellent products. I've just come to rely on Seagate gear, and it's never let me down.

Installing Your Hard Drive

Installing a hard drive is a simple task. First, connect the cables to the back of the drive. You'll need to connect a power supply cable and a data cable. Next, connect the data cable to the proper connector inside the PC. For a single hard drive, this should be the connector labeled SATA 1 or IDE1. For multiple drives on an IDE channel, make sure to set the master/slave jumper appropriately. Then, simply mount the drive in the hard drive bay as discussed in Chapter 3. Figures 8-4 and 8-5 show the cables on the rear of a SATA drive, and the data cable connected to a motherboard, respectively.

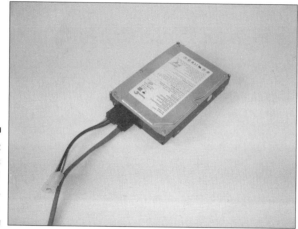

Figure 8-4:
Cables
connected
to a SATA
hard drive.

Figure 8-5:
The SATA
cable
connected
to the
mother-
board.

Chapter 9

Eyeing Optical Drives

* *

* *

*Y*our computer is looking delicious! You have a monster motherboard, a powerful processor, reliable RAM, but enough with the alliteration. I cover internal storage in Chapter 8; now it's time to add removable storage in the form of an optical drive.

By an *optical drive,* I mean one of those drives with the ejectable tray that you plop CDs and/or DVDs onto. System memory stores data in transistors, and hard drives store data magnetically on their spinning platters. CD and DVD disks are called optical storage for a reason — they store their data in tiny little pips that a laser within a CD-ROM drive, or a DVD-RW drive, or a DVD player, or a CD player reads. Writeable CD/DVDs allow a laser in a writer drive (often called a *burner*) to adorn them with those little laser-readable pips.

Optical drive technology is on the move. A slew of standards make the writable DVD market a soupy mess. Manufacturers have come forth with multistandard products, however, making shopping for a drive that much easier.

Optical disks are ideal for a number of tasks:

✔ **Creating music CDs:** You can rip songs off of your existing CDs with programs like Windows Media Player, and acquire new songs and albums from music sites like iTunes and Napster. You can then assemble your songs into play lists, again using software like Windows Media Player, and burn your own mixes to new CDs.

✔ **Backing up your data:** Writeable CDs, DVDs, and new dual-layer DVDs afford a large amount of storage for your important files. Hard drives can crash any time, so you'll want to back up everything from game saves to accounting files.

✔ **Sharing large files:** If you don't have a network, or if you'd like to share a huge file that's too fat to e-mail, burn it to an optical disk. Most optical drives can read files burned to appropriate disks — for example, most CD-ROM drives can read disks burned by a CD-RW burner.

In this chapter, I explore the wonders of optical data technology and help you decide on a drive to purchase for your wonder rig.

Choosing an Optical Drive

Shopping for one or more optical drives can be a confusing endeavor. Drives boast a number of specifications, while conforming to a sprawling network of read/write specifications. The good news is there are all-in-one drives that support virtually every standard, and that's what I recommend for you. But first, I want to show you some of the specs you'll encounter.

Note: I concentrate here on ATAPI optical drives (see Figure 9-1). ATAPI stands for *Advanced Technology Attachment packet interface* and is compatible with the 40-pin IDE interface discussed in Chapter 8. The other alternatives are SCSI optical drives and external optical drives that use USB or FireWire to connect to the computer. Serial ATA optical drives are rare today, and won't be common (and inexpensive) for a couple more years.

Figure 9-1:
An ATAPI
DVD drive.

Making sense of the all-important X factor

All drives are rated in a reading and writing categories with an X number. Basically, the X means a multiple of the original speed of the specification.

Thus, a CD-ROM drive that reads at 52X reads CDs 52 times faster than the original CD-ROM specification. On combo drives, you'll find a whole slew of X ratings: reading DVDs, writing DVDs, reading CDs, writing CDs, re-writing media, and so on.

In general, you want to look for high X ratings for every category.

Getting the lowdown on seek, access, and transfer rates

You'll encounter specifications called *random seek time, random access time, sustained transfer rate,* and *burst rate.* Here's what these mean:

- **Random seek time:** This represents the time it takes for the laser head to find the data requested. Typically, seek times run between 100 and 180 milliseconds depending on the format of the optical disk. *The lower the time, the better.*

- **Random access time:** Seek time is a component of access time. It indicates the time from the instruction to find data to when the data are actually starting to be read. It can run from 100 to 200 milliseconds.

- **Sustained transfer rate:** This indicates how fast the drive can transfer data at a sustained rate. Rates vary widely by the format, anywhere from around 2,500 kilobits per second (Kbps) to over 20,000 Kbps. *The faster the better.*

- **Burst rate:** This is how fast the drive can transfer data at its absolute, nonsustainable peak. UltraDMA (which most common ATAPI optical drives support) bursts at 33.3 megabits per second (Mbps).

Understanding optical drive formats

All optical drives can read some sort of media. Good old-fashioned CD-ROM drives can read CD-ROMs and music CDs. DVD-ROM drives can read CDs, CD-ROMs, DVDs, and DVD-ROMs.

Burners can write to various media. CD-RW drives can write music CDs and CD-ROMs. Recordable DVD drives of all types can record both of the DVD recordable formats, and to CD-RW. So if you have a DVD burner, you automatically have a CD-RW burner as well. Combination drives now exist that write to both of the major DVD recordable formats, DVD-RW and DVD+RW. Drives that can record to dual-layer media can record to all the lesser formats.

Does the world still need floppies?

The floppy drive is a relic in the PC world. Its disks only hold 1.44MB of data. The drive is painfully slow. Although it can sometimes be handy to boot a floppy for diagnostic purposes, there are bootable CD-ROMs, too. In fact, Windows XP comes on a bootable CD-ROM. Why would you possibly want a floppy drive?

Floppy drives do have their uses. Dropping a small file on a floppy — a file small enough that you don't need to use an optical disc — can be handy. Furthermore, flashing the motherboard BIOS on a system — something you should do on a regular basis as new BIOS versions iron out bugs and even increase compatibility —

often requires you to create a bootable floppy with the new BIOS file and the flash program.

Also, if you plan on implementing some type of RAID array, Windows requires you to load the driver from a floppy. That's right — you can't load the RAID driver from a CD or from a flash memory card. It has to be on a floppy.

Floppy drives don't cost much; you can get a generic model for under $20. You may never use it, but it's worth the hassle to install one just in case. To install it, follow the procedure in Chapter 3, connect the data cable, and connect the power cable.

Besides reading and writing, most burners can rewrite. Using rewritable media, burners can write and overwrite the same disks. For example, CD-R (the R standing for recordable) discs can only be written to once, while CD-RW (Rewritable) disks can be written and overwritten. The same goes for DVD media: DVD-Rs can be written once, while DVD-RWs can be written to hundreds of times. Note that, for deleting files on an RW disk, you may need third-party software, as Windows XP often has trouble with that procedure.

When new technologies burst forth onto the market, semiconductor companies scramble to create standards to corner the market. Users end up being forced to gamble on which standard will catch on. Betamax owners found themselves out of luck when VHS took over the world. Sony MiniDiscs never quite put a dent into the monolithic rise of audio CDs. Digital cameras are subject to a ridiculous array of memory cards and sticks, all of which are vying for dominance.

The writeable CD format is pretty straightforward: You never have to worry about whether your CD burner will support a given format. Writeable DVDs, however, are in a state of flux. Various companies jumped to create standards, and thus DVD-RAM, DVD-R or DVD-RW (pronounced DVD *dash* R or DVD *dash* RW), and DVD+R or DVD+RW (pronounced DVD *plus* R or DVD *plus* RW) all want superiority.

A lot of parity exists among the standards. They all hold a maximum capacity of 4.7GB (whereas CD-R or CD-RWs hold around 650MB). DVD-R and DVD+R are ideal for creating video DVDs as well as data DVDs. Which standard to use is up in the air; both claim superiority, both are better than DVD-RAM (which I don't recommend using), and neither differs much from the other.

There's more! DVD+RW DL drives are flooding the market as I'm writing this book, and DVD-RW DL drives aren't far behind. The DL stands for *dual layer,* indicating that the drives can write first to a shallow layer and then refocus the laser and write to a second layer, greatly increasing the storage capacity. A dual-layer disc can hold 8.5GB of data. To get the full benefit, you'll need expensive dual-layer discs to go with your dual-layer burner.

And speaking of media, you'll find a ton: Besides DVD+RW DL, you'll find DVD-R, DVD+R, DVD-RW, DVD+RW, and DVD-RAM. You'll even find the media rated for different speeds, in X ratings.

Getting some recommendations from yours truly

Rather than worry too much about the crazy maze of formats and standards, simply buy a multi-format drive DVD/CD writer. One drive does it all. For example, the LG GSA-1420B 12X Super Multi DVD Rewriter writes CDs, audio CDs, DVD-Rs, DVD-RWs, and so on. Another excellent drive is Toshiba's SD-R5372. Both of these drives support DVD+RW dual layer. Dual-layer drives are considerably more expensive than their non-DL counterparts, so you may want to hold off and get a combo drive that lacks DL capability.

As for media, CD-R (write-once) discs are considerably less expensive than rewritable disks, and they tend to be more compatible to other optical drives, CD players, and set-top DVD players. You can buy entire spindles of 25, 50, or more CD-R discs at a time without jewel cases. Having a stash of cheap CD-R discs, as well as a few rewritable disks for backing up software on a rotating schedule, is a good idea.

Your optical drive will likely come with a software suite for authoring media, watching DVD movies on your computer, and using other handy utilities. Most drives also come with the necessary ribbon cable to connect them to the motherboard's IDE port, and they even include a small pass-through cable to connect to your sound card.

So the bottom line is: Get an optical drive rated for every format, get a spindle of discs, and burn like a madman!

Installing Your Optical Drive

I go over the physical installation of an optical drive in Chapter 3. What I don't cover in Chapter 3 are the jumpers, the data cable, the audio cable, and the power cable.

Because an ATAPI drive is, at its heart, an IDE device, and because two IDE devices can share the same cable, you have to make sure the drive's jumper is set correctly. If the drive lives alone on its cable, it can either be set to master or slave — it doesn't matter. If, however, you're installing more than one optical drive, or any two IDE devices on the same cable, one must be set as a master and the other as a slave. There's a jumper block on the back of the drive (see Figure 9-2), and most drives have a diagram of the jumper settings on the label.

Figure 9-2:
The jumper
block on an
optical
drive.

Now it's time to tackle the physical installation of the optical drive. There's not much to it; it's one of the easier installations you'll perform. Just follow these steps:

1. **With the jumper set, connect the data cable to the secondary IDE channel on the motherboard.**

2. **Then pull the other end of the cable through the bay into which you plan to install the optical drive.**

3. **Connect the data cable to the drive.**

4. **Connect the four-wire audio cable to the back of the drive and feed it into the system.**

   You'll connect the other end to the CD-IN port on your sound card. Note, however, that this step is mostly unnecessary today. Almost all software that reads CD music data now extracts it over the ATA bus.

5. **Slide the drive into the bay and secure it with screws (or, if your case uses them, attach the drive rails and snap the drive into place).**

6. **Connect a Molex power connector to the drive and you're in business.**

Chapter 10

Playing Well with Others: Networking

*Y*ou and your computer may be a match made in heaven, but let's face it: The two of you are just so different. You're made of carbon, your computer's made of silicon. You think in seconds, your computer thinks in milliseconds. You eat, sleep, and carry on with your life, and your computer lives to serve. Wouldn't it be nice if it had some friends of its own?

Computers can talk to each other through the wonder that is networking. More and more homes contain multiple computers, and sharing data or even a high-speed broadband Internet connection between them is a common desire. And speaking of the Internet, that massive phenomenon is just one gigantic computer network itself.

The Internet is a gateway to all kinds of information and recreation, from finding out the capital of Denmark (it's Copenhagen!) to looking up phone numbers to killing time on message boards to playing online multiplayer games with like-minded gamers. Unreal Tournament 2004, Doom 3, and other games challenge you to blast away at the avatars of other human beings; massively multiplayer online games (MMOGs) like Star Wars Galaxies and Final Fantasy XI Online entice you to live a complete life online.

To get there, you have to start somewhere. To enjoy connectivity to other computers, or to a broadband Internet connection, your PC has to have the proper equipment installed. In this chapter, I guide you through the world of networking.

Understanding Wireless Versus Wired Networks

Networking requires infrastructure. The bits and bytes that flow from one PC or networked device to another have to have a means to get there. The infrastructure most widely used in LANs today is called *Ethernet,* which is basically a related group of standards by which computers talk to each other.

You have the choice of using wired or wireless networking. Wireless is, by far, the more convenient of the two, but it's also less secure. Modern wired Ethernet uses a physical scheme resembling the arms of a star: Each computer on the network has its own twisted-pair cable connecting it to a port on either a *hub* (see Figure 10-1) or an Internet connection sharing *router.*

Figure 10-1:
An Ethernet
hub.

Hubs, switches, and routers are not the same:

- ✔ Hubs are the lowest common denominator, simply enabling connections between computers.
- ✔ Switches add some smarts, by doing some load balancing.

✔ Routers essentially act as a barrier between networks, usually between your internal home network and the Internet. Routers usually have firewalls built in, to protect your home network from unauthorized intrusion from the Internet.

Twisted-pair cables come in a variety of speed ratings, ranging from category 5 (Cat 5), to category 5e (Cat 5e), to category 6 (Cat 6e). Standard Cat 5 can handle speeds up to 100 Mbps. For full gigabit Ethernet throughput, you need Cat 6. Hubs and routers have a number of RJ-45 ports to accept network cables. Although earlier forms of Ethernet used a *daisy-chain* scheme, in which one long cable stretched from computer to computer to form the network, that scheme is rarely used anymore.

In the case of wireless Ethernet, called Wi-Fi or 802.11*x,* each computer is fitted with a wireless network interface and the signals are routed through an *access point* (see Figure 10-2), or they communicate directly with one another in what's called an *ad-hoc network.* An access point can also double as a broadband router, allowing computers on the Wi-Fi network to share an Internet connection.

Figure 10-2:
A typical
Wireless
access
point/router.

Wired Ethernet transfers data at rates of 10 megabits per second (Mbps), 100 Mbps, or, in the case of gigabit Ethernet, 1,000 Mbps. The most prominent forms of Wi-Fi networks, 802.11b and 802.11g, transfer at 11 Mbps and 54 Mbps, respectively. Note that in most small, home networks, you'll rarely need data transfer rates higher than 10 Mbps.

If you choose to go with a wired network, you'll have to run cable through the location of your network. That can involve unsightly wiring stretching from room to room, or the arduous task of fishing wires through walls and ceilings. Wired networking equipment is generally less expensive than wireless solutions, but the extra money you spend pays for itself in convenience.

Network Hardware

A PC lacking networking hardware is like a house without a telephone — it can't communicate with other entities. Likewise, a wired network can't exist without a hub, and although ad-hoc wireless networks can function without access points, a Wi-Fi network is much easier to administrate with an access point.

Many of today's motherboards come with 10/100 Mbps and even gigabit network interface equipment. The actual RJ-45 connector is found on the rear riser near the I/O ports. Some motherboards come with Wi-Fi equipment, although they're a relatively rare find compared to networks with wired Ethernet controllers.

Wireless access points and routers usually have a few RJ-45 ports built in, similar to an Ethernet hub. If one or more computers on your network is situated near the access point, it may be easier and more cost-effective to cable it to the access point rather than rely on a wireless connection.

For computers based on motherboards that didn't come with your desired network equipment built in, you'll need to purchase a network interface device. Both wired and wireless network interface cards (called NICs), are available as PCI expansion cards (and as PCMCIA cards for notebook computers). Cards for wired networks will contain an RJ-45 port, while wireless devices may have a detachable antenna that you screw to the back of the card after you've installed it into your computer. Figure 10-3 shows a PCI card for a wired network, while Figure 10-4 shows a wireless Ethernet PCI card.

Figure 10-3:
A PCI network interface card for a wired Ethernet network.

Again, I strongly recommend going wireless. A touch of added maintenance and some extra security steps are involved, but the convenience is well worth it. You won't have to run any wires, and if you have a portable PC you can use it anywhere in the house and still have access to your network (and your Internet connection, if you'll be sharing one).

3Com, Linksys, D-Link, and Netgear make the networking equipment that I use and recommend. 3Com makes the best wired network interface cards andLAN hubs, and D-Link also makes excellent adapters. Linksys and Netgear are my favorites for wireless networking equipment like access points, routers, and PC interfaces.

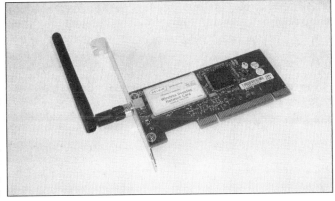

Figure 10-4:
A wireless
PCI network
interface
card.

Setting Up a Network

Years ago, setting up a network was a complex and puzzling affair, but with home networking having become popular, companies have made the once-dark art a user-friendly affair. It can be boiled down to two steps: setting up the hardware and physical connections, and configuring networking in Windows. Just follow the steps outlined here.

Wired networks

To set up a wired network, you'll need the following parts:

✔ **A network hub or Internet sharing router with enough ports for each computer on the network.** Note that you can stack most hubs by connecting one to the next to create a system of hubs.

✔ **Twisted-pair network cables of the appropriate lengths for each computer, and one for connecting the router to the broadband connection if you're sharing one.** Cat 5 is good enough for most home networks, but you'll want Cat 6 if you really want to go gigabit.

✔ **Network interface devices for each computer.** They can be built in to the motherboard or be expansion cards.

After you have all the necessary parts, follow these steps to set up a wired network:

1. **Pick a nice, central location for the hub (or router, if you're sharing an Internet connection).**

   This can be near one of the computers in the network or in a different area entirely.

2. **Install network cards in each of the computers that needs one.**

3. **Run the twisted-pair network cables from each computer to the hub.**

4. **If you're sharing a broadband connection, connect the router's WAN port to the cable or DSL modem.**

5. **Run the Windows XP Network Setup Wizard on each computer.**

   See "Windows XP's Network Setup Wizard" later in this chapter.

Wireless networks

To set up a wireless network, you'll need the following parts:

✔ **A network access point or wireless router if you're sharing an Internet connection.** I don't recommend ad-hoc networks.

✔ **Wireless or wired network hardware for each computer in the network.**

✔ **In some cases, you may need one computer with a wired network card to use to set up the access point or router.** Check your access point or router's configuration instructions.

After you have all the necessary parts, follow these steps to set up a wireless network:

1. **Choose a spot for the access point or router.**

2. **If necessary, wire a PC to the access point/router with a CATV cable.**

3. **Set up the router.**

   You'll have to consult your router's documentation, as procedures differ. In general, you'll

   - Log in to the access point/router via a Web browser.
   - Change the router's default password and SSID (Service Set Identifier, or the name you give to your wireless network).
   - Follow the rest of the setup procedure.

4. **If you'll be sharing an Internet connection, connect the router's WAN port to the cable or DSL modem.**

5. **Install wireless adapters in each computer on the network.**

6. **Configure each PC with the SSID so that it can find your access point/router.**

7. **Configure your wireless network's security features (see "Securing Your Internet-Connected Computer," later in this chapter).**

8. **Run the Windows XP Network Setup Wizard on each computer.**

   See the following section, "Windows XP's Network Setup Wizard."

Windows XP's Network Setup Wizard

The Windows XP Network Setup Wizard is truly an excellent tool that makes setting up a network an exercise in simplicity. Just follow these steps:

1. **Choose Start ⇨ All programs ⇨ Accessories ⇨ Communications ⇨ Network Setup Wizard.**

   The Network Setup Wizard opens.

2. **Click Next.**

3. **Click Next again.**

   The wizard will look for an Internet connection, and then ask you to select a connection method.

4. **Select the appropriate Internet connection (see Figure 10-5).**

   If you're not sure which is appropriate, click the Learn More about Home or Small Office Network Configurations link.

5. **Click Next.**

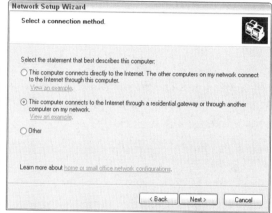

Figure 10-5:
Run the
Windows
Setup
Wizard to
configure
your
network.

6. **Enter a computer description (for example, "Dad's Computer" or "Den" or something descriptive of the PC).**

7. **Enter a computer name (the name it will be known as on the network).**

8. **Click Next.**

9. **Enter a workgroup name.**

   For simplicity's sake, every computer on a home network should be in the same workgroup. The default is MSHOME.

10. **Click Next.**

11. **Select whether to turn on file and printer sharing.**

    If you plan to share a computer's resources, you should turn them on.

12. **Click Next.**

13. **Glance through the summary, and click Next.**

    The wizard will make the settings you requested.

14. **Decide what to do about the other computers on your network.**

    If you have computers running Windows 9x or Me, you can create a diskette that includes a program to run to make each one compatible with your network. If not, just choose to end the wizard.

You'll need to run the Network Setup Wizard on each computer in your network.

Showing it off at a LAN party

In Chapter 1, I touch on the wonders of low-latency gaming. Latency is the lag created by sending information from one computer to another and waiting for a response. It's measured in milliseconds via a command called *ping,* and the lower your ping time, the less you'll notice latency issues. Latency can degrade the gaming experience with skips, freezes, and difficulty aiming at other players.

Thankfully, lag is limited to Internet gaming. LANs are extremely low-lag environments, which inspires gamers to haul their computers to one location to get down with some seriously low-latency gaming. Whether it's a massive fest with hundreds of gamers in a hotel ballroom sponsored by PC parts manufacturers, or just an informal little gathering in the comfort of your own home, LAN parties offer other benefits besides low latency.

Most important, they give you an opportunity to proudly display your modded PC. Comparing techniques, trading ideas, and generally enjoying the sport of modding with like-minded gamers is fun!

Another nice perk in LAN fests is the immediate reaction you get when you line up an opponent in your sights and squeeze off a head shot. There's nothing like hearing a cry of anguish in the same room when you thwart an enemy.

Securing Your Internet-Connected Computer

The Internet is like a big city. There's a lot to do there, and there are tons of wonderful places to go. But like any big city, it has an element of crime. Some people want to break into your computer for nefarious purposes — to steal your data, to wreck your file system, or even to take control of your computer and use it for their own desires.

You should run two types of programs on every Internet-connected computer:

- **Antivirus software:** Antivirus software, such as Norton AntiVirus, McAfee VirusScan, or the free AntiVir (download it from www.free-av.com). Viruses are malicious programs that can cause havoc with your data. They can be grouped into three categories: worms, Trojan horse programs, and viruses themselves.

    Worms and viruses live to propagate themselves and infect as many computers as they possibly can. They often spread themselves as e-mail attachments; when the malicious attachment is run, it usually sends copies of itself to every address in the infected computer's e-mail address book. Some worms have destructive "payloads," too; they may eat up system resources, making the computer less responsive, or they may even destroy data. Trojan horse programs act as little quiet servers through which hackers can take total control of your system. They can then swipe data or use your computer to attack other computers.

Always run an antivirus program, update it frequently, and be mindful of the e-mail attachments you open and the files you download. Scanning everything you acquire from the Internet for viruses before you launch it is a good habit to get into.

✔ **Firewall:** Your computer's connection to the Internet consists of thousands of ports. Think of ports as network "channels," each with its own identifying number. Many ports have their own purpose — e-mail is transmitted through one port, Web surfing through another, and so on. Hackers can invade your computer through unchecked ports. Firewalls serve to close those ports and prevent unwanted access to your machine. Windows XP Service Pack 2 (SP2) contains a robust firewall; Norton and McAfee also offer firewalls, or you can also get a very good one called ZoneAlarm for free from Zone Labs (www.zonelabs.com). Note that some Internet connection routers have their own, built-in hardware firewalls; if yours does, you don't have to run a personal firewall on every computer in your network.

Wired networks have one advantage over their wireless counterparts: They're not susceptible to snooping from afar. If you were to take a Wi-Fi equipped laptop on a drive through a city, you'd be surprised at the number of wireless networks that you could easily join when you got in proximity of their access points. You could then leech Internet access from or even steal data from networked computers.

You'll need to take some special precautions to secure your wireless network from outsiders. You can make these changes through the access point/router's interface, and in some cases you'll also have to run the setup utility on your client PC's network equipment to make changes in kind. The methods vary from one access point and NIC to the next, so follow the instructions in the documentation. In general, you'll do the following:

✔ **Change the SSID.** Don't use the factory default SSID. Hackers know the defaults and using them makes your network easy to invade.

✔ **Don't broadcast the SSID.** Access points can broadcast the SSID so that Wi-Fi equipped computers can pick it up. This makes it easy for snoopers to find out your network's SSID. You'll have to manually enter the SSID on each client computer's network setup interface in order for them to find the access point.

✔ **Enable WEP and WPA.** WEP stands for Wired Equivalent Privacy. It's an encryption scheme that, unfortunately, is fairly easy to crack. That's why WPA (Wi-Fi Protected Access) was developed. Each lets you enter a passcode, which is used to create an encryption key. The key must be the same on the access point and the client PC for the two to be able to communicate. Without your passcodes, hackers can't access your network.

Chapter 11

Thinking Outside the Box: Peripherals

*E*xcept when you're sticking optical discs in your PC's DVD drive or pressing the power or reset button, you don't actually do much with the box itself. All the interfacing between you and your PC is done through external peripherals. These include common goodies like speakers, keyboards, and mice; more-specialized equipment like flatbed scanners, photo scanners, and microphones; output equipment like printers and photo printers; displays like CRT and LCD monitors; and the list goes on. External gadgetry can even include storage devices like self-contained optical drives and external hard drives. Let's not forget gaming controllers: joysticks, gamepads, and driving wheels enhance flight sims, arcade games and racing titles.

At the bare minimum, you'll need three external peripherals to communicate with your PC: a keyboard, a mouse, and a display. Anything beyond that is gravy, although some devices (like speakers) are more commonly used than others (like scanners).

All this gear and more is connected to your PC through various I/O (input/output) ports. PCs contain a whole slew of ports — from rarely used legacy connectors to new, high-speed interfaces. Connector ports can be integrated on the motherboard's rear riser, mounted in the case's front panel, or on the backs of PCI, AGP, and PCI Express expansion cards. I discuss some of the ports in earlier chapters of this book, but in this chapter, I go into more detail.

To get an idea of the stuff you can hook up to your PC, walk down the hardware aisles of your local computer superstore. You'll see all manner of things, many of which you can play around with before you decide to buy. For instance, most computer stores have big displays of joysticks that you can grip, wiggle around, and see how your hand fits them. The same often goes for mice and keyboards.

Although reading reviews of gear that you'll use all the time, like keyboards and mice, is a great way to help you decide what's right for you, nothing beats actually trying the stuff out to see how it feels. A mouse that fits a reviewer's hand perfectly, eliciting a rave review, may not feel comfortable to you. Play around with the display gadgets at the computer store to see what fits your hands and what feels unnatural.

The Port Report

In the world of PCs, there are ports for keyboards, ports for mice, multifunction ports, ports for displays, ports for many devices — it's surprising that there isn't a port that pours fresh, hot coffee into a mug for you. In fact, that gives me an idea. . . .

Ports can be loosely divided into two groups: legacy ports that have been around for a long time, and modern ports that have been developed in the past few years. The two categories have some things in common, though. Most ports in a computer are driven by controllers that handle the task of swapping data through the port itself. Thus, an Ethernet port has an Ethernet controller that drives it, a USB port has a USB controller, and so on. Physically, ports consist of a number of electrical contacts, whether they're in the form of protruding pins or flat contacts.

Getting to know your "older" ports

In the following sections, I give you a look at classic ports that are holdovers from days gone by.

Serial ports

Also called RS-232 ports or COMM ports, these little ports are rarely used anymore. Serial ports come in two sizes: the common 9-pin array (see Figure 11-1), and 25-pin ports that are all but gone from the face of the Earth. Serial ports on the PC are *male ports,* meaning that their pins stick out for connection to a female plug. Serial ports have been part of computerdom for decades, and they're notoriously slow.

Figure 11-1:
The bottom
two ports
are serial
ports; the
larger port
on top is a
parallel port.

They're controlled by a chip called a UART chip, which stands for Universal Asynchronous Receiver/Transmitter. Although efforts were made throughout the life of these ports to update their technology and increase their data transfer rate, it maxes out at a measly 115 kilobits per second (Kbps). Serial ports send data one bit at a time, which is a very inefficient way to transfer data.

Why are serial ports still around? Believe it or not, the occasional peripheral still uses them. I have an Olympus camera that, unlike most digital cameras that interface with USB ports, only interfaces with a serial port. If I fill up a big memory card, it can take 15 minutes to transfer my photos to the PC — whereas it might take a USB port a minute or so.

Most motherboards have two nine-pin serial ports on the rear I/O port riser. Chances are, you'll never use them.

Parallel ports

Unlike serial ports, parallel ports (also called printer ports) are still in use today, mainly for — you guessed it — printers. This 25-pin female connector usually resides near the serial ports. Unlike serial ports, parallel ports transmit data 8 bits (or one byte) at a time. They max out at about 100 kilobytes per second (Kbps). Refer to Figure 11-1 for an illustration of a parallel port.

There are several modes of operation for parallel ports: Standard Parallel Port (SPP), Enhanced Parallel Port (EPP), and Extended Capabilities Port (ECP). All current motherboards can operate the parallel port in any of those standards, which differ mainly in how they shuttle data to and from the system. A given printer may require a certain mode, which you can set in the motherboard's BIOS.

MIDI/game ports

This 15-pin female port normally comes as part of a sound card, often on its own separate gate — although some motherboards include them on the I/O riser. MIDI composers still use the port to input and output MIDI signals to and from instruments like keyboards. Through the use of MIDI sequencing software, like Voyetra's Record Producer series, MIDI composers can create songs with relative simplicity. The port's other purpose, however, has gone the way of the dodo. It was also used as a game port for connecting gaming input devices like joysticks and gamepads. Nowadays, all such hardware uses USB ports for connectivity. Figure 11-2 shows a MIDI/game port.

Figure 11-2:
A MIDI/
game port.

VGA ports

These 15-pin female ports are still in wide use today for nondigital displays, such as CRT and some LCD monitors. They appear on the back of graphics cards. In some cases, graphics cards may only physically have DVI ports (see "DVI ports," later in this chapter), and come with DVI-to-VGA port adapters for backward compatibility. Even though VGA ports have been around for quite some time, they're not outmoded at all. They can transmit imagery to the display as fast as any graphics card can crunch it. Figure 11-3 shows a VGA port.

PS/2 ports

Most motherboards have a pair of little, round, color-coded ports designed for use with mice and keyboards. The mouse port is green, and the keyboard port is purple. Notebook computers often have one PS/2 port that works with either a mouse or a keyboard. Figure 11-4 shows PS/2 ports.

With the advent of USB mice and keyboards, these ports may start disappearing from motherboards. A few motherboards have already done away with PS/2 ports, but I think that's a bit premature. Although USB mice are very prevalent, many current keyboards still rely on the PS/2 port.

Figure 11-3:
A VGA port.

Figure 11-4:
PS/2 ports.

Modem ports

If your computer is equipped with a modem, it'll have a little telephone port called an RJ-11 port. You connect a Plain Old Telephone Service (POTS) telephone cable into this socket, and you stick the other end in a phone jack. (Ordinary modems won't work with digital phone systems.)

Introducing modern ports

Although the ports I discuss in the previous sections are adequate for their purposes, they're not exactly the wave of the future. More modern ports include Ethernet ports that can transfer data at a gigabit per second, USB 1.1 and 2.0 ports, IEEE 1394 FireWire ports, DVI ports for digital displays, and more.

USB ports

Serial, parallel, and game ports reached the upper limits in terms of usefulness and data transfer rates long ago. The computer world was in need of a new external connector that could transfer data faster and more efficiently. A group of technology manufacturers developed Universal Serial Bus (USB), and it's really caught on. Several USB specifications exist, but we're concerned with USB 1.1 and USB 2.0.

USB ports are little and flat. USB 1.1 has two operating speeds: 1.5 megabits per second (Mbps) and 12 Mbps. Although that's certainly an improvement over the serial port's 115 Kbps, it wasn't fast enough for high-speed devices like external hard drives. USB 2.0 stepped up the transfer rate to a whopping 480 Mbps, and it's backward compatible to USB 1.1, so you can plug *any* USB device into a USB 2.0 port and it will work. Figure 11-5 shows USB ports.

Common devices that interface with USB ports include mice, keyboards, game controllers, external storage devices, digital cameras, handheld computing devices, and more. USB ports can provide a small amount of power for devices, but things with motors like hard drives require their own AC juice.

One USB controller can handle a theoretical maximum of 127 devices! You can expand your computer's USB capability through the use of hubs, which are little boxes with more USB ports. Hubs simply connect to an existing USB port on the computer or another hub, and they typically have four or eight ports, or seven like the one shown in Figure 11-6. By connecting hubs to the computer and more hubs to the hubs, you can create a big USB *tree*.

Note that there are powered and nonpowered hubs. To connect USB powered devices into USB hubs, you'll need a powered hub.

Figure 11-5:
USB ports.

Figure 11-6:
A seven-port
USB hub.

Although connecting lots of devices via hubs is nice, not having to spend money on hubs is even nicer. When USB first hit the streets, most mother-boards only had two USB ports; nowadays, motherboards have four or more USB 2.0 ports. You can find out all about USB at www.usb.org.

IEEE 1394 FireWire ports

Pioneered by Apple, the IEEE 1394interface, also called FireWire or i.Link, is a high-speed serial bus for external peripherals. Although it came before USB, there are far more USB devices than FireWire devices. Stuff that connects to FireWire ports include digital camcorders, external hard drives, external optical drives, other removable media drives, digital music players — the list goes on.

The original spec of FireWire transfers data at a maximum of 400 Mbps; IEEE 1394b, which is slowly making headway in the computer industry, peaks at 800 Mbps with faster speeds emerging. The 1394b spec is backward-compatible for 1394a equipment, so you can plug any FireWire device into a high-speed port. There are three types of connectors: four-pin and six-pin from the original FireWire spec, and nine-pin for 1394b. If you search around, you can find cables that bridge the various connectors — for instance, a nine-pin to four-pin cable, so you can connect any FireWire device.

Hot swappin'

Both USB devices and FireWire devices are *hot-swappable,* meaning you can plug them in and detach them while the computer is on. Windows will detect the change and take the appropriate action. The first time you install a USB or FireWire device, you may have to install drivers. After that, you can swap it at your leisure and Windows will know what to do.

For instance, I leave my USB scanner detached from my USB port when I'm not using it. However, if I suddenly develop the need to scan something, I plug it in. Windows says, "Aha! You've just plugged in your scanner!" and then I can use it. When I'm done, I unplug it and Windows says, "So long, scanner!" and it's not missed.

Like USB, FireWire buses can support many devices. Rather than use hubs, you actually daisy-chain devices together to make one long bus. For example, if you have an external FireWire hard drive and a DVD-RW drive, you can plug the first device into the port on your computer and the second device into the first one.

Ethernet ports

In Chapter 10, I fill you in on networking and suggest that you go wireless. If you aren't there yet, or if you are but you want to plug a computer physically into an access point, you use the Ethernet port. This is an RJ-45 port, shown in Figure 11-7, designed for a CATV Ethernet cable, and it's operated by an Ethernet controller on the motherboard or the expansion card.

Although RJ-45 Ethernet ports have been around for years, I didn't lump them in with older ports because they've adapted with the needs of networks. Old Ethernet transferred data at 10 Mbps, while newer technologies can truck bits along at 1 gigabit per second (or 1,000 Mbps).

DVI ports

DVI stands for Digital Visual Interface and its ports appear on the back of graphics cards. They're designed to interface with digital displays, like some flat-panel monitors and projectors, but with an adapter some types are backward-compatible with analog displays like CRT monitors.

DVI technology uses Transition Minimized Differential Signaling (TDMS), a standard for transmitting images, and it can be divided into single- and dual-link. The key difference is the size of the image it can display. Furthermore, there are three types of DVI interfaces: the rarely used DVI-A, which transmits to analog devices like CRT monitors; DVD-D, which is purely digital; and the commonly used DVD-I, which can do either.

Figure 11-7:
An Ethernet
port.

The Goods: External Peripherals

The list of things you can hook up to your computer is all but endless.
Scores of manufacturers produce an endless array of gadgets and gear,
some of which is absolutely necessary to computing and gaming, some of
which is optional equipment, and some of which is gimmicky and altogether
unnecessary.

Before you start shopping for gear, lay out a budget. So much of what I cover
here is available in a huge variety of price ranges. You can get a mouse for
under $10 or more than $60; you can spend $20 on a keyboard or $50. Often,
the difference in price doesn't equate to quality as much as it does to extra
features that you may or may not really care about. What's more, you can
often save a lot of money by shopping online. I like to go to a computer store
to check out the merchandise, decide what I want, and then go home and find
it cheaper at www.newegg.com or www.buy.com.

I don't have the space in this book to present a guide to every peripheral you
can get your hands on, but I go over those that your computer requires, and
some more common gear. For instance, you need a keyboard and mouse —

you can't interface with Windows without them (well, if you want to get technical, you *can* navigate Windows without a mouse, but it's not worth trying to do). You must have a monitor of some sort. You don't need a speaker system, but going without one would be ridiculous.

Interfacing with your computer: Input devices

You can communicate with your computer through a number of devices, from your basic keyboard and mouse to joysticks and driving wheels. Specialized input devices also exist, like drawing tablets for artists and CAD operators, voice recognition software, and more.

Keying in

The most ubiquitous input device is the keyboard. You probably already have a few lying around; every computer you can purchase comes with one. Every keyboard contains the standard alphabet and number keys, a numerical keypad, special keys like print screen, delete, page up and page down keys, 12 function keys, and many more, including, thanks to Microsoft, the Windows key. Keyboards range from simple 104-key arrays to multimedia keyboards full of special buttons that launch e-mail applications, open browser windows, control Windows volume, and more. Figure 11-8 shows a multimedia keyboard.

TIP

Keyboard shortcuts

Using the Ctrl, Alt, and Windows keys, you can perform a number of common tasks quickly with your keyboard that you'd normally have to use the mouse to tackle. Various applications have their own keyboard shortcuts, while there are quite a few common to all Windows applications.

There are far too many keyboard shortcuts to list here, but some of the more common ones include the following:

✔ **Alt+F4:** Close the current window

✔ **Ctrl+X:** Cut the highlighted text, shortcut, program, or other object

✔ **Ctrl+C:** Copy the highlighted text, shortcut, program, or other object

✔ **Ctrl+V:** Paste whatever's on the Clipboard

✔ **Ctrl+Z:** Undo the last command

✔ **Ctrl+Y:** Redo the last command

✔ **Alt+Tab:** Toggle through open windows

✔ **Ctrl+Esc:** Open the Start menu

You can find a pretty complete list of keyboard shortcuts in Microsoft's Knowledge Base at http://support.microsoft.com/default.aspx?scid=kb;en-us;q126449.

Figure 11-8:
This buttons-studded mega-keyboard is the Logitech Media Keyboard.

Besides the Windows key, Microsoft gave us another keyboard innovation in the Microsoft Natural Keyboard, which is supposed to be more ergonomic than standard straight keyboards. Curved, contoured, and split down the middle, it has won over some users and alienated others. I hate the split-keyboard concept — I could never get used to it. My wife thinks it's terrific. It's purely subjective.

Wireless keyboards allow you to control a computer from across the room; they're ideal for home theaters connected PCs. Typically, a base unit plugs into the computer, while the keyboard is battery powered. Both infrared (IR) and radio frequency (RF) devices are available; RF is more convenient because it doesn't require a direct line of sight.

Despite all the gadgets and extra buttons and other jewels that encrust high-end keyboards, I find that I prefer a plain, straight, standard keyboard with big keys that provide nice tactile feedback. One of my favorites is the Key Tronic KT800, which you can grab for under $20.

Mousing about

Nestled next to your keyboard, your mouse is your right-hand (or left-hand, as the case may be) device. Mouse technology has evolved considerably since the device was first introduced in 1981.

Mod by Del Belyea

This clear acrylic case was inspired by the acrylic mouse pad known as GlowPad at Metku Mods (http://metku.net). The effect of the glowing edges looked cool, and I knew the lighting effect could be carried up the sides and around the top of a small case if the acrylic remained one piece as it wrapped around. A wood form was made with the dimensions for the components needed to fit inside. The corners of the wood form were rounded with a router. I used a paint stripper type of heat gun to make the acrylic pliable and wrapped a sheet of $\frac{1}{4}$-inch acrylic around the form. A piece of smoked acrylic was fitted for the front and the back panel is made from 0.040 aluminum. The red lighting comes from four LEDs mounted under the motherboard, pointed toward the bottom edge of the wraparound piece.

Mod by James (Corg8d) Anderson

"Heavy Metal" was my first attempt at doing a mod from the ground up. I am very much a car enthusiast as well as a computer geek, and "Heavy Metal" became the merging of those two interests. The version as it stands now is powered with each wheel having a dedicated 4.5-horsepower DC motor. It steers like a tank, has a top speed of 22 miles per hour, and can get there in a hurry. Even though "Heavy Metal" weighs in at over 250 pounds, it's still very nimble and usually catches spectators off-guard. For more information on the build of "Heavy Metal," including a video of it in action, head over to www.badgerpackaging.com/heavymetal.

Mod by Doom_Prophet

For "Radio Mod," I found an old radio/amp on the side of the road that was put out for trash. The problem with it was the radio tuner no longer worked. I loved the front plate and the wood-grain cover it had. So I decided to measure it and see if I could fit a micro ATX motherboard inside along with my PCI cards. There was just enough room. The radio was long enough for me to put a full-size PSU and hard drive next to the motherboard. I used the knobs on the front of the case to control fan speeds and even lighting. I also used a 2-x-24-character LCD display on the front to display temperatures and anything else I wanted.

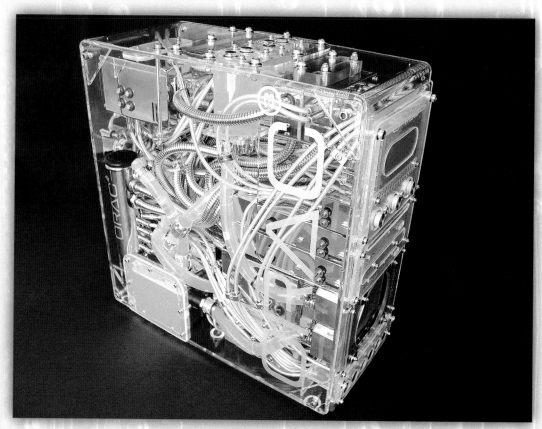

Mod by Peter Dickison

The inspiration behind this mod, "Orac³" came from the computer Orac, in the old sci-fi series *Blakes*-7. Besides the case, every internal component was extensively modded, sticking strictly to the themes of chrome, stainless steel, neon green, and transparent Perspex.

I chromed or built chrome covers for everything, including the motherboard and PCI cards. Wires were hidden inside stainless shower hoses or mesh-lined aquarium tube, custom chrome junction boxes and chrome jack plugs distribute power, and everywhere LEDs are embedded into the green Perspex panels to enable them to subtly "glow" around the edges. Over 400 stainless fasteners were also used in the build, and the case is water-cooled with twin reservoirs attached to a custom mounting plate.

I paid a lot of attention to the small details, even down to things like backlit DVD buttons and custom case feet — a total transformation of case and components.

Mod by Brent A. Crosby

This machine started as mild mannered "Dr. Jekyll," a 1U Internet appliance case that is designed to hold the Crystal-fontz CFA-633 LCD. We modified it into the crazed "Mr. Hyde." Cooling is a major issue in a 1U case. Twin Delta blowers behind laser-cut grills, a Dynatron 1U HSF, and custom ducting keep the heat under control. These monster fans can be monster loud, so the CFA-633's fan-control software is used to slow the fans down when maximum cooling is not needed. Blue cold cathode lamps along the sides and intense red LEDs in the Delta blowers complete the look.

Mod by Tailin (www.kitsunecases.com)

The "Red Dragon" was cut using #409 cut-off wheels and a #9909 tungsten cutter. The other dragon was cut out of $\frac{1}{8}$-inch Plexiglas using a scroll saw. It was painted on the underside and centered in an enlarged cutout on the top panel. I sculpted a scaled pattern into a thin layer of clay on the top panel and then covered it in fiberglass resin. I cut a fireball design into the front panel and mounted a Bulgin power in the center. The entire case was painted Toreador Red. Black was then airbrushed around the edges of the cutouts and at the bottom of the case to fade the paint to a deep red-black.

Mod by Brent Ross (a.k.a. AMD_Ju|\|k13)

The computer case of "Upside Down Case" is modified from a ThermalTake Xaser II. I wanted to do something a bit different with this dragon-style case so I decided to rebuild it from the ground up. The first step was to disassemble the case by removing all panels and drilling out 95 percent of the internal rivets. Then I turned the back plate and motherboard tray upside-down. Third, I reattached the bottom and top and installed the cross braces to their new position on the bottom section of the front panel. Taking the top off of an old case I fabricated a heat shield that would go across the cross braces to create two compartments. The top compartment houses the motherboard and optical drive cage, the bottom power supply, and hard-drive cage. In doing this, I have effectively created two cooling compartments, which improves overall cooling of the computer. The finishing touches were to paint the heat shield black and add a black cover to the upper drive cages; along with a 12-inch red CCFL and three red LED spotlights. The total price of this mod was under $50, a very good investment. The full work log on this mod can be found on GideonTech.com (www.gideontech.com/content/articles/242/1).

Mod by BrainEater

The "Mod Thinktank" started life as a Lian-Li pc-65 case. The case was disassembled down to the frame, and a "fish tank" of glass and aluminum was built to fit inside. The top of the tank forms the motherboard mount for my old Pentium 3 rig. The motherboard, CPU, RAM, cards, and PSU are all fully submerged in a dielectric fluid called Midel 7131. The back of the tank forms a 500-watt Peltier assembly which cools the liquid. There is a small submersible pump to circulate the liquid. The machine weighs 95 pounds and draws just over 1 kilowatt when running.

Conventional mice track movement with rollers activated by a heavy rubber ball that hangs below the mouse. It rolls as you move the device about, and the movements are translated by the computer to move the mouse cursor around Windows. The problem with ball mice is that the ball can pick up crumbs, dust, hairs, eyelashes, and other contaminants that degrade the accuracy of its motion. You have to clean the mouse ball every so often to keep the mouse operating happily.

Ball mice are disappearing, however, thanks to the advent of the optical mouse. These mice have a hole in the bottom through which a light-emitting diode (LED) shines, and a sensor analyzes the reflection. The sensor tracks the minute changes and translates them into fluid motion. As optical mice have evolved, they've become more precise, transferring more positional data faster for better responsiveness and scanning a larger area for increased fidelity. Mice like Microsoft's IntelliMouse Explorer (shown in Figure 11-9) and Logitech's MX510 are gamers' favorites.

Recently, Logitech released the MX1000, a cordless mouse with yet another new technology (see Figure 11-10). Instead of relying on an LED, it beams an actual laser onto the mousing surface and analyzes its reflection for changes. Whereas LED mice aren't reliable on glossy material or repetitive wood grains, a laser mouse works on just about any surface you can imagine.

Figure 11-9:
Microsoft's
IntelliMouse
Explorer.

Figure 11-10:
Logitech's
MX1000
laser-
powered
mighty
mouse.

Like wireless keyboards, cordless mice are available. They exist for both short-range operation at the computer and long-range operation across the living room.

Mice have various gadgets including wheels for scrolling Web pages and documents, and varying numbers of buttons. Tilting scroll wheels are relatively new, allowing you to scroll not only up and down but also from side to side. The buttons are generally programmable through the mouse's driver interface. I like lots of buttons, which I use for tasks like opening Windows Explorer with a single click.

Shop for a mouse by feel. You'll find that some mice fit your hand better than others. Left-handed mousers are at a disadvantage, because most mice are created for right-handed people, contoured for the right palms and fingers. Generally, if you want to use a mouse on the left side of the keyboard, you'll have to look for a symmetrical mouse. If you look hard, you may find a few left-handed mice, but lefties are rarely embraced by the major mouse manufacturers.

Gaming controllers

Logitech, Saitek, Thrustmaster, CH Products, and plenty of other manufacturers release a steady stream of joysticks, wheels, gamepads, and other
gaming controllers. Although gamepads are popular in the console world,
because they're the de facto controllers that come with Xbox, PlayStation, and
GameCube devices, they're not as widely embraced in the PC gaming world.

Some games cry out for specialized controllers, however. Racing simulations
and action-oriented driving games offer a highly enhanced experience when
played with a good driving wheel. The realism and fun factor soars compared
to playing them with, heaven forbid, the keyboard or even a gamepad. Trust
me: After you've tried playing Need for Speed Underground with a wheel, you'll
wonder why you didn't do it sooner. Driving wheels include options like lots
of buttons, butterfly and stick shifters, pedals, and more. My favorite racing
wheel is the Logitech MOMO Racing Wheel (shown in Figure 11-11).

Figure 11-11:
A Logitech
MOMO
racing
wheel.

Military flight simulators are all about a good joystick. Although you can play them with a gamepad or, if need be, a keyboard, a full-featured joystick drives home the experience. Look for joysticks with lots of buttons, twisting motion, and a throttle. Most come in compact, single-unit designs, but some, like Saitek's X45 Flight Stick (shown in Figure 11-12), have two separate pieces: a throttle and a stick. For my money, that's the ultimate device for playing games like Falcon 4.0.

Gamepads are good all-purpose controllers, and they're a must for sports games like EA's NHL and NBA series. Most come with lots of buttons and triggers. Dual-analog thumb pads, like the ones found on console controllers, are common.

Game controllers usually come with profiling programs that let you customize the controllers' behaviors for different games. You can create your own elaborate control schemes for each of your titles. I love this feature; I've been known to spend more than an hour tweaking my joystick for a Jane's flight sim game.

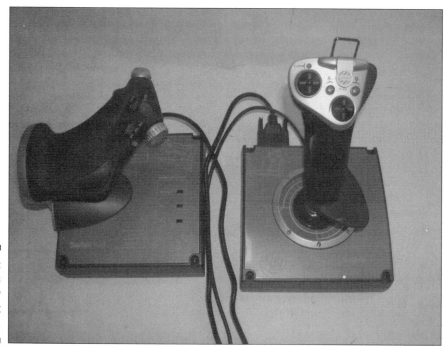

Figure 11-12:
Saitek's heavenly X45 Flight Stick.

The keyboard and mouse as game controllers

Although plenty of controllers are dedicated to the purpose of gaming, computer gamers rely most heavily on their keyboards and mice. First-person shooters and real-time strategy games, two of the most popular genres in gaming, lend themselves heavily to keyboards and mice. If you're a gamer, you're probably particular about your mouse — I certainly am. Current mouse drivers are optimized to let you program the various buttons in games so you can create your own control scheme. Although I'm less picky about my keyboard, I live and die by my Logitech MX510 mouse.

DirectX, Microsoft's suite of gaming APIs, contains DirectInput, the API that deals with, among other devices, gaming controllers. For game gear, it recognizes any number of buttons and a set of four axes. When you think of a joystick, the x-axis is manipulated when you move the stick from side to side, which would bank an airplane left or right. The y-axis deals with front-to-back motion, raising or lowering the nose of the airplane. The z-axis, often controlled by twisting the stick, is also known as the *yaw axis;* it turns a plane left or right like steering a car. A fourth axis, sometimes called the r-axis, is used for throttles.

The well-rounded gamer needs only these three types of gaming controllers — a joystick, a gamepad, and a driving wheel — but dozens of bizarre gimmicky devices have littered the controller industry through the years. From controllers with tilt sensors (so you can wiggle them in the air to attain horribly imprecise control over your game), to a rash of gadgets designed for first-person shooters that never matched the precision of a mouse/keyboard controller, to vocal recognition hardware that lets you bark commands into a microphone, to hand pads designed for real-time strategy games (most of which can be completely controlled with a simple mouse), all kinds of crap has vied for gamers' dollars. Beware when something seems more like a gimmick than a feasible input device, because it's probably nothing more than a novelty.

Joysticks, wheels, and gamepads are extremely subjective. As with mice and keyboards, what feels good to one set of hands may be uncomfortable to another. Experiment with display models before making a final decision, and be sure you can exchange the product for something else if you end up hating it.

Visual feedback: Displays

Now that you have a way to tell your computer what you want it to do, you need to be able to see it carry out your instructions. Although looking at an artfully modded computer case can be fun, it doesn't tell you much about the programs you're trying to run.

Of course, you'll need a display, otherwise known as a monitor. There are two types of displays prevalent today: big, deep, heavy cathode ray tube (CRT) monitors, and flat liquid crystal display (LCD) monitors. Each has its advantages and disadvantages.

CRT monitors

These analog monitors resemble classic television sets (not the new flat-panel TVs). They're beefy and bulky, they weigh a ton, they take up a lot of room, and you can easily put your back out positioning one on your desk. They are, however, versatile and responsive, and they're better for gaming than LCD monitors. Figure 11-13 shows a CRT monitor.

Figure 11-13: A CRT monitor with a flat screen.

Inside the depths of a CRT monitor, electron guns fire beams that strike phosphor dots, which are what you're looking at when you stare at the screen. The phosphor dots glow red, green, or blue, combining to make virtually any number of colors of which your video card is capable of transmitting through its display interface.

CRT monitors work at many resolutions. A *resolution* indicates the number of *pixels* (dots that make up an image) across and down, and they're usually in a ratio of 4:3 (for example, 800x600, 1024x768, 1600x1200, and so on). A CRT monitor will have a maximum resolution that it supports, and lower resolutions tend to look just as crisp.

Monitors also have a *vertical refresh rate,* meaning how many times they flash images in a second (measured in hertz). The higher the resolution, the slower the monitor will be able to refresh. Similarly, the faster the refresh rate, the less flicker you'll notice. When refresh rates hit around 75 Hz, you won't notice any flicker at all, and most monitors can display their maximum resolution at a minimum of 75 Hz.

Just because CRT monitors aren't flat-panel displays like LCD monitors are, that doesn't mean that the screen itself can't be flat. Many CRT monitors feature perfectly flat screens. CRT monitors offer larger screens for less money than comparable LCD monitors, making them a more attractive option.

Nearly all CRT monitors have a power-saving mode; you can instruct Windows to suspend their operation after a certain amount of time of inactivity.

Screen sizes of monitors are measured diagonally. Beware when shopping for a CRT monitor; screen size differs from actual viewable area. The monitor's bezel invariably obstructs part of the screen, so a 19-inch monitor may only have an 18-inch viewable area.

Another consideration is dot pitch. The *dot pitch* is the distance between those little phosphor dots, measured in millimeters. The narrower the distance, the sharper the display. Look for a dot pitch no wider than 0.27 mm; lower is better.

A series of buttons or maybe a jog-dial knob on the front of a CRT monitor lets you control a bunch of options, like brightness, contrast, horizontal and vertical display size, display position, the shape of the display, and more. Look for a monitor with robust controls.

Top monitor manufacturers include Viewsonic (and its sub-brand Optiquest), Samsung, Sony, Philips, and others. Look for a monitor with a flat screen, a decent dot pitch, good controls, and the biggest screen you can afford.

In gaming, the difference between a 17-inch and a 19-inch monitor is considerable.

LCD displays

Believe it or not, LCD monitors share a few characteristics with their CRT counterparts. They have lots of controls for adjusting the color, size, and positioning of the image. They're energy-conscious, shutting down after a period of inactivity. However, these digital displays differ from CRT monitors in more ways than they're similar.

The screen of an LCD monitor is made up of, literally, liquid crystals. Each pixel in the monitor has its own crystal. Electrical current causes liquid crystals to bend and glow. Color filters supply the color saturation.

Because each pixel gets its own crystal, LCD monitors have a characteristic called the *native resolution,* which is the actual resolution at which the pixels in the image transmitted from the graphics card match the pixels in the monitor. For instance, if an LCD is made up of an array of a row of 1,280 liquid crystals by a column of 1,024 liquid crystals, its native resolution would be 1280x1024. Its native resolution is also its maximum resolution.

Unfortunately, some older LCD monitors don't do a very good job of displaying resolutions smaller than their native resolutions. They have to interpolate the image and do their best to display it faithfully, but the results usually involve visual artifacts, a poor display, and, sometimes, unreadable text. Current LCDs do a better job, but CRT monitors still look better at large varieties of resolutions.

That's bad news for gamers. We like to be able to adjust the resolution of our games to achieve ideal frame rates. For example, I play most games at 1024x768 with some antialiasing, but Doom 3 is such a greedy monster that I play it at 800x600 to achieve a decent frame rate. Being tied down to a native resolution is not ideal when you're a gamer. Although the artifacts aren't very noticeable in high-motion graphics, static writing, like that of a game's heads-up display (HUD), will show distortion.

Another consideration that gamers need to bear in mind is an LCD monitor's *pixel response time.* Simply put, that's the amount of time it takes for the crystals in the display to go from black to bright, and it's measured in milliseconds (ms). Response times greater than 16ms can cause ghost images to form in games with speedy graphics — as well as anything that involves a lot of motion, like DVD viewing.

LCD monitors are terrific for mainstream computing — doing things like word processing, spreadsheets, taxes, e-mail, Web surfing, and similar stuff. For gaming, however, I recommend a CRT monitor. Just be sure to wear a lifting belt when you set it up.

Spectacular speaker systems

Your sound card without speakers is like a set of lungs without vocal cords to pump air through. Whether you're into listening to tunes, watching DVD movies, playing games with 3-D sound, or listening to the little Windows *ding* when you do something the operating system doesn't like — or even if you just want some extremely cool looking peripherals — you need a speaker system.

Years ago, PC speakers were an afterthought. Many were nonpowered, dependent on the 2-or-so watts of power put out by the sound card, and sounded like the audio was coming from the bottom of a well. Finally, somebody got the idea that PC users would like to hear decent audio. Altec-Lansing was one of the first companies to make really nice PC speakers. Now, the world is populated by dozens of companies that make speaker systems just for PCs.

When you're shopping for a speaker system, you have a lot to consider. Foremost is the number of *satellite speakers* (those are the actual speakers with the exception of the subwoofer, the big box that plays bass tones). Sound cards support four, five, six, and even seven satellites (called 4.1, 5.1, 6,1 and 7.1 speaker systems — the first number indicates the satellites and the second means the system has a subwoofer). Of course, you'll also have to think about where you're going to *put* all those speakers. I hang my rear speakers from the ceiling, but then again my office is in the basement where I can pound all the nails into the floor joists that I want to.

A close second consideration is the speaker system's power. The power is rated in wattage; the more wattage, the louder the speakers' capability to play sounds.

There are two wattage ratings:

- ✔ **Root Mean Square (RMS):** This is a realistic measurement that indicates the sustained power of the speakers.

- ✔ **Peak Maximum Power Output (PMPO):** This is rarely quoted by reputable speaker manufacturers. It's the theoretical maximum wattage the speakers could possibly achieve for a split second before they explode.

Ignore PMPO wattage. If the speaker manufacturer doesn't publish its wattage in RMS, you have every right to be suspicious.

Although all speaker systems have the necessary minijacks to connect to the various output ports on a sound card, some also include Sony-Philips Digital Interface Format (S/PDIF) input for digital audio. S/PDIF ports can be coaxial RCA-style or optical. If your sound card has an S/PDIF out port, and your speakers have S/PDIF capability, you should use it.

Some speaker systems have Dolby Digital and/or DTS decoders. When you watch DVD movies on your computer, you can take advantage of the atmospheric, three-dimensional sound provided by those formats. Think of that scene in *The Matrix* in which Neo dodges the bullets that the agent fires at him. You can hear those bullets zing past your head with a Dolby Digital setup.

The speakers' controls are an important factor. Besides volume, you may want tone control (bass and treble), and control over fade, balance, and more. Most speaker systems have a separate control pod; otherwise, the controls are usually on the right-front speaker. Some speakers also include a remote control, handy if you use them in a living room situation. Another groovy option is a headphone jack, within easy reach so that you can play with your computer late at night while your family or roommates are upstairs sleeping.

I've listened to 4.1, 5,1, 6,1 and 7.1 speaker systems and, beyond 5.1, the level of accuracy doesn't grow all that much. I'm happy with a 5.1 system, but if you want to get the full effect of a 7.1-capable sound card, you may opt for a 7.1 speaker system.

Feel the force

A great deal of gaming controllers have a technology called *force feedback*. Wheels and joysticks contain motors that can actually move the control device based on conditions within games. Gamepads have vibrating gear inside their handles.

Force feedback can be a boon or a bust, depending on how well the game developer implements it. Ideally, a game should provide subtle tactile feedback to help you maintain control of the vehicle or avatar you're operating in the game. Too often, however, force feedback is thrown

into a game at the last minute and, instead of relaying helpful tactile information, it jolts the stick or wheel yon and hither, making the game harder to control. Thankfully, most games let you turn force feedback off if you want.

My Logitech MOMO Driving Wheel has force feedback, and games like the Need for Speed and the NASCAR series implement the technology quite well. I've never cared for force feedback in joysticks because so few flight sims do a decent job with it. Your mileage may vary.

TIP

I'm a big fan of Logitech's Z series of speakers. I have the Z-680 5.1 speaker system (shown in Figure 11-14) hooked up to my gaming machine. Creative Labs markets a whole bunch of speaker systems with all numbers of satellite systems; the Inspire series is the pick of that litter. A great many reviewers, however, consider Klipsch's multimedia speaker systems to be the very best products for the PC, and I agree. The ProMedia Ultra 5.1 is an incredible, clean-sounding, powerful system.

All the rest

In the previous sections, I show you just a smattering of the peripherals you can connect to your PC. Because this is a modding book about creating a fun PC, I'm not going to get too deeply into the officey stuff — but I do want to go over a few other goodies you can get into.

If there's something you want to do with your computer, there's probably a peripheral that does it.

Figure 11-14:
Logitech's
Z-680
speaker
system.

Printers

High-speed laser printers, color inkjet printers, color laser printers, and photo printers are all useful in their own ways. You can share printers across a network so that any computer on the network can print it. In fact, some printers come with network hardware built in — there are even Wi-Fi enabled printers that you can put anywhere in the house and use through your wireless network.

Scanners

I use my scanner all the time. It's an old USB flatbed, but it still works. I scan pictures, book and magazine passages, documents, and even graphics cards for providing images in reviews that I write. With a scanner and the proper software, you can scan text and import it into a word processor like Microsoft Word for editing. You can scan images to post on your Web site. The possibilities are endless.

External storage

USB and FireWire drives of all sorts are available to connect to your computer, from hard drives to optical drives (see Figure 11-15). Although they're portable, they require their own AC power — so they're not handy to bring on the plane. But they make up for that in ease of use — you can add storage without having to open your computer.

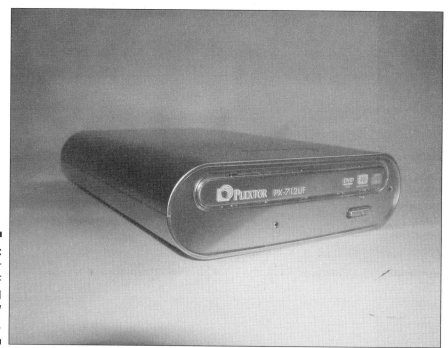

Figure 11-15:
The Plextor
PX-712UF
External
DVD+/-RW
drive.

Installing Peripherals

Hooking up external devices is simple by design. You just connect the device and, if necessary, install the drivers.

Follow the device's instructions regarding the driver installation. Windows has its way of prompting you to provide media with drivers on it, but some devices require you to cancel this procedure and run a custom installation procedure. Note especially that many USB-connected devices require you to install the driver before you attach the hardware.

Some gear, like PS/2 mice and keyboards, monitors, and printers connected to the parallel port, should be attached while the computer is turned off. When you turn the computer on and boot up Windows, you can then install the drivers. Standard 104-key keyboards don't require drivers, but those multi-media keyboards with all the extra buttons do. Mice will work without drivers (Windows drops in a generic mouse driver), but for full functionality and programmability you should install the proper software. Monitors come with information files — not drivers, per se, but files that tell Windows things like their various refresh rates and maximum resolutions.

Hot-swap devices, like USB and FireWire gear, can be plugged in while the computer is running. The first time you plug one in, Windows will detect the new device and, if it requires drivers, initiate its driver installation procedure. Follow the directions that came with the device. Some devices, like external hard drives and digital cameras, don't require drivers at all; Windows XP recognizes them as storage volumes and allows you to use Windows Explorer to move, copy, or delete data just as you do with your main hard drive and removable media.

After the drivers for a hot-swap device have been installed, you don't have to install them again. When you plug the device into the USB or FireWire port, Windows recognizes the device and activates the drivers.

Chapter 12

Software: The Reason Your Computer Exists

*A*s an intricate work of ingenious, precision electronics, a computer is a beautiful thing. I think the microcomputer should be considered a man-made wonder of the world: To get all those microscopic transistors firing with the utmost accuracy down to the nanosecond is astonishing when you think about it. That's how much of a nerd I am — I wax philosophical about computers.

All that spectacular hardware is completely useless, however, without something to do. Software provides the computer with the tasks it must accomplish to please its user. Computer software comes in many categories:

✔ **Operating systems:** These are the central set of programs that make the computer go, allowing you to interface with it to launch other programs. The operating system I concentrate on here is Windows XP.

✔ **Utilities:** Used to maintain a healthy and happy computer, utilities do things like eliminate old, unused files from the hard drive, check the drive for errors, watch out for viruses, quarantine spam e-mail, and more. Windows XP comes with a basic set of utilities, but many third-party utilities line store shelves.

✔ **Applications:** These are the meat of the software you'll run on your computer. They're the programs that let you get stuff done, like checking e-mail, tracking expenses, burning optical disks, balancing your checkbook, banging out documents, and so on.

✔ **Web browsers:** Microsoft's Internet Explorer isn't the only game in town. In fact, it's constantly being updated because hackers tear it apart to find and expose security holes. Check out Opera, or my favorite, Mozilla Firefox, for alternatives to Internet Explorer.

✔ **Multimedia programs:** Ditties like Windows Media Player, WinAmp, QuickTime, Voyetra Record Producer, Ulead VideoStudio, and many, many others let you play music, create MIDI tunes, edit video, watch streaming video from the Web, and generally enjoy the sound and video features of your computer.

✔ **Games:** I'll say it again: Games are what computers are for. Yes, I am using my computer to write this book in order to earn money to keep a roof over my head. But, to be brutally honest, I'd rather be playing Half-Life 2. I'd rather go to a LAN fest for a night of Unreal Tournament 2004 than, say, go to a movie.

As we roll along through this chapter, I help you install a fresh copy of Windows XP, get it up-to-date, install device drivers, and generally get your computer ready to install the software you plan to use. I'm sure you've installed your share of programs, so I won't get into the details of that mundane and simple task.

Why I don't recommend Linux (or other operating systems)

Another operating system is growing a cult following and a decent install base — tiny compared to Windows, but those who use it are passionate about its strong points. That operating system is called Linux, and it's available in a bunch of different versions called *distributions*.

I know I'm going to catch hell for this from Linux fanboys all over the globe, but I strongly recommend using Windows XP as your operating system. It's stable, it's versatile, and unlike Linux (and other operating systems, like Solaris, Unix, and others), it's compatible with the widest array of PC software and hardware. I concede that more and more hardware vendors are releasing Linux drivers, and that some good open-source software for Linux exists for accomplishing basic workstation chores. A fairly decent amount of games get released for Linux, but a great many don't.

Linux can be difficult to get into for novice and casual users. Getting a Linux distribution to run on an x86 platform often requires a fair amount of improvisation and technical wizardry. Although Linux is amazingly customizable, building your own kernel isn't something that every user wants to do before he can start to actually use his computer.

I want to be able to get a new PC up and running in an hour or so. I want to use virtually any hardware I can get my hands on. I want to play any game I'd care to, without having to hope it comes out for my operating system or wait six months after a Windows release to get my hands on a version that will run on my system. I'm a Windows user, and I'm proud. Experiment with Linux if you want, but I'll stick to XP.

Installing Windows XP

In this section, I assume you want to install a fresh, clean, new copy of Windows XP onto your hard drive. That's really the best way to go. Although you can upgrade from Windows 98 or Me, you'll pull along a whole bunch of baggage in terms of registry bloat, old software, and so on. If your hard drive is new, I help you create a big partition on it and drop Windows XP into place.

If you already have important stuff on your hard drive, I strongly suggest you back it up, because if you follow my instructions you'll wipe the hard drive clean.

I'm a firm believer in wiping a computer clean and installing a fresh copy of the operating system every year or so. Windows bloats. It collects lots of little files from programs that you install that sit on the hard drive; the Windows Registry (a database that stores information about the hardware and software on your computer) keeps entries that it doesn't need anymore; uninstalling software doesn't truly remove all remnants of it, leaving files and registry entries that you no longer need. The bottom line is that letting Windows get old and fat hurts performance. It takes longer to load programs; it's less responsive; it's, well, muddled. My test machines get refreshed on an almost constant basis, and I back up and wipe my main work computer annually.

Turn to "Preliminaries: Setting up the hard drive," later in this chapter, for instructions on how to wipe out your hard drive and start fresh. ***Remember:*** Be sure that everything you want on your hard drive is backed up somewhere else before you wipe it out — starting fresh means you lose everything on your hard drive.

Installing a new Windows XP operating system takes several steps, but the installation procedure is mostly user-friendly. If you've ever installed an operating system based on Windows NT, such as Windows NT 4.0 or Windows 2000, the process will look familiar to you. Installing Windows 98 or Me bears less resemblance to installing XP.

For this walkthrough, I use Windows XP Home Edition. You can still follow along if you're using Professional Edition; the installation procedures are extremely similar. Home Edition is sufficient for any consumer-oriented tasks, including gaming; there's no performance difference between the two operating systems. Professional Edition includes more-robust security, encryption, support for dual-processor systems, and a few other odds and ends.

Now batten down the hatches — we're going in!

Booting the Windows XP CD-ROM

The Windows XP CD-ROM is bootable. That means the computer can boot up off the CD-ROM in your optical drive. Booting the Windows CD-ROM automatically launches the Windows setup procedure.

The first thing you have to do is tell your computer's BIOS that you want to boot the CD-ROM. You have to adjust the boot order so that, when it's looking for a bootable device, the BIOS looks at the optical drive before it checks the hard drive.

Do this by entering the BIOS setup program:

1. **Turn on the computer.**

2. **Watch the POST screen (black background with white text) for a prompt to enter Setup.**

   You'll probably be instructed to hit the Delete key, but the key you're supposed to hit may be different.

3. **Check your motherboard's instruction manual to find out where in the BIOS setup program you set the boot order or boot priority.**

4. **Navigate to the proper screen.**

5. **Tweak the settings so that your optical drive is the first boot device and the hard drive is second.**

   Figure 12-1 shows the boot device priority screen on an Intel motherboard BIOS setup program.

6. **Exit the BIOS setup program, saving the new settings.**

7. **Allow the computer to boot.**

8. **Watch for a prompt that says something like** `Press any key to boot the CD`.

9. **Bang any key, and Windows will launch its setup procedure.**

If you're using a SATA hard drive and the motherboard's native BIOS doesn't recognize SATA, you'll have to load drivers. Watch for a prompt to hit F6 and then insert the floppy disk that came with your motherboard or PCI SATA controller. Check your motherboard's documentation to see if special drivers are required to recognize SATA hard drives.

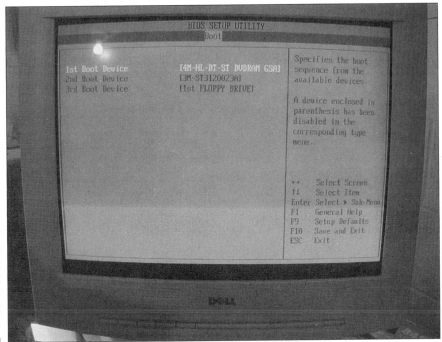

Figure 12-1:
Set the boot order so that your optical drive is first in line.

Preliminaries: Setting up the hard drive

After you've launched the setup procedure (see the preceding section), the Windows setup program loads a whole bunch of drivers. You'll see a blue screen with status updates along the bottom telling you which drivers are loading. Windows needs drivers to interface with your computer's hardware.

If you have a second, physical hard drive installed (as a D: drive, for example), you may want to physically unplug it before starting the Windows install. There are two reasons for this:

 ✔ You won't accidentally format the wrong drive.

 ✔ If you delete the old boot partition and reinstall, you'll find that your second drive has become the C: drive and your boot drive the D: drive. Mostly, this is a nuisance, but a few programs don't like the boot drive being the D: drive.

Eventually, the setup program presents a screen that says `Welcome to Setup` (see Figure 12-2). Continue on with the following steps:

1. **Select the option to set up Windows XP now, and hit the Enter key to proceed.**

   The setup program messes around for a few seconds and then assaults you with the end-user license agreement (see Figure 12-3). It's full of important information about your agreement with Microsoft regarding how you use Windows. It's a fascinating read . . . okay, *not.*

2. **Although I'd never tell you not to read this important document, I will say that, at your leisure, you can hit F8 to accept the agreement and proceed with setup.**

   Windows setup now checks out your hard drive situation. In my case, I'm wiping a hard drive with a previous installation clean. Therefore, I'm going to delete the partition on the hard drive and create a new one, by following steps 3, 4, and 5.

   Note: If your drive doesn't already have a partition on it, you'll skip ahead to Step 6 (you can tell your drive doesn't already have a partition on it because the screen you see will look like Figure 12-7).

3. **On the screen in Figure 12-4, I hit D to delete the partition.**

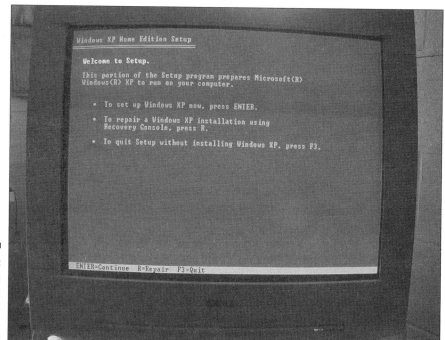

Figure 12-2:
The
Welcome
to Setup
screen.

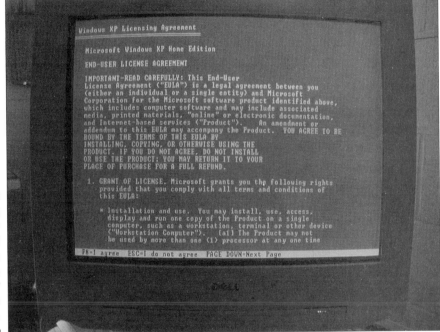

Figure 12-3:
The mighty
batch of
legalese
that is the
end-user
license
agreement.

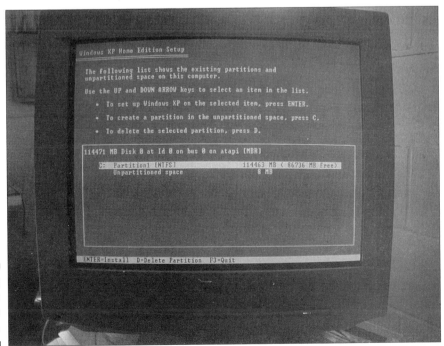

Figure 12-4:
I'm going to
delete this
partition.

4. **On the screen in Figure 12-5, I confirm my decision by hitting Enter.**

5. **On the screen in Figure 12-6, I press L to confirm my decision *again* (Windows really doesn't want you to delete a partition by accident).**

   Next, setup show you a screen similar to the one in Figure 12-6, only this time it shows a big block of unpartitioned space (see Figure 12-7).

6. **Hit Enter to set up Windows in the unpartitioned space.**

   Windows creates a partition and then informs you that the partition has to be formatted (see Figure 12-8). You'll have two options: to format it in NTFS (NT File System, the protocols through which Windows interacts with the hard drive), or to quick-format it in NTFS.

   A full format checks the drive thoroughly for problems like bad sectors (very rarely, a hard drive will contain areas that aren't writeable). Hard drives can develop bad sectors with prolonged use.

7. **Select either the regular-format or the quick-format option and hit Enter.**

   I suggest avoiding the quick format and going for the full format, even though it takes a long time on a large drive.

   A status bar crawls while Windows is formatting the partition (see Figure 12-9).

8. **Grab a magazine and get comfortable.**

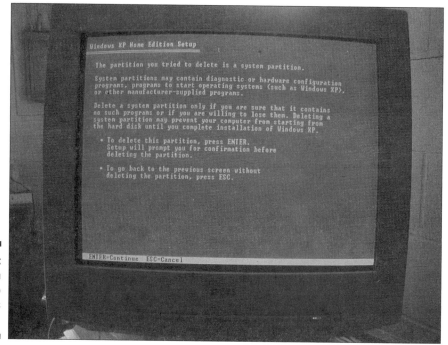

Figure 12-5:
I said, I'm going to delete this partition!

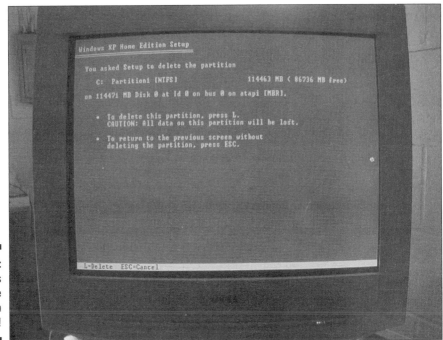

Figure 12-6:
For Heaven's
sake, delete
the partition
already!

Figure 12-7:
Set up
Windows in
the unpar-
titioned
space.

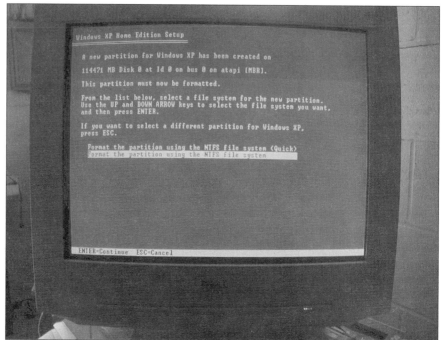

Figure 12-8:
Choose a
format
option —
quick or
thorough.

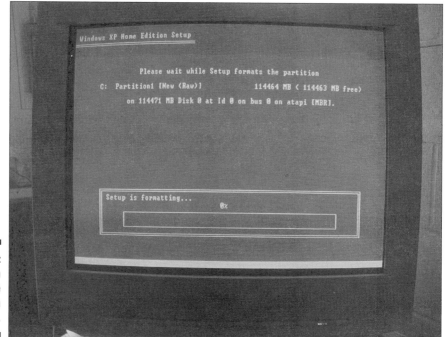

Figure 12-9:
Formatting a
large drive
takes a
long time.

Gathering information

When the drive is finally formatted, Windows setup will churn away and load a GUI with mouse support. Notice the steps listed down the left side of the screen and the estimated time remaining in the Windows installation.

The first screen you'll encounter asks you about international conventions. By default, Windows sets its language setting to English (United States) and its location to United States. It also assumes you have a U.S. keyboard layout. Here's where to go from there:

1. **If you want to change the international conventions settings, go for it; if you're happy with the defaults, click Next.**

   The next screen has two text fields: Name and Organization.

2. **Type in a name and, if you want, an organization, and then click Next.**

3. **Next, enter the 25-character product key that came with Windows, and click Next.**

   It's divided into five groups of five characters to make it easier to get through the code accurately.

   The next screen asks you to enter a network name. The default name it slaps into the text field is usually a random jumble of ASCII.

4. **Enter a name, and click Next.**

   You'll want to name the computer something that will make it easily identifiable on a home network — perhaps something location-specific like DEN, or the name of the person who uses it, like EURIPIDES.

   It's time to tell your computer what time it is.

5. **Set the date, the time, and your time zone, and click Next.**

   Leave the field that offers to automatically adjust for daylight saving time checked for convenience — unless you hate daylight saving time (or you live in an area that doesn't follow it).

   Now the Windows setup program does some work on its own. It installs the network stuff, sets the parameters, and then asks you if you want to customize the network.

6. **Click either Typical Settings or Custom Settings, and click Next.**

   In most cases of home networking, the typical settings work just fine: They allow you to share files and printers, and they install TCP/IP (a network protocol used for routing data throughout the network).

The setup program starts copying operating system files from the CD-ROM to the hard drive. This part takes a while, so relax and have a refreshing beverage. Feel free to read the feature billboards that the setup program plasters on the screen as it copies files.

After a while, Windows reboots the computer.

7. **Windows needs to boot the hard drive, not the CD, so when you see the prompt to press any key to boot the CD, control yourself and don't do it.**

Finalizing the setup procedure

After you go through all the steps in the preceding section, you're confronted with a black screen with a little dialog box that informs you that Windows is going to change the resolution of your screen. Here's where to go from there:

1. **Click OK.**

   The screen resolution changes from 640x480 to 800x600.

   Another dialog box gives you 30 seconds to accept the new resolution.

2. **Click OK to accept the new resolution.**

   Setup is almost done. The next thing you're confronted with is the "Welcome to Microsoft Windows" presentation. It wants you to spend a few minutes setting up your computer.

3. **Click Next.**

   Windows wants to find the Internet. It checks for connectivity. If it doesn't find any, it'll ask you how the computer connects to the Net. Depending on your hardware, you're given several choices. For instance, if your PC is directly connected to a cable or DSL modem, you can tell Windows just that. If it's connected to a LAN with an Internet connection, you can let Windows know.

4. **If you don't want to set up an Internet connection at this time, click Skip; otherwise, make your selection and click Next.**

   Windows needs to be activated. Windows Product Activation (WPA) gives you 60 days to activate your copy of Windows before you can't use it anymore. You can connect via the Internet or by making a phone call.

5. **Because I know that my Ethernet controller needs drivers before Windows can use it and thus access the Internet, I'm going to say No, remind me every few days and click Next. If you're not sure whether Windows can get to the Net, select No, Remind Me Every Few Days; otherwise, select Yes, Activate Windows over the Internet Now. Then click Next.**

Now you can set up user names. Windows can create separate user accounts for each person who uses the computer, so each person can customize his desktop and applications.

6. **Enter at least one name and click Next.**

At last, you come to the screen that tells you you're all done.

7. **Click Finish.**

You're taken to the Windows desktop.

You're now ready to start using Windows . . . after you do a few other things, like install all your hardware's device drivers and use Windows Update to bring your copy of Windows up-to-date.

A little icon in the *system tray* (the little bar next to the clock on the bottom-right of the Windows desktop) informs you if you need to activate Windows. Another icon in the system tray tells you that you can take a tour of Windows (which is mildly informative). If you've never used Windows XP, take the plunge and take the tour. It's geared toward the basic user, so it may be below your level, but it shows some of XP's more interesting features.

Installing Device Drivers

If you consider the sheer number of devices that are available to add to a PC, Windows has a huge array of hardware it has to deal with. If Microsoft built compatibility into Windows for every graphics card, sound card, network interface device, modem, motherboard chipset, and so on, the operating system would come on about 12 CD-ROMs and take up most of your hard drive. Windows *does* come with quite an array of drivers, but it can't possibly keep up with the flood of equipment released every week.

Keeping drivers up-to-date

After you've installed the driver software that came with your devices, you should hit the Web and visit the manufacturers' sites for each of your computer's devices. Go to the download section and look for updated drivers for your gear. Companies release driver updates on a regular basis, building more functionality, better performance, better stability, bug fixes, and other benefits into new driver releases. Yes, it can be a pain to download all those drivers and go through the installation process all over again, but you should keep your drivers current. Check for new drivers for your devices at least once a month.

Instead, Windows relies on manufacturer-provided device drivers to tell it how to use some of the gear in your system. Some stuff, like Integrated Drive Electronics (IDE) hard drives, optical drives, and memory, don't require drivers from the manufacturer; Windows knows what to do with them. Other equipment, like motherboards, graphics cards, sound cards, SATA controllers, and external stuff I discuss in Chapter 11 do need drivers, and before you're ready to start using Windows you need to install them.

A *device driver* is basically a translator. Devices have sets of commands that tell them what to do, when to do it, and how to do it. Windows has its own set of commands, and it doesn't care what the device thinks of them. The drivers translate Windows commands into the specialized commands used by the device. You may not appear to need drivers for some devices (for example, you can operate a Windows desktop without installing manufacturer-provided drivers for the motherboard and graphics card, because Windows uses generic drivers to interface with them until the proper drivers are installed). However, you'll encounter performance degradation, unusable features, and incompatibilities until you install the proper drivers.

Most manufacturer drivers have their own setup programs that run just like software installation procedures, dropping the drivers for their devices into place. In some cases, however, you may have to install the drivers by Windows conventions. This procedure can differ based on how the device's drivers are provided. The instruction manual for the device in question will tell you step-by-step how to install the driver.

The order in which you install your devices' drivers doesn't matter — with one exception: *You should install the motherboard drivers first.* Motherboard drivers may include a core chipset driver, drivers for storage device interfaces, drivers for onboard Ethernet controllers, and even programs that optimize how Windows interfaces with the board. Install any drivers that came with your motherboard before doing anything else.

Note: You'll probably have to reboot between each driver installation. The process can grow tiresome, but you have to do it.

After you've installed the motherboard drivers, proceed to install your graphics card drivers, network interface drivers, sound card drivers, mouse drivers, keyboard drivers (if you have a keyboard that requires them), and so on. Again, you'll most likely have to reboot in between each installation. With each driver installation, your computer will become more and more useful. After you install your sound card drivers, for instance, you can hear things through your properly connected speaker system. Your mouse will become fully functional after you install its drivers. After you install the drivers for your Internet connection (be it through a modem, through a direct connect to a broadband appliance, or through a shared connection on a LAN), you'll be able to surf the Web. After you install your graphics card drivers, you can change your screen resolution and refresh rate to whatever you consider suitable.

Activating and Updating Windows

If you've read and done everything in this chapter to this point, Windows still isn't ready for use. Microsoft is constantly improving its operating system by patching security holes, releasing software updates, and even coming out with major upgrades called *service packs*. You need to activate Windows and get it up-to-date before you start to use it.

Activating Windows

If you didn't activate Windows when you first installed it, you should activate after you've got Internet access:

1. **Choose Start ➪ All Programs ➪ Activate Windows.**

   You'll see a screen like the one in Figure 12-10. It gives you three options: to activate Windows over the Internet, to activate Windows by calling a toll-free number, or to hold off on activating for now.

2. **If you have Internet access, choose the first option; if not, choose the second. Then click Next.**

3. **If you want, register with Microsoft.**

   Registering is optional, and I never do it.

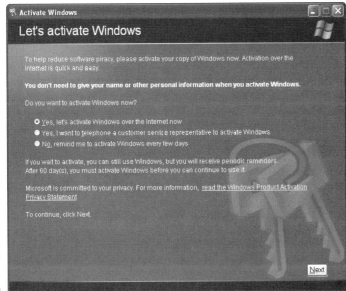

Figure 12-10:
Activate Windows within 60 days of installation.

The importance of DirectX

I cover APIs and DirectX earlier in this book, but it warrants attention here, because, like Windows itself, keeping DirectX up-to-date is important for gaming. As of this writing, the latest version of DirectX, version 9.0c, was included as part of Service Pack 2. You can manually check for DirectX updates every so often by visiting www.microsoft.com/directx.

DirectX is a series of APIs (application program interfaces) designed to foster excellent, responsive, and high-quality multimedia and gaming in Windows XP. DirectX includes graphical APIs, audio APIs, video APIs, input APIs, and more. APIs consist of code that makes it easier for hardware manufacturers and application programmers to design their wares. For instance, in theory, a game programmer can program to DirectX rather than include support for every graphics card, sound card, and joystick it could possibly encounter. As long as the game uses DirectX properly, it will work with DirectX-compliant hardware.

With your drivers up-to-date, Windows up-to-date, and DirectX up-to-date, you're finally ready to use your operating system! Install your games, applications, utilities and other software and get computing!

Updating Windows

When you finally have all your drivers in and up-to-date, and when you've activated Windows, you should run Windows Update and get all the latest service packs, security patches, and other important updates to the operating system.

Note: You'll need Internet access to use Windows Update.

When you're ready, follow these steps:

1. **Choose Start ⇨ All Programs ⇨ Windows Update.**

   Internet Explorer will launch and take you to the Windows Update Web site (see Figure 12-11).

2. **Click Express Install to automatically download the most critical updates automatically, or Custom Install to pick and choose which updates you want to add.**

   Depending on the version of Windows XP you installed, it may already have several updates. The latest major update to Windows XP was Service Pack 2, which introduced new security features like a robust firewall, a pop-up blocker for Internet Explorer, and many other enhancements. Since Service Pack 2 was released, more security patches have been made available to Windows Update. Optional accessories are also available, like Windows Media Player 10.

Figure 12-11:
Windows
Update.

3. **Allow Windows Update to download and apply Service Pack 2, and all critical updates.**

   Some updates, Service Pack 2 included, must be installed separately and can't be grouped with other updates. In other cases, you can apply several updates at the same time.

4. **Run Windows Update over and over again until there are no more critical updates available.**

Using Automatic Updates is a good idea. Automatic Updates is a module of Windows that periodically checks the Windows Update site for critical updates, downloads them in the background, and installs them for you or informs you that you have updates to install. You can configure Automatic Updates by clicking **Start**, right-clicking **My Computer** (or by right-clicking on My Computer right on the desktop), clicking **Properties**, and clicking on the **Automatic Updates** tab.

Part III
Modding for Speed: Tweaking and Overclocking

The 5th Wave   By Rich Tennant

In this part . . .

The roots of modding lie in making computers work as quickly and efficiently as they possibly can. Unfortunately, with their default settings, most PC BIOSes and, certainly, Windows XP, don't operate at full capacity. This part discusses how to fine-tune a computer's BIOS to get the utmost in core performance, how to modify Windows for the peak computing experience, and how to push your components past their factory specifications in a process known as *overclocking*. Overclocking is like getting a free upgrade: You can make your CPU and graphics card perform faster, like more expensive parts — but getting them to do it with peak stability is a challenge. When you're done with this part, your PC should be flying at its absolute peak in terms of power.

Chapter 13

Modding and Maintaining the BIOS

. . . .

In This Chapter

▶ Understanding the BIOS setup program

▶ Getting a grip on the many BIOS settings

▶ Keeping your BIOS updated

. . . .

*B*asic Input/Output System (BIOS) is a chip that contains the first instructions so that the computer knows what to do when it wakes up. It performs a Power-On Self-Test (POST) and looks for bootable media (such as the operating system on the hard drive). The BIOS setup program contains lots of options that affect how your computer does what it does, and those options are saved on a chip called a Complementary Metal Oxide Semiconductor (CMOS).

I told you how to get into the BIOS setup program. . . .

When you first power up the PC, the POST screen, which is black with white lettering, displays. If you pay attention, you'll see a prompt that most likely says Press DEL to enter setup. This means you should bang the Delete key (sometimes repeatedly) if you want to initiate the BIOS setup program. In very rare cases, you may have to hit a different key. Intel motherboards, for example, ask you to hit the F2 function key.

In Chapter 12, I mention a few of the BIOS settings, such as selecting the boot order so that you can instruct your computer to boot the Windows XP CD-ROM in order to install the operating system. But the BIOS contains lots of other settings — controlling everything from how fast keys repeat when you hold them down to where to look for a graphics card, from delicate memory timings to PC power management . . . and much, much more.

In this chapter, I give you a look at a typical motherboard BIOS — that of the DFI LANParty PRO875B — and walk you through some of the more common settings that you may want to tweak. The BIOS on this board was developed by a company called Award, which makes BIOS chips used in dozens of motherboards. Depending on your selection of motherboard, you'll encounter some differences, but a great many BIOSes resemble this one.

Making Sense of Your BIOS Options

BIOS settings contain a lot of options, many of which are holdovers from days gone by. Lots of the settings just don't matter anymore. Other, more pertinent settings can directly affect the operation of your computer.

Although I try to explain the most important settings in the next few pages, you should live by this law: *If you're unsure what a setting does, don't change it.* Some of the BIOS settings alter how the motherboard uses its components, and mishandling them can cause adverse effects.

Standard CMOS features

The first page of the BIOS through which we're strolling is called standard CMOS features. This is where you can set the date and time, configure hard drives, and inform the computer of the nature of its floppy drive.

Setting the time

Most BIOSes operate in military time, so 8:00 PM is 20:00. I recommend leaving the hard drive settings alone; the BIOS auto-detects the hard drives each time it boots up. If you do explore the hard drive parameters, be careful. Some of the options, like cylinder, head, landing zone, and others are for legacy hard drives (and, in this case, by *legacy* I mean *ancient*).

Setting up the floppy drive

If you have a floppy drive, it will most certainly be the A: drive, and it will definitely be a 1.44MB 3.5-inch drive. Years ago, different types of floppy drives existed, including big 5.25-inch drives that took big black disks that were quite literally floppy.

Setting up the video option

If you have a video option, it will usually be selectable to EGA/VGA, CGA, and MONO. It should be set to EGA/VGA; CGA and monochrome graphics cards haven't been around for at least a decade.

Halting on errors

A Halt On setting lets you tell the BIOS when to stop booting in the event that it encounters an error. Such errors include a missing keyboard, a missing diskette drive, and a video problem. You can tell it to cease operation if it encounters one of those problems, or to simply boot up no matter what. I recommend halting on errors so you know if something fails or is unplugged.

Advanced BIOS features

The next page of the BIOS setup program is much meatier than the standard CMOS features page. Options include, but are not limited to, the following.

Flash protect

You update the BIOS through a method called *flashing* it. If something goes wrong with the flash process, however, it can render your computer unusable. Flash protect doesn't allow the BIOS to be flashed. You have to disable it in order to update the BIOS, but while it's turned on, it keeps the BIOS safely unwriteable.

Boot priority

Here is where you can tell your computer what order to check your drives for a boot partition. To speed up boot time, set your hard drive in front of your other drives. If you have to boot a floppy or a CD-ROM, you can always change this option.

L1, L2, and L3 cache

You can disable your CPU's cache, but I can't imagine why you'd want to. For peak performance, be sure all cache levels are enabled.

Quick power-on self-test

You can speed up the boot process by enabling this option. The BIOS will perform a less thorough, but much faster, POST when the computer is turned on. Because even a full length POST isn't a reliable diagnostic for hardware problems (it only caches the most pronounced predicaments), I keep this option enabled.

RAID or SCSI card boot

On the LANParty board, which contains a RAID controller and SATA capability, there are three settings for this option. High Point RAID will boot the drives connected to the RAID controller; ICH5 RAID will boot a SATA device; and PCI SCSI Card will boot a SCSI drive connected to a PCI host adapter.

USB flash disk type

This interesting option lets you determine how the BIOS will recognize one of those little USB based "drives" that contains flash memory. You can set it to IDE or floppy; the advantage of one over the other is unclear.

Swap floppy drive

Back in the olden days, many computers had two floppy drives. With two identical drives, disk duplication was really quick and easy; a computer could also accept both 5.25-inch floppies and 3.5-inch floppies with the proper drives installed. This holdover option tells the BIOS to flip-flop the A: and B: drives. Because modern computers have one floppy drive (if they have any at all), this option is outdated.

Boot up floppy seek

With this option enabled, the BIOS will try to determine whether the floppy disk is 40 or 80 tracks. Because modern floppy drives are all 80-track, there's no reason to enable this option.

Boot up NumLock status

This tells the computer whether you want NumLock on or off by default. NumLock on causes your numerical keypad to respond with numbers; with NumLock off, it acts like arrow keys.

Typematic rate status

Enabled by default, this option affects how the BIOS tells Windows to handle a key held down. Enabled, there will be a pause, and then the key will repeat. The next two settings — typematic rate and typematic delay — affect the speed at which the key repeats and the length of the delay before it starts to repeat.

Security option

If you password-protect the BIOS, this setting affects when the password is needed. Setting it to System means the machine won't boot and access to the BIOS setup program is denied without the password. Set to Setup, the system will boot, but the BIOS setup program is password-protected.

Advanced chipset features

This section controls features not of the BIOS, but of the chipset itself. They are more advanced than the BIOS features and include options that tell the system how to use its RAM.

DRAM timing selectable

RAM contains logic that imparts information about it to the BIOS, including the size of the module and its timing settings. Setting this option to By SPD (Serial Presence Detect) will tell the motherboard to use the RAM at its native — and stable — settings. You can set this to Manual, which will allow you to tweak the following variables:

- **CAS latency time:** CAS stands for *Common Access Strobe.* The CAS latency indicates how long the system has to wait before the RAM is in a ready state to transfer data. Lowering this may speed up memory transfers, but it can also degrade system stability.

- **Active to precharge delay:** This indicates how long a row of memory is active before it can become inactive and ready for new data. Lowering this setting can improve performance marginally, but again you may sacrifice stability.

- **DRAM RAS# to CAS# delay:** RAS stands for *Row Access Strobe.* When the memory controller selects a memory row; it has to wait a few cycles before the columns in the row can be read. Lowering this delay can increase RAM performance.

- **DRAM RAS# Percentage:** After data have been read from the memory, the controller deactivates the row — after waiting a few cycles. The lower this setting, the faster — but again stability may be forfeited.

No magic formula for picking the perfect memory timings for peak performance exists. It takes a lot of experimentation. If you're not up for it, leave the DRAM timing selectable option to By SPD, which is a small chip on the memory module that tells the system how fast it can run. Your system will be stable.

System BIOS cacheable

Way back when hamburgers cost a nickel, operating systems communicated with the hardware via the BIOS. Caching the BIOS into the processor's L2 cache sped up this process. Now that operating systems like Windows XP communicate directly with the hardware, there's no reason to enable this option.

Video BIOS cacheable

Similarly, there's no reason to cache the video BIOS because, again, Windows doesn't communicate with the hardware through the BIOS. Disable this feature.

AGP aperture size

This setting indicates how much system memory can be allocated to the AGP graphics card. It doesn't *reserve* the memory for the graphics card; it just states the maximum amount of memory the card is allowed to use. Tweaking this setting won't affect graphics performance. If your graphics card has a lot of RAM (say, 256MB), keep AGP aperture size low, around 64MB. If your card is low on RAM (64MB or less), jack up the AGP aperture size to 128MB or more.

DRAM data integrity

Some memory is capable of error checking and correction (ECC). Set this option appropriate for the type of RAM you're using.

Integrated peripherals

This section is where you tell your motherboard which of its integrated devices you want turned on and which of its you won't need. You can also change how some of the integrated peripherals operate.

OnChip IDE device

This submenu lets you activate or deactivate onboard IDE devices, including PATA and SATA devices. Some options you may encounter here include the following:

- ✔ **Primary and secondary IDE controller:** You can enable or disable your motherboard's IDE controllers. If, for instance, you're using a SATA hard drive and you have only one optical drive connected to the primary IDE controller, you can disable the secondary IDE controller.

- ✔ **PIO Mode:** You should leave these options set to auto. PIO stands for Programmed I/O, and several modes have evolved over the years. The BIOS can determine what's best for your IDE devices.

- ✔ **UDMA Mode:** These options should never be disabled. You want your IDE devices to operate in Ultra-DMA mode, so leave this set to Auto.

- ✔ **On-Chip Serial ATA:** This option should be set to Auto, unless you're not using SATA, in which case you can disable it. Other selections include Combined Mode (which lets you use up to four devices between the SATA and IDE ports), Enhanced Mode (which allows up to six devices), and SATA only.

OnChip PCI device

Another submenu, this area allows you to enable or disable PCI devices like USB ports, USB 2.0 ports, AC'97 onboard audio, and more. Disable the ones you know you won't use (for instance, if your computer has a PCI sound card, you should disable the onboard audio).

Onboard super IO device

This heavily populated submenu lets you tweak all kinds of stuff:

- ✔ **Onboard FDC controller:** This option lets you toggle the floppy drive controller. If you're not using a floppy drive, disable it.

- ✔ **Onboard serial port 1:** If you may use a serial port device, leave this option set to Auto; otherwise, disable it. You can manually set an I/O address and IRQ for the device, but there's no real need to.

- ✔ **IrDA options:** There are many options for IrDA (Infrared Data Association). IrDA is rarely used; it just never caught on.

- ✔ **Parallel port options:** You can set the resources for the system's parallel port or disable it entirely. If you leave it enabled, you can set its functionality to SPP, EPP, ECP, or EPP + ECP. Check your printer's documentation to see what type of parallel port it requires, and adjust this option as needed. If your printer uses USB, you may want to disable this.

- ✔ **Init display first:** This option lets you choose between PCI and AGP to tell the BIOS where to look first for your graphics card. Of course, you'll want to set it to AGP.

Power management

You can instruct your computer to draw less power after a certain amount of inactivity. These options work hand in hand with the Windows power management settings to determine how to save power.

ACPI function

ACPI stands for *Advanced Configuration and Power Interface.* You should set this option to Enabled to make power management possible.

ACPI suspend type

The choices here on the LANParty board are S1(POS), called the power-on suspend function, which allows the computer to suspend operation while leaving some devices powered; and S3(STR), which allows the computer to suspend its operations to RAM and shut down its components entirely.

Video-off method

This option instructs the BIOS how to suspend the monitor's operation. You should use DPMS (display power management signaling), which lets Windows determine the suspend state of your monitor.

Soft-off power button

You can shut down the computer with the power button. This option lets you determine if the shutdown procedure starts immediately when you hit the button, or if you have to hold it down for 4 seconds to start the shutdown procedure.

Various wake/resume on events

You can instruct your computer to come out of a suspend mode given various events, including modem rings, LAN queries, and more.

Power lost resume state

Here you can instruct your computer about what to do if it loses electricity. You can tell it to remain off, to turn back on, or to resume its last state. I suggest you instruct it to remain off, in case power outages continue to occur. Brownouts can damage the power supplies of computers that are left on.

PCI and PnP configuration

Plug and Play was once thought to be a pipe dream. Could Windows really be intelligent enough to configure devices on its own? Could motherboards be made to take care of their own resources? The happy answer turned out to be a resounding "Yes!" and now you can enjoy amazing ease of use in adding peripherals to your computer.

The options in this section should be left to Auto. Let the motherboard and operating system work out the PCI configuration and resource control. Leave the option Reset Configuration Data to Disabled; there's no need to force a reset of the Extended System Configuration Data (ESCD) each time the computer boots.

PC health status

You'll see a couple of options on this screen, but it's mainly filled with data showing the temperature of the CPU, various fan RPM speeds, voltages, and so on. This data can be fed to a Windows-based monitoring program so you can keep tabs on the health of your system from within XP.

CPU fan protection

The BIOS can monitor the CPU fan rotation. If the fan seizes up, the CPU is in immediate danger of overheating. If you enable this option, the system will shut down if the fan stops turning.

Shutdown temperature

Enabling this option lets you choose a temperature at which the system will shut itself down to avoid damage from overheating. You need the Windows monitoring software installed for this to work. This is especially handy if you're overclocking your CPU — setting a shutdown temperature can protect it from burning out.

Overclocking

Most BIOS setup programs have a page at which you can control things like the front-side bus speed, the clock multiplier, voltages, and more. I cover these details of overclocking in Chapter 15.

Keeping the BIOS Up-to-Date

Just as you monitor your hardware drivers, checking for updated versions on a regular basis, so should you make an effort to keep your motherboard BIOS up-to-date. New BIOS versions can increase system stability, bring added features, fix bugs, and more.

You can download the latest BIOS revisions from the motherboard manufacturer's Web site. When you discover a new version, you should download it and prepare to flash your BIOS. The flash procedure will vary by motherboard maker. Some manufacturers, like Intel, provide Windows-based utilities that, when activated, reboot the computer, flash the BIOS, and boot back into Windows, all automatically. Other manufacturers have you flash the BIOS the old-fashioned way: You download the new BIOS revision and a flash utility and copy them to a bootable floppy diskette. Then you boot into a command prompt and type a command to activate the flash utility. The motherboard manufacturer's Web site will have detailed instructions in flashing the BIOS.

Write down or print out the instructions on the manufacturer's Web site. When you boot the floppy, you won't have access to a Web browser to read them. *Remember:* Follow the instructions carefully.

No matter what you do, *do not power down the system while the BIOS is being flashed!* An incomplete flash procedure can render the BIOS unusable — thereby magically transforming the whole computer into a $2,000 paperweight. If this happens, you'll have to contact the motherboard manufacturer to arrange a repair. When the BIOS flash utility is running, don't go near the AC cable or the power button!

Chapter 14

"Modding" Windows for Speed

● ●

In This Chapter

▶ Knowing why you may want to fine-tune Windows XP

▶ Tweaking Windows's performance options

▶ Dumping unwanted Windows programs

▶ Getting rid of adware and spyware

▶ Disabling unnecessary services

▶ Optimizing and maintaining storage devices

● ●

*Y*ou bought the best hardware you could afford in order to build up a speedy system. You've optimized the BIOS, installed Windows, updated all your system's device drivers, and you've actually got a working PC on your hands. Congratulations!

Windows XP is a fine piece of operating system engineering, and it's pretty speedy and efficient with its default settings. You can, however, make adjustments here and there to make it faster and more responsive. You can speed up the boot process, tweak performance options, weed out programs you don't need, prevent some annoying applications from loading at startup, keep your hard drive running at its peak, and a whole lot more.

Understanding the Need to Tweak Windows XP

Operating systems exist simply to allow people to use computers. They're the layer of software that gives users the ability to install and run programs, store things on the hard drive, rip CDs, surf the Web, e-mail Grandma Eunice, and so on. In the case of Windows, it's the graphical user interface (GUI) that lets you tell your PC what to do.

But operating systems are more than that. Windows is also the captain in charge of how your computer works. It affects the way every piece of hardware in the system operates, from the hard drive to the graphics card. With Windows responsible for so much, it's no wonder that it embeds a number of ways to optimize it.

Here's another thing to think about. Windows is designed to run on virtually any PC equipment that meets its system requirements. That means it has to deal with hundreds of motherboards, graphics cards, sound cards, network interface cards, modems — and on and on. It's also designed to work out of the box in any number of environments: the homes of consumers, the desks of cubicle jockeys, the workstations of power users, the shop floor, the hardcore gamer's desk, the dorm room, the school computer lab, and endless other places where computers spend their time.

It's for that reason that Windows XP makes a *lot* of assumptions as to how it's going to be used. It installs all kinds of programs and services (which consist of code that runs in the background to allow various processes to take place) to be prepared for any eventuality. It also decides how it's going to look visually, how it's going to handle *virtual memory* (which is a file on the hard drive that, in the eyes of running programs, mimics system RAM), and more.

Some programs that you download or buy and install make their own assumptions. They decide that part of their code should be running in the background at all times, often to speed up the load time of their main application. Those background applets increase the time it takes Windows to fully load at startup, and they eat up system resources, which can degrade performance.

You can make a whole bunch of adjustments to Windows to weed out running code that you don't need, to handle resources more efficiently, and to generally streamline the operating system and make it run better. You don't necessarily *have* to; it works great out of the box. But if you can make it even better, why wouldn't you want to?

Windows XP's Built-In Optimization

Windows knows that you want it to operate at its peak performance. Like a good little doggie, it aims to please. That's why it periodically updates itself based upon its observations of the way you use it: It makes your favorite programs run faster, it tries to cut down on its startup time, and it simply wants to make your life easier.

Windows uses a technique called *prefetching* to accomplish its self-optimization. It observes the programs that launch at startup and the programs you use most often, keeping track of them in a file called layout.ini. It then writes data critical to your habits into a cache, and when it boots up or starts to launch an application, it reads the prefetch data to expedite the process.

Furthermore, Windows knows that data that are on the outer edge of the hard drive platters are read faster than data in other locations. Every three days or so, when the computer is idle, it rearranges the location of boot files and commonly accessed files to speed up the loading process. It also does this when you use the Disk Defragmenter utility.

Sometimes, the prefetch folder, which is located at `C:\Windows\Prefetch`, gets gunked up with old files. This can cause a slight determent in performance. Every few weeks or so, navigate to that folder (see Figure 14-1) and clean out everything except the layout.ini file. You won't lose any data; Windows will re-create any files it needs to use its prefetching abilities.

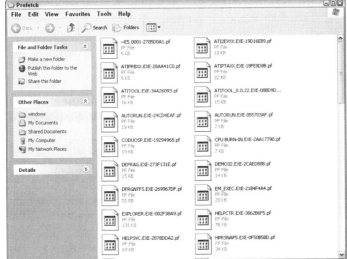

Figure 14-1:
The Windows prefetch directory.

Tweaking the Windows Performance Options

Microsoft anticipated the desire of the world at large to tool around in Windows and adjust performance settings. Windows includes a basic set of GUI-related options in a little applet called Performance Options. It's there that you can trade pleasing visual effects for a more responsive computing experience.

Tweaking the Performance Options can boost Windows's responsiveness on older computers that lack the power of modern equipment, but you may not notice a big difference in performance if your PC is loaded with an Athlon 64 or a Pentium 4 Extreme Edition. However, you should still check out the Performance Options selections, because they affect how the operating system looks; you'll be able to experiment with the visual effects to find the most pleasing arrangement. I used to work with this guy named Mike who was attached to Windows 2000; when XP came out he loaded it up and declared, "It's Windows Candyland Version!" He was grateful when I showed him the Performance Options applet, where you can turn off the eye candy and achieve a bland, practical look.

To invoke the Performance Options applet:

1. **Right-click My Computer.**

2. **Select Properties.**

   The System Properties window appears.

3. **Select the Advanced tab.**

4. **Under the Performance heading, click the Settings button.**

   You'll see a window that looks like the one shown in Figure 14-2.

   Four radio buttons let you decide how to use the performance options. They are:

   - **Let Windows choose what's best for my computer:** This option ostentatiously allows Windows to figure out its own settings, but it seems to leave all the detail options turned on no matter what.

   - **Adjust for best appearance:** This one turns all the eye candy on.

   - **Adjust for best performance:** Likewise, this one turns all the visual effects off (as shown in Figure 14-3).

   - **Custom:** You choose which of the various options stay on.

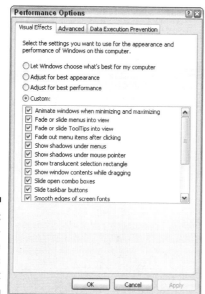

Figure 14-2:
The Perfor-
mance
Options
applet

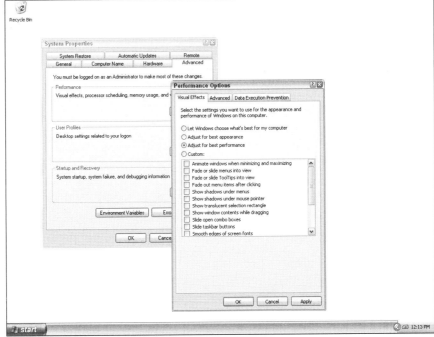

Figure 14-3:
This is the Windows desktop with all the visual effects turned off. Kind of bland, isn't it?

You can fill in the check boxes next to each effect to enable them, or clear them to turn the effects off. Experiment to see how your system behaves. The visual detail settings available to turn on or off are:

- **Animate windows when minimizing or maximizing:** When you minimize or maximize a window with this setting turned on, you'll see it shrink down toward its taskbar button. Otherwise, the window simply disappears leaving only its taskbar button.

- **Fade or slide menus into view:** Turned on, this effect animates menus, such as drop-down lists or the Start menu, to gradually appear. With it turned off, menus simply pop into existence.

- **Fade or slide tooltips into view:** *Tooltips* are those little floating hints that sometimes appear when you pass the cursor over a button or other item. They can either be animated into view, or simply snap into appearance.

- **Fade out menu items after clicking:** This determines whether menus gradually fade after you click on an item or simply disappear.

- **Show shadows under menus/Show shadows under mouse pointer:** Windows can display a shadow beneath menus and the mouse cursor to give a slight 3-D effect.

- **Show translucent selection rectangle:** When you band-box to select items (by holding down the mouse button and dragging it to form a rectangle), the rectangle can either be a translucent blue with the feature enabled or simply a square of dotted lines with the feature turned off.

- **Show window contents while dragging:** When you drag a window around the desktop, this setting will preserve it in its visual state. With it turned off, the drag box will simply be dotted lines.

- **Slide open combo boxes:** This option determines whether combo boxes slide open smoothly when clicked, or whether they just pop open.

- **Slide taskbar buttons:** When your taskbar is getting full and you open another program, the buttons will either slide over (with this feature enabled) or just pop aside.

- **Smooth edges of screen fonts:** If you have a flat-panel monitor, this option can make screen fonts, especially ClearType fonts look really spiffy.

- **Smooth-scroll list boxes:** This affects whether list boxes scroll smoothly or jump.

- **Use background image for each folder type:** Folders like My Pictures and My Music have a very light, easy-to-miss watermark in the bottom-right corner. You can enable or disable this feature.

- **Use common tasks in folders:** As you navigate through Windows directories, you may notice a vertical bar on the left side of the window with a bunch of hyperlinks (see Figure 14-4). You can get rid of that bar by disabling this feature.

Figure 14-4:
The vertical bar on the right with the options View System Information, Add or Remove Programs, and so on, is the common taskbar.

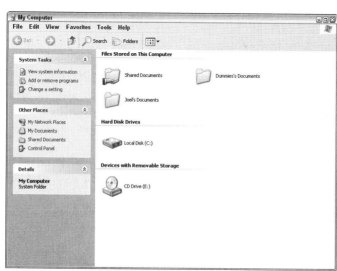

- **Use drop shadows for labels on the desktop:** The labels under desktop icons can be fitted with cool looking shadows, or you can disable this feature.

- **Use visual styles on windows and buttons:** That Gummy Bear look — the rounded edges of buttons and title bars, the deco Start button, and other friendly visuals — can be disabled for a sterile, square feel reminiscent of older versions of Windows.

While I'm on the subject of visual appearance, there's another dialog box I'd like to show you. It's the Effects dialog box in the Display Properties applet. Call it up like this:

1. **Right-click in an area of the desktop free of any icons.**

2. **Select Properties.**

   The Display Properties window appears.

3. **Select the Appearance tab.**

4. **Click the Effects button.**

   The Effects dialog box appears (see Figure 14-5).

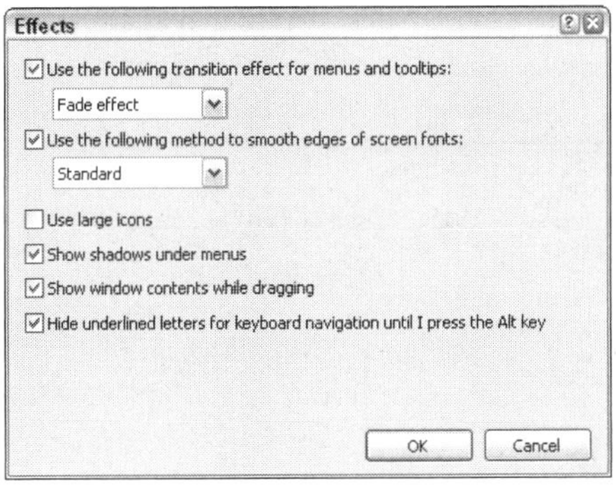

Effects	? ☒
☑ Use the following transition effect for menus and tooltips:	
Fade effect ⌄	
☑ Use the following method to smooth edges of screen fonts:	
Standard ⌄	
☐ Use large icons	
☑ Show shadows under menus	
☑ Show window contents while dragging	
☑ Hide underlined letters for keyboard navigation until I press the Alt key	
OK Cancel	

Figure 14-5:
Effects
dialog box.

The Effects dialog box has the following options, which don't necessarily affect performance as much as they affect the visuals:

- **Use the following transition effect for menus and tooltips:** You can disable the effects altogether by unchecking the check box, or choose to fade or scroll menus and tooltips.

- **Use the following method to smooth edges of screen fonts:** You can disable font smoothing by unchecking the check box, or choose between standard and the higher-end ClearType — but you'll only notice a major difference on a flat-panel monitor.

- **Use large icons:** I can't imagine why you'd want to — it increases the size of your desktop icons so fewer will fit in any given space.

- **Use shadows under menus:** This feature determines whether menus cast 3-D–like shadows.

- **Show window contents while dragging:** This is exactly the same as the option in Performance Options dialog box.

- **Hide underlined letters for keyboard navigation until I press the Alt key:** With this feature enabled, you can access the menus (File, Edit, and so on) by holding Alt and clicking the letters indicated by the underlines that appear (see Figure 14-6).

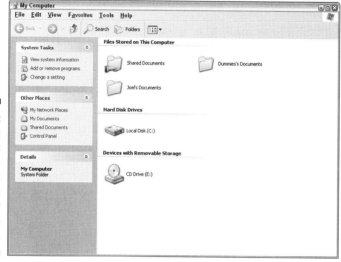

Figure 14-6: Note the underlines beneath some of the letters in the menu bar for keyboard navigation.

Eliminating Unwanted Windows Programs

Windows comes with a myriad of programs, many of which you may have no use for. It's easy enough to tank a bunch of Windows modular components through the Windows Components Wizard. Launch it by following these steps:

1. **Choose Start ⇨ Control Panel (or Start ⇨ Settings ⇨ Control Panel).**

2. **Click Control Panel.**

3. **Click Add or Remove Programs.**

4. **Click Add/Remove Windows Components.**

   The Windows Components Wizard appears (see Figure 14-7).

Figure 14-7:
The
Windows
Components
Wizard.

Surf through the wizard and decide what you want to banish from Windows. Check out the Accessories and Utilities heading (click the Details button to drill down and see more options). Feel free to uncheck any of the accessories — MSN Explorer, Outlook Express (if you don't want to use it for e-mail), Windows Messenger. You probably don't want to uninstall Internet Explorer, but you can if you want. The rest you should leave alone.

When you've unchecked those that you want to part with, click Next and watch as Windows removes the offending matter from your hard drive. When it's done, your computer is a little bit leaner.

Preventing Unwanted Items from Starting

One of the most annoying things that programs do is assume that you want little parts of them running in the background all the time. Many popular applications do this, like Microsoft Office, QuickTime, Real, Quicken, and many others. Most such programs are represented by little icons in the system tray, down on the bottom-right near the clock.

Some applications you *want* running in the background, such as antivirus programs, firewalls, and driver applets for graphics cards, mice, sound cards, and other gear. But there are plenty of programs you don't want running unless you *choose* to run them.

Even worse, you could end up with what's commonly known as *adware* and *spyware* on your computer. This annoying and potentially intrusive software runs in the background and does nasty stuff like hog system resources, invoke pop-up ads, collect information about how you use your computer, and it often leverages a serious performance hit against your system.

In the following sections, I show you how to halt the startup of background apps that you don't want or need and how to get rid of that spyware.

Using the System Configuration Utility

One of the most totally handy and cool utilities ever to find itself as part of the Windows operating system is the System Configuration Utility. A one-stop shop to safely prevent various applications from loading at startup — and therefore speed boot time and free up system resources, increasing performance — it gives you a simple list, lets you uncheck items you don't *think* you need, and safeguards you from making a mistake: Changes aren't permanent. You can always go back and recheck an item if you find one of your programs ceases working properly.

Fire up the System Configuration Utility by choosing Start ➪ Run and then typing **msconfig** and hitting Enter. The System Configuration Utility window, shown in Figure 14-8, appears.

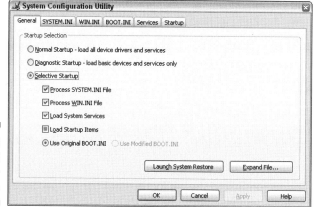

Figure 14-8: The System Configuration Utility.

Select the Startup tab (see Figure 14-9). Leave the options on the other tabs, which include General, SYSTEM.INI, WIN.INI, BOOT.INI, and Services, alone. (I tell you how to lose unwanted services in the "Disabling Unnecessary Services" section of this chapter.)

You'll be treated to a window that shows a list of line items with check boxes next to each one. Some may appear cryptic, like CTHELPER (which, actually, is a SoundBlaster driver module). Others may be easier to identify, like Quicken Scheduler.

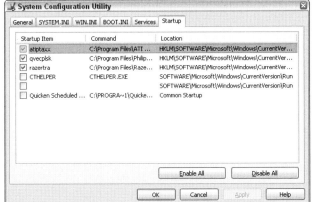

Figure 14-9:
The System
Configura-
tion Utility
Startup tab.

Look carefully at each item. Try to identify each item as well as you can. If it's obviously part of an application that you can launch manually (like Quicken) or that launches on its own when needed (like Real), disable it. If it appears to have something to do with your firewall or antivirus program, leave it running. Here's the beauty of the System Configuration Utility: If you're unsure, go ahead and uncheck it.

Ignore the buttons beneath the list (Enable All and Disable All); you'll want to be choosy.

When you're done, click OK. Windows asks if you want to reboot your computer; you'll need to reboot for the changes to take effect. When Windows starts back up, you'll see the dialog box shown in Figure 14-10. Select the check box and click OK.

Figure 14-10:
The infor-
mational
dialog box
that appears
after you
reboot after
using the
System
Configura-
tion Utility.

Now you'll have to be observant to see if one or more of your programs stops working. If something doesn't work, methodically recheck the check boxes in the System Configuration Utility's Startup tab, one at a time, reboot and retest the program in between each one. After you've identified the module that the troubled program was reliant upon, you know to keep it enabled. Disable what you don't need.

Removing spyware and adware

Getting rid of aggravating spyware and adware isn't as cut and dried as disabling other programs or running the Control Panel's Add/Remove Programs applet. Such shady software is designed to remain hidden from your watchful eye; it's made to be difficult to remove. To get the job done, you'll need to download a removal utility.

My favorite is Ad-Aware SE Personal, a free-for-personal-use tool from Lavasoft. It's available at `www.lavasoftusa.com/support/download/`. Download it and install it. When it's done installing, leave checked the check boxes asking if you want to do a full system scan, if you want to update it, and if you want to display the instructions. It will update itself to spot the latest offending applications, launch its search tool (see Figure 14-11), and show you its help file.

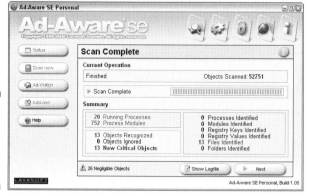

Figure 14-11: Ad-Aware is scanning this computer.

Ad-Aware is very thorough. It scans memory, folders, files, and the system registry for any trace of spyware and adware. When it's done, it'll offer up a report showing you everything it found that it identified as intrusive software. Simply click Next to quarantine the files and registry keys Ad-Aware deems hostile. If Ad-Aware makes a mistake and quarantines something benign or critical (which, by the way, I've never had happen), you can access and restore the quarantined items. Later, you can open the quarantine list and delete the quarantined entries when you're sure you no longer need them.

Disabling Unnecessary Services

Windows XP uses a service model to get things done. A service is a little program that runs in the background that allows Windows to do certain things, like download Windows updates automatically, handle plug-and-play devices, and share files, folders and printers. Although most services don't take up much memory, some do, and tweaking purists like to streamline Windows by disabling any services they don't feel they need.

Windows takes a lot of liberty in trying to anticipate everything you want to do with your computer, and therefore enables a whole batch of services (or at least leaves them ready to wake up when they're needed), some of which may be irrelevant to your computing whims. The operating system provides an applet, appropriately called Services, that lets you change the startup habits of the various services installed on your computer. You can launch the applet by choose Start ➪ Run, typing in **services.msc,** and hitting Enter (see Figure 14-12).

If you want to tweak services, do it here — *not* in the System Configuration Utility.

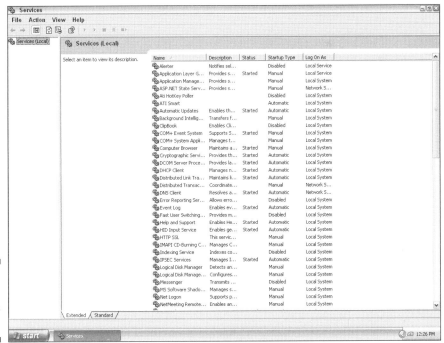

Figure 14-12:
The
Services
applet.

To change the startup behavior of a service, simply right-click the service in question and click Properties. A dialog box like the one shown in Figure 14-13 will appear.

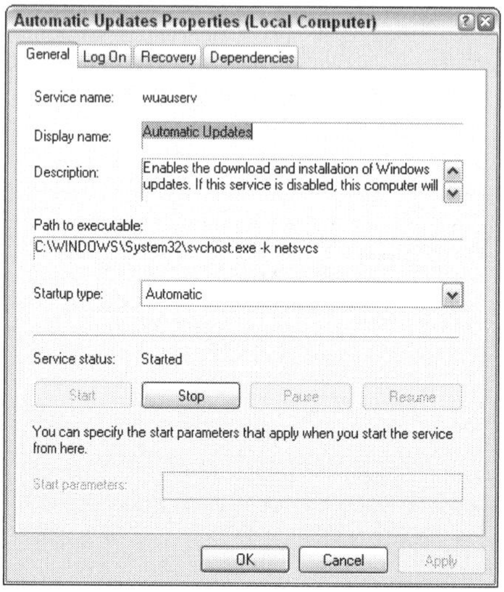

Automatic Updates Properties (Local Computer)

General | Log On | Recovery | Dependencies

Service name: wuauserv

Display name: Automatic Updates

Description: Enables the download and installation of Windows updates. If this service is disabled, this computer will

Path to executable:
C:\WINDOWS\System32\svchost.exe -k netsvcs

Startup type: Automatic

Service status: Started

[Start] [Stop] [Pause] [Resume]

You can specify the start parameters that apply when you start the service from here.

Start parameters:

[OK] [Cancel] [Apply]

Figure 14-13: A properties sheet for a service.

Focus on the General tab. Here, you can start or stop the service, and change the startup type with the drop-down list to one of three states:

- **Automatic:** The service will start when Windows starts.
- **Manual:** The service won't necessarily start when Windows starts, but it can be turned on by a user or another service dependent on this one.
- **Disabled:** The service will not start, even if another service or a user action tries to invoke it.

Disable a service first by stopping it if it's started, and then by selecting Disabled from the drop-down list.

Although I'm going to discuss some of the services you can disable, you should never change the startup behavior of a service that you're unfamiliar with. You can potentially disable components necessary to your computing experience. If you're not sure, don't touch!

The list in the Services window contains the name of each service, a description of what it does (for the full description, left-click on the service and it will be displayed in the window next to the list), its status (whether it's started), its startup type, and logon information which you need not be concerned with. Here is a list of services that, at your discretion, you may want to disable.

✔ **Automatic Updates:** Only advanced users should disable this service. It allows the computer to check the Windows Update site and download updates on its own. If you choose to disable this service, be sure to check Windows Update manually on a regular basis.

✔ **ClipBook:** This allows information in the Clipboard to be shared across a network. It's almost unilaterally unnecessary in any given situation.

✔ **Computer Browser:** This services maintains a list of computers on the network and reports it periodically to the "master browser" and "backup browser." If your computer is not on a network, you don't need this service. You can still browse a network even with Computer Browser disabled, as long as one computer on the network has it running.

✔ **Error Reporting Service:** If Windows or a program crashes, it can trigger this service to alert you to send an error report to Microsoft so the engineers can mock you. Actually, it doesn't send any identifying information to Microsoft, but I still find it unnecessary.

✔ **Fast User Switching Compatibility:** Fast user switching allows you to jump from one account on the computer to another without logging the first one off. It's not necessary when only one person uses a computer, and some people don't like it on shared PCs.

✔ **IMAPI CD-Burning COM Service:** If you have a CD-ROM burner, this service lets you easily burn data and music CDs. If you don't have a burner, obviously you don't need this service.

✔ **Indexing Service:** This one's a notorious system hog that just about every Windows tweaking guide recommends you disable. Basically, it keeps track of all kinds of data about files and their contents in an index, which speeds up the Windows search function. However, it eats up a big chunk of RAM even when it's idle. I strongly recommend disabling this service.

✔ **Messenger:** This service is for sending messages between clients and servers. It's not necessary in a home environment, even on a home network.

✔ **Net Logon:** Used for logging onto a network with a domain controller, this service is unnecessary in home and home networking situations.

✔ **NetMeeting Remote Desktop Sharing:** How often do you say to yourself, "Gosh, I wish I could share my desktop with a remote computer by using NetMeeting!" You don't? Disable this service.

✔ **Portable Media Serial Number Service:** This service polls any portable media player connected to your computer for its serial number. There's probably a reason for this, but I've never found it referenced anywhere. Disable it if you want, but if your iPod stops working set it back to manual.

✔ **Print Spooler:** This one takes up a lot of memory but is almost always necessary. If you print from your computer to a local or network printer, this service must be active. If you never print, disable it or set it to manual.

✔ **Secondary Login:** This service allows processes to be started under "alternate credentials." There's rarely a reason for this ability in a home environment.

✔ **Server:** This allows sharing of resources like files and printers over a network. If your computer isn't sharing anything, you can disable it.

✔ **System Restore Service:** This important service, which is another resource pig, allows Windows to create restore points, to which you can revert the operating system should it become hosed for some reason (say, a faulty driver or a botched program installation). Only power users should disable this service. If you don't mind the possibility that bad software could cause you to have to reinstall Windows rather than roll back to a restore point, you may disable this service.

✔ **WebClient:** The description indicates that this service is for creating and modifying Net-based files, but I've never missed it after I've disabled it. Just in case it's necessary for something, I tend to set it to manual.

✔ **Windows Time:** The Windows clock can log on to an Internet time server to maintain accuracy. It's not really necessary.

Note that this is absolutely not a complete list of Windows services; I only list the ones that can safely be disabled. If you want an exhaustive list of Windows services, you can find an excellent resource at `www.blackviper.com/WinXP/servicecfg.htm`. Note also that not all services come from Microsoft. Device drivers and software can install services of their own. In most cases, you won't want to disable them.

Optimizing and Maintaining Storage Devices

The vitality of your system depends quite a bit on how efficiently it accesses, reads from, writes to, and maintains its storage devices. You can streamline the process of maintaining the page file, which is used for virtual memory; keeping files from becoming fragmented, resulting in a degradation in performance that grows more severe as this task is neglected; and ensuring that Windows is accessing its optical drives as efficiently as possible.

Tweaking the paging file

Windows likes to make things easy on the novice user by doing as much as it can by itself. One of the things it likes to take care of without your intervention is the maintenance of the paging file. Unfortunately, it doesn't do a very good job.

Windows likes to dynamically change the size of the paging file on the fly. That can cause problems in two ways:

✔ **While it's adjusting the size of the file, the hard drive is busy.** When you do things in Windows that require drive access, they have to compete with the operating system hogging up the hard drive's attention. That results in a very noticeable performance hit.

✔ **By dynamically increasing the size of the paging file, Windows opens it up to the possibility of fragmentation.** *Fragmentation* is the phenomenon of a file becoming scattered across the platters of a hard drive. As a hard drive writes data, it uses the first space it encounters. If it fills up that space, it moves on until it finds another chunk of free space. If it's writing one file, that file ends up spanning different areas of the hard drive. Reading and manipulating that file requires the drive heads to move around a lot, which causes — you guessed it — a performance hit. A fragmented paging file is a performance nightmare.

You can do one of two things. You can eliminate the paging file, but that's rarely a good idea. Even if your system has piles of RAM, you still may encounter situations that require still more memory — and without a paging file to swap data out to, you'll end up getting all kinds of error messages. If there's even a chance you could find yourself working with an extremely high resolution, uncompressed photograph file, or doing 3-D rendering, or converting a long movie file from one format to another — and other such demanding tasks — you should have a paging file.

The other thing you can do is take the reins of the paging file away from Windows. To do so, you determine the ideal size, and then you set the minimum and maximum page file size to the same number. Do that by following these steps:

1. **Right-click My Computer.**

2. **Click Properties.**

   The System Properties window opens.

3. **Select the Advanced tab.**

4. **Under the Performance heading, click Settings.**

   The Performance Options dialog box opens.

5. **Select the Advanced tab.**

6. **Under the Virtual memory heading, click Change.**

   The Virtual Memory dialog box (shown in Figure 14-14) opens.

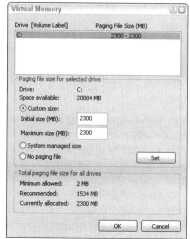

Figure 14-14:
The Virtual
Memory
dialog box is
where you
tweak the
paging file.

The easiest way to determine a good, static size for your paging file is to look at the bottom of the dialog box under the heading Total Paging File Size for All Drives. It lists a minimum size, a recommended size, and the amount of hard drive space currently allocated as the paging file. Some tech journalists devise complex formulas to figure out how much of a paging file you need; I don't. I recommend you simply double the recommended size. That's all there is to it.

Select the Custom Size radio button. Then type in the size of your paging file, in megabytes, in both the Initial Size box and the Maximum Size box. Click the Set button, and click OK. You've just created a static paging file. You may be prompted to reboot the PC.

If your computer contains two hard drives (not two partitions on the same drive, but two physical hard drives), you may see a slight performance boost by moving the paging file to the secondary drive. Note, in the Virtual Memory dialog box, the list of drives at the top of the window. First, click the drive that the paging file currently resides on. Select the No Paging File radio button and click Set. Then click on the secondary drive. Select the Custom Size radio button. Then type in the size of your paging file in both the Initial Size box and the Maximum Size box. Click the Set button, and click OK.

Defragging the hard drive

Just as the paging file, left to Windows to manage, can become fragmented, so can all your programs. The longer you run Windows without using the Disk Defragmenter tool, the worse the fragmentation can become. A fragmented drive is an inefficient drive, and you'll notice a performance degradation that grows gradually more severe as the drive becomes more fragmented.

You should defrag the drive a *minimum* of once a month; I recommend doing it once a week. To defrag the drive, choose Start ➪ All Programs ➪ Accessories ➪ System Tools ➪ Disk Defragmenter. You'll see the Disk Defragmenter, as shown in Figure 14-15.

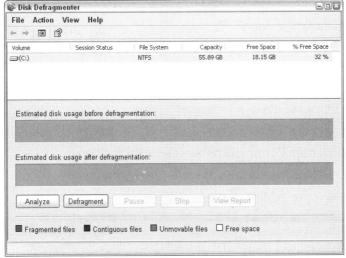

Figure 14-15:
The Disk
Defrag-
menter.

Your system's hard drives are shown. There are also a couple of buttons. Ignore the Analyze button. Windows can take a look at the drive and tell you whether it thinks it needs defragmenting. Windows is pretty conservative about this; it often tells you the drive doesn't need to be defragged, when it actually could benefit from a defrag. To start the defragmentation process, simply click the Defragment button. The drive will churn away for a while — the larger and more stuffed the volume, the longer it'll take. Be patient; it can take more than an hour on large hard drives.

Although some third-party defragmentation utilities have tools for defragmenting the paging file, Windows doesn't include such a tool. There's a quick, free way to defrag the paging file that takes just a few steps:

1. **Right-click My Computer.**

2. **Click Properties.**

   The System Properties window opens.

3. **Select the Advanced tab.**

4. **Under the Performance heading, click Settings.**

   The Performance Options dialog box opens.

5. **Select the Advanced tab.**

6. Under the Virtual memory heading, click Change.

   The Virtual Memory dialog box (refer to Figure 14-14) opens.

7. In the Virtual Memory dialog box, click the drive that the paging file currently resides on.

8. Click the No Paging File radio button and click Set.

9. Reboot your computer.

10. Defrag the hard drive with the Disk Defragmenter.

11. Right-click My Computer.

12. Click Properties.

    The System Properties window opens.

13. Select the Advanced tab.

14. Under the Performance heading, click Settings.

    The Performance Options dialog box opens.

15. Select the Advanced tab.

16. Under the Virtual memory heading, click Change.

    The Virtual Memory dialog box (refer to Figure 14-14) opens.

17. Click the Custom Size radio button.

18. Type in the size of your paging file in both the Initial Size box and the Maximum Size box.

19. Click the Set button.

20. Click OK.

21. Reboot if prompted.

Enabling DMA mode for ATAPI drives

DMA mode refers to a speedy, efficient method of accessing the various storage devices. Sometimes, slave drives on IDE channels are set to the outdated PIO mode. This can greatly slow the transfer of data, it can cause terrible DVD performance, and it can generally screw with your Windows user experience. All modern ATAPI drives are capable of DMA mode data transfer, so you should ensure that all your drives are set to take advantage of it.

1. Right-click on My Computer.

2. Click Properties.

3. Select the Hardware tab.

4. **Click the Device Manager button.**

   The Device Manager will open (see Figure 14-16).

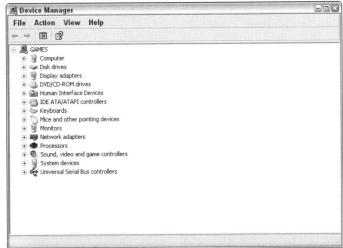

Figure 14-16:
The Device
Manager.

5. **Expand the entry labeled IDE ATA/ATAPI controllers.**

6. **Right-click on the Primary IDE Channel entry.**

7. **Select Properties.**

   The Primary IDE Channel Properties sheet will appear (see Figure 14-17).

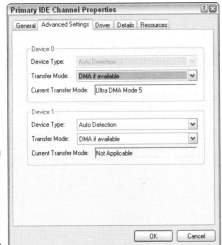

Figure 14-17:
An IDE
channel
properties
sheet.

8. **Select the Advanced Settings tab.**

9. **Make sure that, under both the Device 0 and Device 1 tab, the Transfer Mode drop-down list entry reads DMA If Available.**

10. **Right-click on the Secondary IDE Channel entry.**

11. **Select Properties.**

    The Secondary IDE Channel Properties sheet will appear.

12. **Select the Advanced Settings tab.**

13. **Make sure that, under both the Device 0 and Device 1 tab, the Transfer Mode drop-down list entry reads DMA If Available.**

Chapter 15

Overclocking: Blasting Through the Factory Specs

*W*hat if you could upgrade your PC's gear for free? What if you could perform this upgrade without the need to obtain new parts and swap stuff out? What if you could make a $200 graphics card behave like a $300 model? Wouldn't you want to?

Depending on the parts installed in your system, you may be able to do just that. Overclocking, once a dark art pursued only by the most hardcore of computer enthusiasts, has all but gone mainstream. *Overclocking* is the act of pushing your PC's components to work faster, harder, more efficiently — and hotter.

Though overclocking, you can make a CPU that operates at 3.2 GHz run at, say, 3.4 GHz instead. You can goose the memory speed on your computer's graphics card to overcome the infamous memory bottleneck, and you can pump up its core chipset to work like a card that cost far more than yours did.

Overclocking is not without dangers. By increasing the frequencies at which your components operate, you subsequently increase the heat that they generate. Heat is the sworn enemy of electronics. It causes the metal traces (circuits) inside the chip to move. When two traces touch, the chip can fail. Overclocking can also void the warranties of your components, so if something goes belly up before its time, there's not much you can do besides replace it out of your pocket.

Understanding Overclocking

The components in your PC — notably, the CPU and graphics card — are designed to work at a certain level, at a certain frequency. Sometimes, this is called the *rating,* because, interestingly, the specified frequency is arbitrary. All semiconductor parts have some "cushion" built into their ratings, because the manufacturers need to account for environmental issues, like CPUs being crammed into very small cases with little airflow. So many components can operate at higher frequencies than the specification calls for. That, in a nutshell, is overclocking.

You perform the nuts and bolts tasks of overclocking by jumping into your PC's BIOS setup program (for CPU overclocking), or by tweaking driver settings or using a third-party program (for graphics-card overclocking).

The most important thing to remember when it comes to overclocking is that you've got to make every effort to keep your overclocked parts cool! Through extreme cooling, you'll not only be able to achieve greater clock frequencies while keeping your rig stable, but you'll also protect your equipment from premature aging.

Overclocking doesn't make sense. Don't companies that make hardware want you to have to pay more for faster parts? The answer to that is complicated: They would prefer that, if you want the performance of, say, an *Ultra* part over a *Pro* part, you fork over the extra dough. However, they also acknowledge the fact that, like it or not, hardcore performance nuts are going to overclock and there's nothing they can do about it. Thus, in some cases, they actually embrace the overclocking community.

But why can parts run faster than they're supposed to? There are two theories, both of which are probably true to some extent.

- ✔ **Manufacturer overspec:** Manufacturers want their parts to be stable. Therefore, they probably ensure that their CPUs or GPUs can run faster than they're actually supposed to as a sort of quality buffer: If a part can run with stability at, say, 800 MHz, it will definitely run stable at 650 MHz. This habit, known as *overspec,* allows overclockers to achieve higher clock frequencies than the factory specification calls for.

- ✔ **Labeling for demand:** Intel and AMD are constantly creating CPUs that are faster than the ones already on the shelves. Sometimes, demand for a slower CPU than the ones being created at the factories calls for rating new chips at slower speeds: say, if a 2.8 GHz processor is in demand, a company may label its more abundant 3.2 GHz processors to default and run at 2.8 GHz. Companies rarely admit when this happens, but there are several instances when it's known to have occurred.

Overclocking Methodology: How to Overclock

The key to overclocking is to take it slowly and test, test, test. It's a step-by-step process that requires a lot of time and patience, and you shouldn't ever rush it or assume stability without proper testing.

 Before you start overclocking, read Chapter 16 about cooling your computer and its parts. Factory coolers are sufficient for running CPUs at spec and, sometimes, for minor overclocking, but to achieve overclocking that results in a true performance increase, you'll have to partake in more extreme cooling. There are air, electronic, and water cooling solutions for your consumption; investigate them before you begin an overclocking project.

When you overclock, you'll want to quantify the performance gains that your system experiences. You do that through the magic of benchmarking, which I discuss in Chapter 6.

Here are the steps to take during an overclocking project.

1. **Before you start, back up all your data files that you'd miss if they disappeared forever.**

   Chances of losing data due to overclocking are very slight, but it can happen.

2. **Benchmark your system and write down the results.**

   Keep the results in a neat chart.

3. **Perform a very slight overclock.**

   Increase the frequency of the target part just a bit.

4. **Test for stability.**

   Run a strenuous program — a graphics-heavy game for a graphics card, or a burn-in test that maxes out CPU utilization for your CPU. Test for stability for *at least* a few hours, preferably for 24 hours.

5. **If the system doesn't crash and there are no visible glitches on- screen, repeat steps 2 through 4.**

6. **When stability becomes an issue (when the PC crashes during a burn-in or when graphical artifacts appear in a game or graphical benchmark), you've gone too far.**

   Back up the system to the last *stable* frequency and be happy with your efforts.

Stability testing is of utmost importance, so don't skimp. If you don't test for stability for a long enough interval, you could end up experiencing crashes, hangs, dropouts, problems in games and multimedia applications, and other annoyances.

Testing for Stability: What Do You Use?

The key to stability testing is to push the overclocked part to its maximum potential for a long period of time to see if it can handle the load. To do this, you'll use a program to beat the bejeezus out of the poor CPU or GPU until it either crashes, or it passes muster.

For CPU overclocking, popular programs to use include SETI @ Home (http://setiathome.ssl.berkeley.edu/) and the Distributed.net client (www.distributed.net), both of which push CPU utilization to maximum. Another option is to use looping demos of Quake 3 Arena or another advanced game.

I recently found a wonderful, tiny program called CPU Burn-In (http://users.bigpond.net.au/cpuburn/), which heats up a CPU to the hottest it can get at the current settings (see Figure 15-1). You can set it to run for as long as you like, and monitor the PC for hangs, crashes, or reports from the program with which it will alert you if it detects any signs of instability.

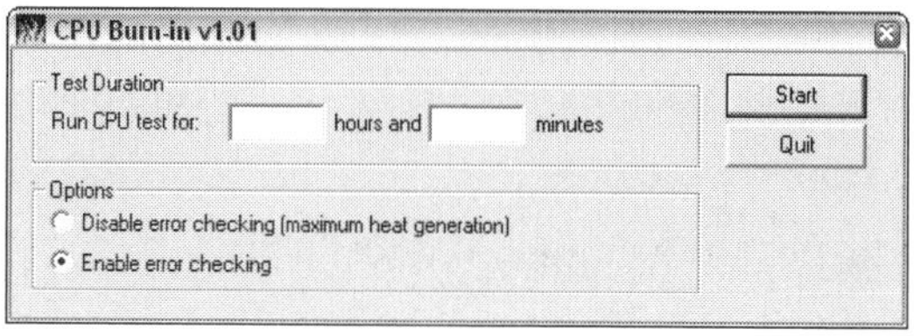

Figure 15-1: CPU Burn-In is a nice little program for pushing your CPU to its limits.

For graphics overclocking, you'll want to use a game or the latest version of 3DMark (currently 3DMark05, available at www.futuremark.com). 3DMark05 is especially handy because you can set it to loop its graphic-intensive game environments. You'll have to keep an eye on the screen for visual glitches: Blacked-out textures, warping artifacts, and other problems can indicate that your graphics equipment is running too hot.

Choose the right computer for overclocking. Don't overclock your primary household PC — the one on which you do your taxes and e-mail and accounting and that kind of stuff. You should overclock a PC that you consider a test or high-performance box — one that you wouldn't mind being out of service for a while, and one that you can work on without destroying the productivity of your house.

CPU Overclocking

The frequency of a CPU is determined by two factors: the motherboard's bus frequency and the CPU multiplier. Combine the two and you have the CPU's current operating frequency. For instance, a bus clock of 133 MHz, and a multiplier of 15 would result in about a 2.0 GHz CPU. Note that the FSB is often "quad-pumped" so that, say, a 200 MHz FSB is effectively running at 800 MHz, but you'll want to deal with the native bus frequency.

There are two types of CPU overclocking:

- **Bus overclocking,** in which you manipulate the frequency of the front-side bus to increase the CPU's operating frequency
- **Multiplier overclocking,** in which you change the multiplier (by intervals of 0.5) to change the CPU frequency

However, in many cases, the only option open to you is bus overclocking. That's because processor manufacturers often "lock" their products' multipliers. Thus, you can't increase (or decrease) the multiplier of your CPU. That doesn't prevent you from overclocking it; it only means that you're relegated to FSB overclocking.

In some cases, you can unlock the multiplier, either by choosing the right motherboard or by other means. I urge you to research your own CPU at sites like HardOCP.com, Overclockers.com, AnandTech.com, and others. To include information on the sheer volume of processors past and present would fill a book this size in its own right.

If you're unsure of your CPU's frequency — which is entirely possible if you have an Athlon XP or Athlon 64 because AMD's CPU monikers no longer indicate their true operating frequency — you can right-click on My Computer and click Properties. The page lists the clock rate.

Bumping up the frequency and/or multiplier

Most motherboards have a special area in the BIOS setup program especially for overclockers. For example, my SOYO KT400 Dragon Ultra has a page called SOYO Combo Feature (see Figure 15-2) that features an area to set the FSB frequency, tune the voltages, tweak the multiplier, and more. Similarly, my ASUS A8V motherboard setup program has a spot called System Frequency/Voltage Configuration (see Figure 15-3) where you can make such adjustments.

To overclock your system's CPU, go into the proper page in your motherboard's BIOS setup program and bump up the bus frequency or, if possible, the multiplier. Calculate what the CPU operating frequency will be after your modifications. Raise the CPU frequency by a small interval — definitely no more than 100 MHz.

When bus overclocking, pay attention to the frequencies of the memory and the AGP and PCI clocks (see Figure 15-4). You don't want to change them very much at all. There's usually a control for tweaking them — say, CPU to PCI divider or a separate option for them altogether. Your PCI clock is 33 MHz natively and your AGP clock is 66 MHz; the memory clock, if your system is using DDR memory, will be half of the memory speed (for example, 400 MHz memory will run on a 200 MHz clock). Consider looking for a motherboard that lets you lock the PCI/AGP and other clocks that you don't want to alter.

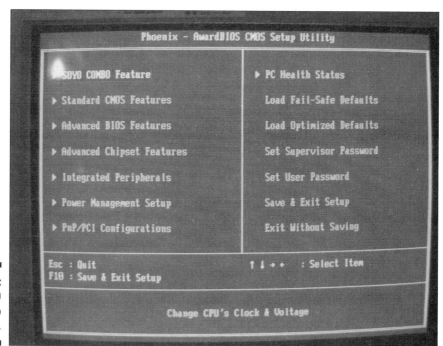

Figure 15-2: The SOYO Combo Feature.

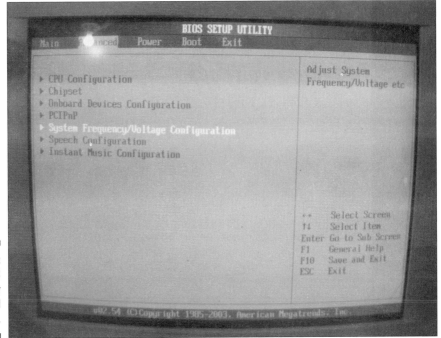

Figure 15-3:
The ASUS frequency control option.

BIOS SETUP UTILITY

Main   Advanced   Power   Boot   Exit

▶ CPU Configuration
▶ Chipset
▶ Onboard Devices Configuration
▶ PCIPnP
▶ System Frequency/Voltage Configuration
▶ Speech Configuration
▶ Instant Music Configuration

Adjust System Frequency/Voltage etc

→←   Select Screen
↑↓   Select Item
Enter Go to Sub Screen
F1   General Help
F10 Save and Exit
ESC Exit

v02.54 (C)Copyright 1985-2003, American Megatrends, Inc.

Figure 15-4:
Keep a close eye on the PCI and other bus frequencies as you bus-overclock your CPU.

SOYO COMBO Feat

System Performance	Turbo
CPU Frequency Mode	Manual
Frequency 1MHz Stepping	134
CPU To PCI Divider	/4
DRAM:AGP:PCI Clock	201 : 66 : 33
DRAM Clock	200 MHz
CPU Ratio Select	Auto
CPU Voltage Select	Default
DDR(2.5V) Voltage Select	Default
AGP(1.5V) Voltage Select	Default

Make your modifications, save the changes to the BIOS setup program, boot into Windows, and test for stability.

Tweaking voltages

Sometimes, when you run a CPU at a higher clock frequency than that which its manufacturer intended, you may run into the fact that it requires a bit more voltage than it needs at spec. There's no way to tell for sure if this is the case; if you run into instability during your stability tests, you might bump up the voltage a little bit.

To do this, enter the BIOS setup program and look for an option to tweak the CPU voltage, sometimes called VCORE (see Figure 15-5). Know your CPU's original voltage before you select a new one, and only change it by a few decimals. Too much voltage *will* overheat the processor.

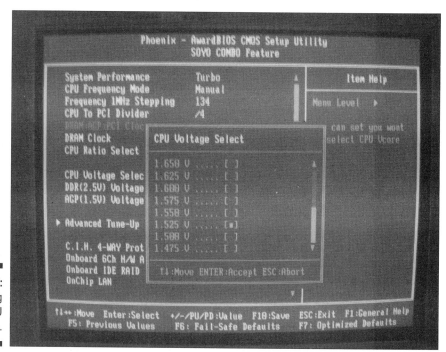

Figure 15-5:
Tweaking the CPU voltage.

If you end up overclocking your memory and/or AGP buses, you can often increase the voltages to them as well. Be very conservative when tweaking voltages, because too much voltage always means too much heat.

Stability testing and benchmarking

I hate to repeat myself, but in this case I'm going to: Between each overclocking session, you have to test for stability. This is not an option; an unstable system can lead to crashes, hangs, glitches, and even data loss. Then of course, you should benchmark the system to see if your efforts have resulted in a performance gain.

Even after you've done these steps, if you're a gamer, you may want to engage in an extended gaming session with a game that pushes the limits of your system, like Doom 3 or Half-Life 2. By doing hands-on stability testing, you'll notice things like minor graphical glitches and other oddities that may be telltale signs of an unstable overclock.

. . . And repeat!

When you've run through a cycle (overclocked, tested, and benchmarked), do it again! Push your system's CPU as far as it can go. Don't worry too much about doing permanent damage to the CPU or the motherboard; if any problems arise, in most cases, you can simply back off the aggression of your settings and everything will be all right again.

Graphics-Card Overclocking

Overclocking your PC's graphics card is a bit different from pushing your CPU to its limit. Instead of doing your dirty work in the system's BIOS setup program, you use graphical interfaces within Windows to tweak frequency settings.

Furthermore, most graphics cards have two settings that you can mess with: the core chipset frequency and the memory frequency. You'll see different gains tweaking one versus the other. You can also often push one farther than you can push the other.

You'll be surprised at the gains you can see by overclocking your graphics card's memory frequency. Memory technology has struggled to keep up with the abilities of processors, often resulting in a memory bottleneck. Although bumping up the core frequency and leaving the memory alone may be intuitive, do give the memory frequency some warranted attention.

To overclock your graphics card, you'll use the same methodology as described earlier: You'll perform a clock frequency change, test for stability, and benchmark the results. As with CPU overclocking, you'll go in small intervals, just a few megahertz at a time, until your system experiences problems. Then you'll back off to the last stable setting, sit back, have a nice refreshing beverage, and congratulate yourself on a job well done.

Here's the difference: You'll overclock one thing at a time. I suggest using the following procedure:

1. **Benchmark.**

2. **Increase the core chipset frequency by a small percentage.**

3. **Test for stability.**

4. **Repeat steps 1 through 3 until it fails the stability test. Make note of the last good setting.**

5. **Reset the card to its default settings.**

6. **Increase the memory clock frequency by a small percentage.**

7. **Test for stability.**

8. **Benchmark.**

9. **Repeat steps 6 through 8 until it fails the stability test; make note of the last good setting.**

10. **Reset the card to default again.**

11. **Increase the core frequency by a small percentage.**

12. **Increase the memory frequency by a small percentage.**

13. **Test for stability.**

14. **Benchmark.**

15. **Repeat steps 11 through 14 until it fails the stability test; make note of the last good setting.**

16. **Using your benchmarks, find the best settings for both core chipset and memory frequencies.**

17. **Experiment further until you've found the ideal settings and the limits of your graphics card.**

ATI overclocking

To overclock an ATI-based graphics card, you'll need a third-party program that lets you tweak the frequencies (ATI's reference drivers don't have such an applet). My favorite is the little, perpetually-beta ATITool, available at www.techpowerup.com/atitool/.

Download and install the application. When you run it, you'll be presented with a little window like the one shown in Figure 15-6.

To change the card's frequencies, simply use the mouse to slide the sliders, or click in one of the boxes above the sliders and type in a number. Then click the Set Clock button. The program has other features: You can create and save profiles, create a "safe range," and tweak other attributes. I'd ignore the Find Max Core and Find Max Mem buttons; they seem to indicate the maximum settings for your card, but they don't include a long, comprehensive stability test.

Figure 15-6:
The graceful
little ATITool
lets you
tweak your
Radeon
or other
ATI card
frequencies.

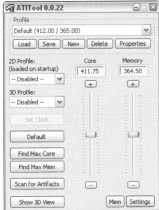

NVIDIA overclocking

NVIDIA's drivers do include an application for adjusting the core and memory frequencies, but you have to unlock it. To do so, you have to edit the Registry. Follow these steps:

1. **Choose Start ➪ Run.**

2. **Type** regedit **in the box and hit Enter.**

   The Registry editor will appear.

3. In the left pane, navigate to HKEY_LOCAL_MACHINE\SOFTWARE\ NVIDIA Corporation\Global\NV Tweak.

4. Click on NV Tweak in the right pane.

5. In the left pane, right-click and choose NEW and then DWORD Value.

6. Type Coolbits.

7. Right-click on the new Coolbits entry and click Modify.

8. In the Value Data box, enter 3.

9. Click OK

The new Coolbits settings appear in the Registry (see Figure 15-7).

10. Close the Registry editor.

11. Reboot.

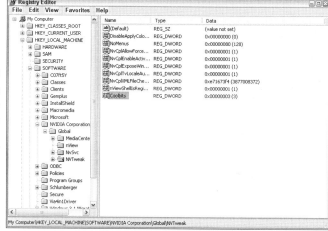

Figure 15-7:
The new
Coolbits
setting in
the registry
unlocks the
NVIDIA
overclocking
page.

To get to the new frequency settings page in the NVIDIA display applet, do this:

1. Right-click on an empty area of the desktop.

2. Select Properties.

3. Select the Settings tab.

4. Click the Advanced button.

5. **Select the tab that indicates your graphics card.**

6. **On the little sidebar on the left, click Clock Frequencies (see Figure 15-8).**

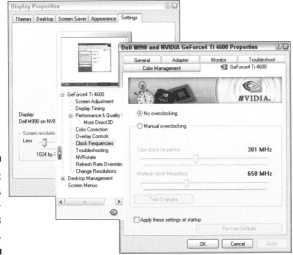

Figure 15-8: The NVIDIA clock frequencies page.

You can now tweak the core chipset and memory clock frequencies by clicking on the Manual Overclocking radio button and sliding the sliders. If you click the Test changes button, the applet will perform a quick test, but don't substitute that for a long-term stability test.

Part IV
Cooling, Cutting, and Painting

The 5th Wave   By Rich Tennant

"Oddly enough, it does improve performance. But you've got to make sure the nitromethane mixture is just right, or you'll crash the disk drive and crap out the valves."

In this part . . .

This part involves modifying or replacing stock parts to chill out your PC, to beautify it, and to make it something that's truly a spectacle. I cover cooling, which is absolutely necessary for overclocking stability. You can replace the stock coolers on your CPU and your graphics card with better-performing after-market coolers that use air, liquid, and electronics to drive heat away from the processors. I talk about adding case fans by cutting blowholes right through the computer's case. Continuing on the cutting motif, there's a whole chapter on chopping a window into the side of the PC case. I tell you some simple ways to add amazing lighting effects to the case, and, finally, I go over an easy painting technique.

Chapter 16

Chilling Your Rig

An integral part of overclocking (see Chapter 15) is keeping your system and its components cool. Today's processors won't operate for more than a few seconds without a cooler. If they have a high temperature shut-off system, they'll simply shut down; if not, they'll burn out! Last year, I foolishly fired up an AMD Athlon XP 1800+ without a cooler attached and stood there like an idiot waiting for the POST screen. When it didn't appear, I checked the monitor cable, made sure the monitor was on, all the while allowing the poor CPU to dry-roast its transistors. After a few more seconds, the telltale smell of burnt electronics alerted me to the fact that something was wrong. A little while later, I had to make a very sheepish call to my contact at AMD to beg for another processor.

If you buy your CPU in a kit, it will come with a stock cooler. Such coolers consist of a heat sink, often comprised of a copper core with aluminum fins, and an attached fan to dissipate the heat. Connecting the fan to a power header is just as important as attaching the cooler to the CPU; without the fan, the heat sink itself will grow too hot to dissipate the heat coming from the CPU. The processor will probably shut down or burn out — but it'll take longer than it would without any cooling whatsoever.

Similarly, graphics card GPUs require cooling to protect them from their own heat. Different brands of cards come with different coolers; ATI cards come with basic, stock coolers, while ASUS is well known for including very muscular coolers on its graphics cards.

With CPUs and graphics cards, you're not limited to the stock coolers. Plenty of aftermarket coolers exist to super-chill your system's components, in order to facilitate extreme overclocking. You can cool your PC's parts with air, water, and even electronics.

Then there's the case itself. It's a smallish, enclosed area full of hot parts. Providing good airflow through its confines to keep the ambient temperature cool is important. This is especially relevant if you're using air cooling for your components: If the air in your case is hot, there's no cool air to exchange as the cooling fans dissipate the heat from their heat sinks. In some cases, you can get away with installing fans in the various mounts provided within the case, but sometimes you'll want to cut new blowholes in the case to give it even more air circulation.

Monitoring the Temperature

To keep track of just how hot your system is, you need a good heat monitor. Many motherboards have built-in heat sensors in different places, and Windows applications are available to give you a constant readout of the temperatures detected by each sensor. In many cases, fan speeds are also sensed and offered up for monitoring.

Check the CD that came with your motherboard for a heat monitoring utility. One may be tucked away among the drivers and utilities that came with the board. Although it's an application that runs in the background — and we're very protective of system resources — a heat monitor is justifiable.

For Intel-based motherboards, try Intel Active Monitor, available at `www.intel.com/design/motherbd/active.htm`. It has a friendly Windows interface with readouts for the various temperature sensors, including the case ambient temperature and the CPU temperature.

I have yet to find a substitute for the awesome utility Motherboard Monitor, the final version of which is available at `http://mbm.livewiredev.com/`. Due to difficulties obtaining useful information from motherboard manufacturers with which to further develop the program, the author decided to cease development.

Another option would be to purchase heat-monitoring hardware. Devices like the DigiDoc 5+, shown at `www.frozencpu.com/cgi-bin/frozencpu/tmp-11.html`, are easy to install and come with their own digital readouts, mountable in a 5-inch drive bay.

Research your CPU to find out the maximum temperature at which you should allow it to operate. Then, use a monitor to make sure it stays below that temperature. If it doesn't, you'll have to either stop overclocking it or beef up your cooling strategy.

Keeping Your PC's Case Cool

Putting an exact number on the ideal ambient temperature for the inside of a computer case is difficult. Ideally, it shouldn't get much hotter than 95°F (35°C), and it should remain cooler if possible. Though expensive, refrigerated cases are available. The most common way to keep a case cool is through airflow.

By balancing a number of *intake fans* (fans that pull air into the system) and *exhaust fans* (fans that blow air out of a system), you can achieve a good level of airflow, keeping fresh, cool air from outside the PC circulating through the system. Intake fans bring cool air into the system to replace the warm air that the exhaust fans expel from the case.

All ATX computers have at least one or two fans in the power supply. The ATX power supply specification allows for any number of airflow configurations and fan directions, but ideally power supplies should serve to cool themselves by drawing air in from the computer chassis and blowing it out the rear of the system. Fan direction is rarely given in power supply specifications.

You should arrange fans for good, smooth airflow through the case. Consider placing intake fans at the front and sides of the case, and exhaust fans in the rear. Don't create a chaotic airflow pattern with intake and exhaust fans scattered around without much of a plan. See Figure 16-1 for an idea of good airflow.

Looking at positive versus negative airflow

Fans are rated in cubic feet per minute (CFM), and you may want to take that into consideration as you purchase fans of various sizes to install in your case. Try to have around the same amount of air coming into the system as the amount of air blowing out of it. Differences between the two will result in a positive or negative discrepancy in airflow.

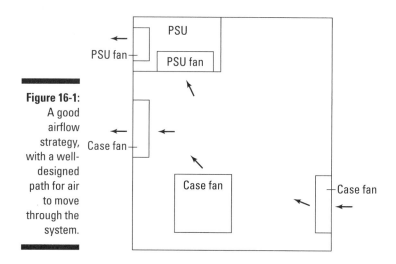

Figure 16-1:
A good
airflow
strategy,
with a well-
designed
path for air
to move
through the
system.

A system with more air being pulled in by its fans than being exhausted has a *positive* airflow discrepancy; systems with more air being blown out by the fans than sucked in have *negative* airflow. That's nothing to panic about. Basically, what it will affect is airflow through ambient breathing holes, open expansion gates, and other places where air can slip into and out of the system. A system with positive airflow will blow air out of cracks and holes in the system. Negative airflow will draw air through those ambient holes.

Each has its advantages. Basically, air being pulled in through ambient holes will further cool a computer case. However, that air will contain dust, and the dust will settle on components and gather on the fans on CPU and GPU coolers. Dust isn't a huge problem (see the nearby sidebar), and I'd rather have a cooler system than a warmer one, so I lean toward negative airflow schemes versus positive. Either way, as long as the discrepancy isn't huge, it's not a big problem.

Adding blowholes

Sometimes, a case may not have enough mounts for sufficient fans to keep the ambient temperature at a decent level. This is especially true in older cases. Although most newer cases have big mounts for 120mm fans in the front at the bottom and in the rear above the expansion slots, older cases may have a mount for an 80mm fan if you're lucky. Back in the olden days (say, around 1998), the airflow generated by the power supply was often sufficient for keeping the system cool enough for normal operation. That's no longer the situation.

Dealing with dust

When I ran a service shop in a small, Rochester, New York–based computer repair and networking company, we used to send out a direct-mail campaign entitled, "Does Your Computer Have Allergies?" The fact is, *all* computers have an allergy: They're allergic to dust.

Dust in as inevitable part of computing. With cases dependent on intake airflow for cooling, they're subject to dust buildup within their fans, and on the boards and other components. Dust can clog fans, reducing their effectiveness, and worse, it can insulate components, interfering with heat dissipation. You've got to do something about it.

You can combat dust in two ways:

✔ **Use air filters for your PC case's intake fans.** You can get air filters wherever you get fan grills.

✔ **Whether or not you use filters, open up the PC and inspect it for dust a few times each year.** If there's dust on your PC's components, consider using a can of compressed air to dislodge it, and a Shop Vac with a wand attachment to suck it up before it settles back in the case. Be thorough; get all the dust out of every nook and cranny. Take care not to suck any jumpers off the board with the vacuum (I've done this). Occasional dust inspection and removal is like an antihistamine for your computer's allergies.

If your case doesn't have at least a pair of fan mounts, consider adding your own. That entails burrowing through the computer case with some sort of cutting implement, drilling holes for fan screws, mounting a fan, and mounting a grill — and, if you want, a filter.

You can add a blowhole anywhere a fan will fit — the top, front, rear, or side of a case. Consider adding one to the side of the case to cool the graphics card and other expansion cards, or adding one to the front of the chassis as an intake fan. For this example, I'm going to cut one into the top of my PC's case.

Decide what size fan you want to add to the system. Fans come in several sizes, including 60mm, 70mm, 80mm, 92mm, and 120mm. They have four holes on each side, so you can mount them either blowing in or out, and they usually come with short, self-tapping screws to drive into the holes. Most come with a three-pin connector, which you can connect to the motherboard for monitoring, and a Molex connector for power.

When choosing a fan, be sure to factor in both airflow and noise. A 120mm fan may require a larger hole, but it will probably turn more slowly than a 60mm fan rated for the same airflow. The net result is less noise for the same amount of airflow.

Deciding how to make the hole

The easiest way to cut a fan hole is with a hole saw for your drill, but hole saws are hard to find for larger fans. You can also use a rotary tool with a cutoff blade to cut the hole — although because it's a rounded hole, it's a tricky cut. Finally, if you have one, you can use a jigsaw. All these tools are available at your local home-improvement store.

For this example, I added an 80mm fan to the top of my case, and I used a 72mm hole saw to cut the actual hole (see Figure 16-2).

Preparing to cut the hole

You'll need a large, well-lit area in which to work. It should be somewhere that you don't mind littering with metal shavings, especially if you plan to use a hole saw, which will throw metal shards all over the place. You should probably have a shop vacuum cleaner at the ready.

Other items to have handy include:

✔ Work gloves

✔ Safety glasses

Figure 16-2:
For my 80mm fan, I'll be using a hole saw for my ⅜-inch drill.

- A drill
- A drill bit slightly wider than the threads of the fan screws
- Clean rags
- A pencil
- A square
- A tape measure
- An awl or metal punch
- A hammer
- A Philips head screwdriver
- Sandpaper or a rotary saw with a sanding attachment
- A fan (of course)
- A fan grill
- A fan filter (optional)

Remove the cover from your computer, and move your computer far away from the place where you plan to cut. Metal shavings on circuit boards are bad news.

Before you cut, you'll need to do a good amount of measuring. I want my blowhole to be in the center between the sides of the case, and back far enough so that the fan doesn't come into contact with the optical drive.

I measure the distance I'll need the fan to be from the front of the case based on clearance from the optical drive (see Figure 16-3). Then, with the square, I measure the width of the case and mark the center. I make a divot with the awl so I can drill there with the hole saw (see Figure 16-4).

Cutting the hole and adding screw holes

If you've never used a hole saw on metal before — or a rotary tool or jigsaw, whatever implement you'll be using — you'll want to take care. If possible, cut from the inside of the case panel outward. Unfortunately, I can't; my case cover is one large piece and I can't get the drill inside to the top of the cover.

Wearing safety glasses and work gloves, drill the hole with light pressure, allowing the tool to do the work. Don't press hard, or the hole saw may get hung up — that can cause problems. (For tips on using a rotary tool, see Chapter 17. I don't have a jigsaw, so if that's what you're using, you're on your own!) With the hole saw, continue drilling until you've cut completely through the metal of the case (see Figure 16-5).

Figure 16-3:
Measuring
the center
of the hole.

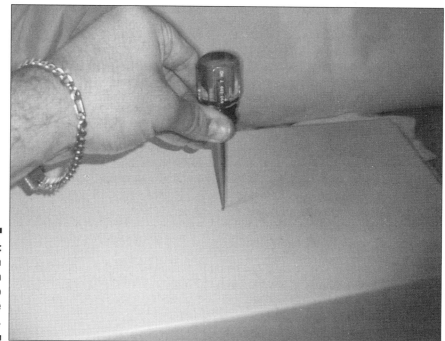

Figure 16-4:
Making a
divot with
an awl to
facilitate
drilling.

Use caution when you handle the cutout piece of metal. It will be hot, and the edge will be jagged and will cut you easily. Similarly, when you're dealing with the edges of the hole itself, take care not to chop off a finger.

Using the sandpaper, or the sanding wheel with the rotary tool, sand around the edges of the hole. It will be sharp, and may be jagged, so sand it smooth. Be sure to wear your work gloves while you sand the hole to avoid cutting yourself. When it's perfectly smooth and all the jagged pieces are sanded off, you're ready to drill screw holes.

The easiest way to mark the positions of the screw holes is to place the fan over the hole, using the square to make sure its sides are parallel to the edges of the case. Use the pencil to mark the position of each hole. Then make a small divot for each hole with the awl. Drill the holes, and, if necessary, sand around them.

Finishing up

Use the rags to wipe off all the metal shavings. Dampen a rag and wipe the entire panel down to make sure you get all the stray metal.

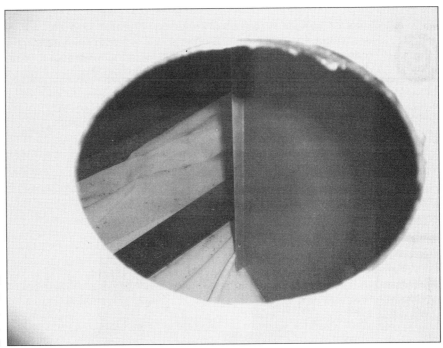

Figure 16-5:
The hole,
cut.

Now, you can install the fan. Be sure to orient it so that it's blowing the direction you desire. Install the fan, the grill, and, if you're using one, the filter. If it's the first time this fan's been screwed into place, you'll have to use a bit of elbow grease; the holes aren't threaded, and the screws themselves tap the threads into the plastic.

Finally, put the case back together, being sure to connect the fan to a power lead. If you want to add any more blowholes, follow the same procedure.

Air-Cooling a CPU

CPUs, sold in kits, come with air coolers. They fasten tightly to the CPU, transferring heat from the top of the processor through the core and out through the fins. A fan, attached to the top of the heat sink, serves to cool the fins, allowing them to dissipate more heat.

The stock cooler is fine for running the CPU at spec, but if you have any interest in overclocking, you'll want to replace it with a more-extreme cooling solution. One way to do this is with a much more robust air cooler.

Look for reviews at various overclocking-oriented Web sites for aftermarket air coolers. One of my favorites is the Silent Tower from Thermaltake. This beast rises 6 inches above the CPU, transferring heat from its copper plate via copper pipes to a massive array of aluminum fins, to which is attached a full 90mm fan (see Figure 16-6).

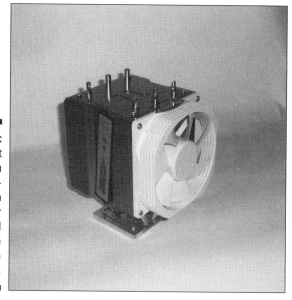

Figure 16-6:
The Silent Tower, from Thermaltake, is an air cooler that could easily take over the world.

The Silent Tower works with any AMD K7 or K8 processor, or any Pentium 4 mPGA478 or LGA775 CPU. You'll actually have to remove the motherboard from the case and install a tension bracket to the bottom of the board, to which you'll screw a top tension bracket.

When you install any cooler, you need to use a thermal transfer layer between the top of the CPU and the cooler itself. This can be thermal tape, which often comes preinstalled on stock coolers, or thermal paste, such as Arctic Silver 5. This ensures good thermal contact between the CPU and the cooler. You need it because the top of the CPU and the bottom of the cooler may have microscopic gaps that allow air, a poor thermal conductor, to get between the two; thermal compound will fill the gaps and allow successful transfer of heat from the CPU to the cooler. Note that you can use too much as well as too little. Ideally, you want a very thin layer of compound between the surface of the CPU and the heat sink surface.

Liquid-Cooling

A far more extreme method of cooling your CPU is through the use of liquid. Commonly referred to as *water-cooling* (although the liquid typically includes coolant of some kind mixed with the water), it's a far more efficient method of chilling out a processor than air-cooling.

A water-cooling system consists of several parts:

✔ A water block, which affixes to the CPU (and the GPU, if you're cooling your graphics card as well)

✔ A water pump

✔ A radiator, for cooling the water before it reaches the processor

✔ Hosing, to create a liquid circuit

Liquid moves from the pump through the water block, where heat is transferred from the CPU to the liquid. It then moves through the radiator, where it's cooled, and then through the fill and bleed system if there is one (this is where you fill the system and bleed out any air), and back to the pump.

You can buy water-cooling parts separately and cobble together a system on your own, which, for a long time, was the only way to water-cool your system. More recently, self-contained water-cooling kits became available and they've become very popular for first time do-it-yourselfers. Kits can contain all-internal or internal and external parts; most notably, the radiator often sits on the top of the case and some minor cutting is required to feed hosing through the case itself and into the cooling system.

For this example, I'm using an all-internal system with everything included. It's the SwiftTech H20-120P, available from FrozenCPU.com and other online retailers, and it includes a radiator mounted to a 120mm fan, a petite pump that rests on the floor of the case, a water block that fits several CPUs (this kit came with clamps for a Pentium 4 mPGA478 processor socket), and all the hosing and other hardware necessary to create an awesome cooling solution (see Figure 16-7).

The parts

The parts of the H20-120P are all created specifically for PC liquid-cooling. They include the following:

- ✔ **A radiator:** A cool blue radiator, fitted with intake and discharge holes, is fitted to a standard 120mm case fan with a Molex connector for power (see Figure 16-8). The fan itself can be mounted to a 120mm fan mount in the front or rear of a case, to draw cool air into the PC to cool the liquid as it flows through. Note that you'll need a 120mm fan mount, whether your case comes with one or you create one yourself.

- ✔ **A pump:** The pump comes with a Molex connector for power from the PC's power supply (see Figure 16-9). It's small and can be mounted, with included sticky foam pad, to the floor of the PC. It comes with a hose already fitted to the inlet.

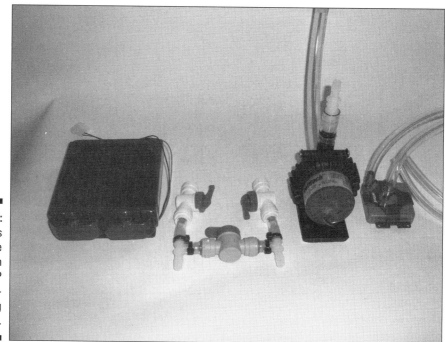

Figure 16-7: The parts of the SwiftTech H20-120P liquid-cooling system.

Figure 16-8:
The radiator
is fitted to a
120mm fan.

Figure 16-9:
The
compact
pump fits in
the bottom
of the PC
chassis.

✔ **A pump:** The pump comes with a Molex connector for power from the PC's power supply (see Figure 16-9). It's small and can be mounted, with included sticky foam pad, to the floor of the PC. It comes with a hose already fitted to the inlet.

✔ **A fill and bleed assembly:** This little assemblage of valves and hose fittings is designed to make filling the liquid-cooling system and removing air from it as easy as possible. It comes with clips to mount into a 5-inch drive bay (see Figure 16-11).

✔ **Hoses:** The kit includes every hose you'll need, ready to be cut to length and fitted into the liquid-cooling system.

Installing the system

The first step in installing a water-cooling system is to decide where to place everything, and then gauging the length of hoses you'll need and cutting them down. You don't want miles of extra hose looping through the chassis, because it will impede airflow and increase the likelihood of crimping.

Figure 16-10:
The heavy water block comes with its hoses already attached.

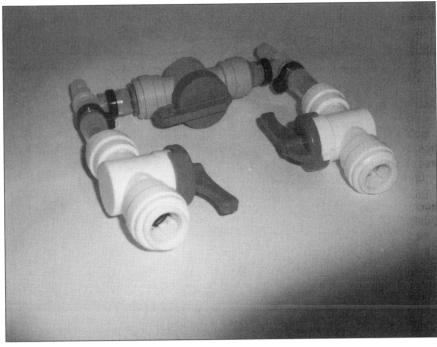

Figure 16-11:
The fill
and bleed
system
mounts in
a 5-inch
drive bay.

I've decided to mount the radiator/fan on the front 120mm fan mount, but I've got a problem: With the bulky radiator attached, the fan won't fit into place (nor will it on the rear fan mount). It *almost* fits, and I can get enough of the fan over the blowhole to afford good air intake, so I'll mount it with sticky-backed foam tape (see Figure 16-12). I can also use a strong glue to keep it securely in place.

I'll place the pump next to a 3-inch drive bay that's mounted permanently on the floor of the chassis (see Figure 16-13). It'll be quite close to the radiator, but that's not a problem. The water block, of course, will attach to the CPU (see Figure 16-14), while the fill and bleed system will go, as the manufacturer suggests, in the case's topmost 5-inch drive bay. Note that, for the water block, the manufacturer strongly recommends that the outlet be *above* the intake, so I've positioned it accordingly.

Next, it's time to connect the hoses. Some of them come preconnected to the various components, while others I'll have to do myself. I'll make sure that, as SwiftTech recommends, the flow goes from the fill and bleed outlet to the pump inlet, the pump discharge to the water-block intake, the water-block outlet to the radiator intake, and from the radiator back to the fill and bleed system.

Figure 16-12:
The radiator
mounted in
the front of
the chassis.

Figure 16-13:
The pump is
in place.

Figure 16-14:
The water block mounted on the CPU.

With the parts installed, I measure out the length of each hose connection, leaving a few extra inches in each case to avoid crimping. I cut the cables with an ordinary pair of scissors; you can also use a very sharp razor knife. Then I seat all the cables (see Figure 16-15).

Make sure that every connection is secure to avoid leaking! I suggest securing the cables tightly with small cable ties.

Filling and bleeding

The next step is to fill the system with liquid. This kit comes with a small bottle of coolant to add to 1 liter of water. I'll use an empty and well-rinsed 1-liter soda bottle to mix the coolant with distilled water (available at any supermarket). The bleed and fill system comes with fittings in the front of the system for temporary hoses used for filling the system.

Before filling the system, however, I have to leak-proof it. The manufacturer suggests this method:

1. **Close the main valve of the fill and bleed assembly.**

2. **Close one of the two valves: the inlet valve or the discharge valve.**

Figure 16-15:
There's enough cable to avoid crimping, but not vast loops of cable monopolizing the interior of the case.

3. **Connect the temporary hoses.**

4. **Suck on the hose connected to the open line to create a vacuum in the system.**

5. **Close the valve.**

6. **Wait 30 seconds, cover the tube with your finger, and open the valve.**

   The tube should adhere to your finger, indicating that the system retained its vacuum. If it does, it's leak-proof.

Do *not* skip the leak-proofing process. The last thing you want is water dripping through your system. It *will* cause problems, including the possibility of permanent damage to your PC's components.

I mixed the coolant and distilled water as instructed. The kit comes with a little bottle of coolant, which I empty into my soda bottle. Then I fill it up with distilled water.

Because the pump is not self-priming, I have to prime it like this:

1. **Open the intake and discharge valves of the fill and bleed system.**

2. **Make sure the main valve is closed.**

3. **Hold the bottle of fluid *above* the computer.**

4. **Submerge the end of the intake tube into the liquid in the bottle.**

5. **Suck gently on the discharge tube.**

6. **Insert the discharge tube into the bottle, but don't submerge the end in the liquid.**

7. **Liquid should start flowing into the system through the force of gravity (see Figure 16-16).**

Next, it's time to bleed the system. I make sure both the intake and outlet valves of the fill and bleed system are open, and the main valve is closed. I then submerge both hoses in the liquid in the bottle. I ensure that the pump and radiator fan are connected to the PC power supply, and, with the system upright, power up the computer. The pump starts circulating liquid.

I let the system run for about a minute. My wife helpfully holds the bottle for me with both hoses submerged. Then I turn the system on its side, faceup. This will allow any trapped air to bleed out of the system. I leave it on its side for a minute or so, and then set it back upright. Next, I open the main valve to let any air in the valve's line escape. Then I close the main valve.

I inspect the system for air bubbles. They'll be easy to see, because the coolant has colored the liquid green. If I don't see any, I can power down the system. I open the main valve and close the intake and outlet valves of the fill and bleed system. Then I remove the temporary hoses.

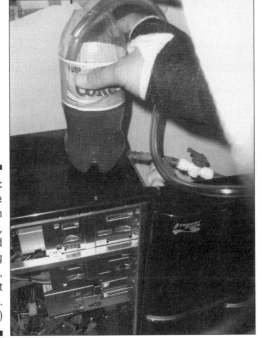

Figure 16-16:
If you prime the system correctly, liquid should start flowing in. (Yes, that's a cast on my hand. Don't ask.)

Installation is complete!

Most water-cooling systems will require a very similar installation procedure. Some, with self-priming pumps, won't require you to suck on the system to prime them. You'll always have to bleed the air out of the system thoroughly; if air reaches the pump, it can impede the flow of liquid through the system, resulting in CPU failure.

You can add to your water-cooling system by buying water blocks for your graphics card's GPU and even your motherboard chipset. If you have to drain the system to install new components, drain it *completely*. Follow the same procedure to leak-proof, prime, and bleed it.

For another perspective on water-cooling, check out this terrific guide at Spode's Abode: `www.spodesabode.com/content/article/watercool`.

Graphics-Card Cooling

The system CPU isn't the only component open to extreme cooling. While you can liquid-cool a graphics card GPU, you can also purchase an aftermarket air cooler capable of much more efficient cooling than the stock cooler. One such product line is the Arctic Cooling Silencer series.

I have an ATI Radeon X800 Pro that I'd like to run as fast as an XT version of the card. With the stock ATI cooler, I can't achieve much success overclocking it, but with the ATI Silencer 4, I can hit amazing frequencies.

To install a new cooler on your graphics card, you'll follow a procedure like this:

1. **Remove the old cooler.**

   In the case of my X800, I had to remove three small screws.

2. **Using rubbing alcohol and a clean, soft cotton rag, remove any thermal compound from the GPU and, if applicable, the memory chips.**

   My X800's stock cooler only cooled the GPU itself.

3. **Apply a new dab of thermal compound to each chip that the new cooler will touch.**

   Thermal compound is often included with the new cooler; the Silencer series does include some.

4. **Install the new cooler.**

Here's how it looked when I did it. I started with a standard ATI X800 Pro and removed the stock cooler and thermal compound (see Figure 16-17).

Figure 16-17:
My X800 Pro
with the
stock cooler
removed.

I applied thermal grease to the GPU and every memory chip, front and back, because the Silencer 4 cools all the chips (see Figure 16-18).

Figure 16-18:
Applying
thermal
compound
to the X800
Pro.

I then installed the Silencer 4. Note that it's huge; you won't be able to fit anything into the expansion card immediately next to the graphics card.

WARNING!

If you install a Silencer on your graphics card, be very careful when you're screwing it into place. The first time I installed one, the threaded rod that the screw attaches to snapped when I applied too much torque. I suggest screwing it snugly with your fingers, avoiding the use of a screwdriver.

When finished, it looks like Figure 16-19.

Figure 16-19: The Silencer 4 installed on my X800 Pro.

Other Cooling Options

You're not limited to air and water cooling, nor are you limited to cooling only your CPU and graphics card.

One CPU cooling solution that's losing popularity to water cooling is electronic cooling. That involves installing a flat, electronic pad called a *Peltier element,* which electronically transfers heat from one side (the cold side) to the other (the hot side). Heat from the hot side is dissipated with an active air cooler (a heat sink and fan combo).

The downside of Peltier cooling is that Peltier elements suck up a lot of power. You'll need a beefy power supply to support a Peltier-cooled CPU. A risk specific to Peltier cooling is that, if you install the element backwards, with the hot side facing the CPU, the processor will burn out in seconds. Similarly, if the fan seizes up or doesn't run for any reason, the chip will quickly overheat. You can find out more about Peltier cooling in this dated but still relevant guide at Ars Technica: `http://arstechnica.com/guide/cooling/peltier-1.html`.

Hard drives, although you wouldn't find yourself overclocking them, tend to run hot — and they get hotter as their spindle rate increases. You can purchase hard-drive coolers that surround the drive in a heat sink, which you mount in a 5-inch drive bay.

Cooling computer systems is a bona fide cottage industry, and the technology is advancing all the time. Keep an eye on overclocking-oriented Web sites and PC enthusiast magazines to stay current on cooling technology. With a super-chilled system and good overclocking technique, you'll be able to achieve mind-blowing performance.

Chapter 17

Adding a Window

. . . .

. . . .

*I*t's time to peer into the inner workings of your system. You can do this in one of two ways: You can throw the case cover away, or, a much smoother option, you can cut a window into the case.

Don't laugh. I have two or three test systems on my bench at any given time, and I don't even know where the case covers are. I tear out components, install new gear, juggle circuit boards, benchmark, overclock, try to get Doom 3 running with maximum detail at a decent frame rate, and so on. Plus, I find it easier to keep my systems cool by leaving the covers off and aiming a table fan into them. The dust factor is high, but it works.

If you've never cut metal before, you're in for a whole new world of fun — that is, if you enjoy working with power tools. If you don't, you probably aren't reading this book. My Dremel rotary tool is one of my closest friends. Some people may suggest that's kind of sad, and to them I say, you've never *met* my Dremel rotary tool. Give it a chance.

Before you start your cut, it pays to do a bit of planning. As with any do-it-yourself project, you want to collect everything you need beforehand and have all your tools handy, including safety equipment like gloves and eyewear.

Turn off the phone, lock the front door, and get ready to engage in what many people consider the quintessential act of modding: chopping the case.

Planning and Preparing for Your Cut

You need to consider several factors before you rush out to buy all your materials. Planning is essential so that you know what to buy, what tools you need, and how you're going to go about your project.

Planning your cut

Unless you've cut a lot of metal, you really should go with a simple design for your first case-cutting project. Cutting takes practice; my Dremel still gets away from me. I suggest making a simple shape with straight edges. If you want to be nutty, round the corners off — but cutting on a curve is tricky. I know it's tempting to want to make a really cool design, like a skull or a dragon, but save that until you've put in some time with your cutting tool.

Get an idea of how large you want your window to turn out. I suggest leaving a couple of inches of metal on each side of the cut so that, if you really botch it, you can recut the case panel. Get a ballpark measurement before you buy your materials so that you know how much of a window to purchase.

Preparing your work area

A clean, comfortable work area does wonders for easing the task of making your first cut. This is not the kind of the thing you should do on the living room floor. You may want to work outside if you don't have room in your house — that's what I do when it's not raining.

Here's what you'll need in a work area:

- ✔ **A flat, clean workbench:** You'll need a surface upon which you can spread out your stuff and do the actual work. A waist-high workbench is ideal, but if you have to use a smaller surface, consider one of those little fold-down portable benches with the built-in clamps. The surface should be sturdy; I don't suggest working on a plank laid across two sawhorses.

- ✔ **Good lighting:** Working in a poorly lit area is a nightmare. A fluorescent, hanging shop light is perfect, as is a sunny day if you're working outside.

- ✔ **Readily available AC:** You'll need a place to plug in your tools, unless you're using cordless equipment.

- **Somewhere to put your tools and materials:** I hate having my tools scattered around all over the place. When I reach for my screwdriver, I want to know exactly where it is. A pegboard is nice to have, but I don't have a place for one. I like those long, wooden toolboxes that you can just toss stuff into. For materials, have a nearby table or a second surface at the ready.

- **Good ventilation:** This is more critical for painting (see Chapter 19), but that burnt-metal smell that chopping steel or aluminum generates is unpleasant.

Gathering your tools

Have all your tools at the ready so that when you need something it's right there. You don't want to have to run down to the basement or out to the garage between every step of your project.

The tools you'll need for case cutting are:

- **A cutting tool:** For the utmost in precision, I recommend a rotary tool like the popular Dremel line. Some people like to use jigsaws, but I find that I achieve more precision with a rotary tool. You'll need one or two types of wheels: a cutoff wheel and, optionally, a sanding band for smoothing the edges after you make the cut. Note that cutoff wheels vary in quality: The flimsy ones that come with the rotary tool will suffice for cutting, but you may go through two or three of them before you finish the job. You may want to visit the local hardware store and buy a few higher-quality cutoff wheels before you get started.

- **A drill (if you plan on securing your window with nuts and machine screws or bolts):** You'll need to drill holes in both the case panel and the window material. You'll also need the proper bit for your fasteners: It should be just a tad wider than the threads of the bolts.

- **A screwdriver and pliers (again, if you plan to use nuts and machine screws of bolts to secure the window).**

- **An awl (if you plan to use . . . you get it by now).**

- **A utility knife or plastic cutter:** You can get your window material cut to order, or you can buy precut sheets and trim them down yourself. You can, if you want, cut them with your rotary tool — which you need to do if it requires curves — but I like to cut it with a knife. You can get a cheap plastic cutter — it won't last, but it'll get you through a few jobs.

- **Sandpaper, if you don't have a sanding band for your rotary tool or if you're not using a rotary tool.**

- ✔ **Safety glasses:** The rotary tool will throw sparks while it's cutting the metal of your case cover. You should always wear safety glasses when you work with power tools.

- ✔ **Leather work gloves:** You'll create sharp and sometimes jagged metal edges through your efforts. You can easily chop your hands open if you're not wearing a pair of cowhide gloves.

- ✔ **A pencil:** You'll need this to draw your window design on the case panel to be cut.

- ✔ **A ruled square:** This is for measuring for the design drawing and for use as a straightedge when you sketch the design on the case panel.

- ✔ **Rags (yes, rags):** You'll have to wipe up the metal soot after you make your cut.

- ✔ **A shop vacuum cleaner:** I insist on a tidy workplace, and you should, too. It's much more pleasant to work in an area free of grime and metal shavings, which you can end up tracking through the rest of the house. When you're done cutting, vacuum your bench.

Securing your materials

In this case, your materials consist of window material, and something to attach it to the inside of your case with.

- ✔ **A window:** For this chapter, I used a sheet of clear plastic called Lexan L10, which is what Home Depot sells in lieu of the better-known Plexiglas brand. I had already measured for my case window so I knew what size I wanted, but the cutting blade on Home Depot's glass cutter was broken so I had to buy a big sheet and cut it myself. Consider getting a window large enough so that it's 2 or 3 inches wider than the size of the window you plan to chop — but it still has to fit in the case.

- ✔ **Something to secure your window:** I like the industrial look of nuts and bolts or machine screws. For this project, I decided to secure the window with machine screws and nuts, one for each corner. I used ¼-x-⅜-inch screws and corresponding nuts. That, of course, requires measuring and drilling holes. For an easier solution, you can buy a roll of Velcro tape, which you can cut into strips and use to fasten the window. Some modders like to use rubber molding, which looks really spiffy but requires incredibly precise cutting. I don't recommend it for your first project. Other people go so far as to use rivets, which are cool, but they require a special riveting tool and they're permanent; to remove them, you have to drill them out.

Preparing Your Case for the Cut

Your next task is to get the case ready for chopping. If your case has separate side panels, you'll want to cut the panel on the left as you're facing the front panel — that's the one that will give you a glimpse into the system. If you cut the other side, all you'll be able to see is the back of the motherboard panel. Similarly, if your case cover is one big piece (like mine, shown in Figure 17-1), be sure you know which side you need to cut.

Mod your case before you install the components. In other words, you should only mod an empty case. The last thing you want is metal or plastic dust coating the working components of a system. The results could be catastrophic when you turn on the system.

If you're modding a case cover for an existing system, leave the PC in a different room. If you really want to mod portions of the case that house fragile PC components, remove all the electronic gear (including the power supply) and stash it somewhere safe and far away from stray metal or plastic particles.

Figure 17-1:
The case I'm going to mod has a single piece cover.

Drawing the design

Before you cut, you'll want to draw out the design you plan to cut so you have lines to follow as you make your cut. Placing the cut exactly where you want it requires meticulous measuring and careful sketching. You should sketch the shape on the *inside* of the panel, unless the case cover is one big piece like mine.

Here is how I sketched in the rectangular cut, with rounded corners, that I planned to create.

1. **Near the top of the case, using the ruled square, I measured the width of the panel.**

2. **I marked the center with a pencil.**

3. **I then measured equal distances from the center in each direction, halting about 2 inches from the edges of the panel, and marked them with the pencil.**

4. **Using the square as a straightedge, I sketched a couple of lines through the pencil marks I had created.**

5. **I then used the square to sketch lines near the top and bottom of the panel to intersect the lines I drew in Step 4.**

   I now had a rectangle sketched out on the case panel, but it looked sort of like a big # symbol.

6. **I erased the extraneous pencil lines, resulting in a clean, centered rectangle.**

7. **Technically, you should use a protractor or a compass to do this, but I cheated and rounded the edges with the bottom of a spray paint can (see Figure 17-2).**

8. **I sat back and admired my drawing.**

Making final preparations

Now that the design is sketched, it's almost time to cut out the panel. I suggest you do one thing first, only if you've never cut metal before.

You'll be cutting out and discarding the shape you defined when you sketched your design. That area makes a perfect place to practice! Draw a few straight lines in the middle of your design and use your cutting tool to cut through the metal. Do this until you run out of room, or you get a feel for your tool and how it operates. If it's a variable-speed tool, experiment with the different speeds and see what seems to work best. I have a five-speed Dremel whose top rotation speed is 30,000 RPM, and I find it cuts metal best at maximum speed.

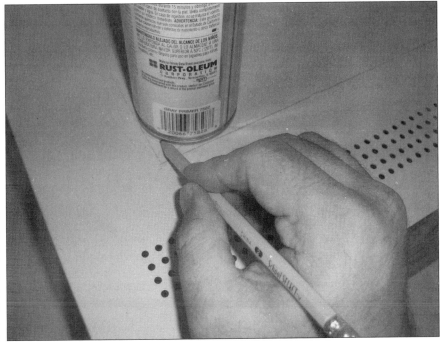

Figure 17-2:
Use
whatever
you have
around to
round the
edges.

If your case has the big, multisided panel like mine does, you'll need to wedge something between the two side panels to give it support: Use a block of wood, a box, or whatever you have around that's handy — and that you won't mind if the cutting tool nicks it.

Cutting the Case

Now it's time to make the actual cut. First, make sure there's no chance of your case panel sliding around on the workbench. If there is, you may want to use something like double-sided tape to secure it. If the blade gets hung up and the case panel slides around, it can ruin your cut.

Now is the time to put on your work gloves and your safety glasses. I absolutely insist that you use them. I will not take no for an answer. If you're using a rotary tool, it will throw sparks as you make the cut, and they can burn your hands and injure your eyes. What's more, if you slip and your hand hits the cutting blade, you could lose a finger; sturdy leather gloves will offer some protection against that. Use safety equipment!

For this walkthrough, I'm going to assume you're using a rotary tool with a cutoff blade.

Set the rotary tool for the speed that felt most comfortable when you made your practice cuts. Pick a straight side of the design to start the cut. Holding the tool with both hands, and with a slow and deliberate motion, place the edge of the cutoff wheel on the sketched line. Using minimal force and letting the tool do the work, follow the line of the sketch carefully (see Figure 17-3).

If you press too hard or try to force the cut, you'll wear out your tool's cutoff wheel in a matter of seconds. Use light pressure, just enough to feel the wheel doing the cutting.

Cut gradually in repeated strokes. Use the first pass to etch a groove along the line of your sketch. Then go back and cut deeper. Repeat until the wheel makes it all the way through the metal.

When you come to the first rounded corner (if you chose to do rounded corners like I did), move extremely slowly. You can easily lose control of the rotary tool when you're cutting a curve. This is where people using jigsaws have the advantage; jigsaws corner a lot better than rotary tools.

Continue cutting in slow, deliberate layers, a few inches at a time. When the cutoff wheel wears down to a tiny little nub, stop cutting and replace it with a new one.

Right after an extended cut, the wheel will be extremely hot! Give it about two or three minutes to cool off before you touch it with your bare fingers. You can try to replace the wheel with your gloves on, but that little, tiny screw that holds the wheel into place is really hard to manipulate.

Even if you're cutting the painted side of the case panel, as you would be if your case has the large, U-shaped panel like mine does, don't panic if the blade gets away from you. It's your first project. You're going to paint the case in Chapter 19, which will effectively hide any gaffs.

Work your way around your design until you reach the point where you started. If it doesn't come apart, you may have not cut all the way through at some points around the drawing. Go back and inspect your work, touching up wherever necessary. When you've cut through the entire thing, shut off the rotary tool and set it aside.

The panel that you've cut away will be hot where you've cut most recently, and it will also have sharp edges. Keep your gloves on when you handle it. Discard it into a trash can, not just a garbage bag where you may forget about it and, later, cut yourself while you're taking out the trash.

You're not done yet. If you have a sanding band for your rotary tool, replace the cutoff wheel with it. If you don't, you'll have to use coarse sandpaper to smooth out the cut edge.

Figure 17-3:
Cutting the
case. You
have no
idea how
difficult it is
to take a
picture with
one hand
while
holding a
rotary tool
steady with
the other.

If you have a sanding band, run it around the perimeter of the cut with gentle pressure. If you press too hard, it can actually grind away the metal, causing divots in the shape of your window. With the sanding band or sandpaper, work the cut edge until it's smooth. Make sure to work out any burrs you encounter. When you're done, you need to clean the case. Use a rag to wipe all the soot off the case. Then moisten a rag and clean the entire case panel thoroughly.

Attaching the Window

Now it's time to secure the window. There are several ways to do it; I'm going to concentrate on easy methods that also allow you to remove the window whenever you please. First, you have to trim down the window material.

Cutting the plastic

If you didn't get the window material cut to size at the hardware store, you'll probably have to pare it down. You can try to cut it with the cutoff wheel of your rotary tool, or you can etch it with a knife and then snap it.

First, measure out the size of the panel you'll need with your ruled square. Using the square as a straightedge, mark the cut lines with a marker.

If you use your rotary tool, be warned: Plastic cuts a lot quicker than metal. You should work in a well-ventilated area, because the plastic will melt and spew fumes while you cut it. Plastic sheets generally come with protective film over them, often with a thick plastic backing. Leave the backing on and cut on that side; if you lose control of the cutoff wheel, it may save your plastic from a nasty scratch.

If, on the other hand, you choose to etch the plastic with a hobby knife or a plastic cutter, you'll need your square as a straightedge. Line up the square with your marker lines, and hold it down. You may want to get someone else to place pressure on it for you, because it's important that it not move while you're making your etch. Run your knife down the plastic along your straightedge nine or ten times. Use a good amount of pressure; you want your etch to be deep.

Now move the plastic sheet so that the etch is just over the edge of, and parallel to, the edge of your bench. Press down on the overhanging portion of the plastic. With sufficient pressure, and if your etch is deep enough, the plastic will snap forcefully right along the etch.

Securing the window

The easiest way to secure your window in place is through the use of Velcro. You can buy a sticky-back roll of Velcro at any home improvement store for a reasonable price; I got 5 feet of it for around $6. That's enough to secure a whole bunch of case windows.

A key advantage of using Velcro is that it's really easy to take out the window for any reason, such as to paint the case. It's also the most forgiving method; there are no holes to drill, no measurements to make — as long as the window fits inside the case panel, you're all set. Stick Velcro strips to the edges of the window. Then attach corresponding strips right to the Velcro on the window. Peel off the backing and press the window into place on the inside of the case panel. That's all there is to it.

If you want to use machine screws and nuts like I have, you have to do a bit of measuring to line up the holes. I'm putting one screw in each corner. Here's one method of measuring for your screw holes if your cut has rounded corners:

1. **Lay your ruled square along so that the inside of one leg runs along one side of the window cut, and the inside of the other leg runs along the perpendicular edge.**

2. **Make a mark right at the inside corner of the square.**

3. **Move the square ½ inch, keeping one of its legs right along one of the window cutout sides.**

4. **Make a mark right at the inside corner of the square.**

5. **Return the square to its original position, and then move it ½ inch with the other leg along the perpendicular window edge.**

6. **Make a mark right at the inside corner of the square.**

7. **Mark to the center between the second two marks.**

   That's where the hole will go.

8. **Repeat the process for each of the other corners of the window cutout.**

Now, using your awl and a hammer, make an indentation at each of the screw hole marks. Using a drill bit just wider than the threads of your bolts or machine screws, drill each hole.

Place the cut plastic sheet over the panel. Line it up so that it's centered over the window. It's imperative that it stays in place throughout this process, so have someone hold it for you if you don't think you can keep it steady. Using the awl without a hammer, make an indentation at the exact center of where the plastic covers each of the holes in the case panel. Drill corresponding holes in the plastic.

Place the plastic on the inside of the case panel, lining up the drilled holes. Insert a screw or bolt through each hole, with the screw head on the outside of the case panel. Secure it with a nut by using the screwdriver and pliers. Tighten it snugly, but not too tightly or you may crack the plastic. When you're done, you can put your computer case back together and, finally, peer in through the side of your case

Velcro and screws aren't the only ways to secure a plastic window into a PC case. Another popular solution is to use rubber molding. That, however, requires precision-cutting the plastic, as it has to fit the window cutout exactly with about ¼ inch of play all the way around. You can get rubber molding from case mod stores and Web sites, including FrozenCPU.com and CrazyPC.com.

Chapter 18

Lighting Up the Case the Easy Way

*Y*our case is cut, its window is in place; now you need something to look at.

A computer case can be a lonely, dark place. The PC's components don't complain, but I bet they think it's eerie in there. Even with a window, you get a tantalizing peak at . . . shadows. You could always shine a desk lamp through the window so you can enjoy the cool look of your motherboard and graphics card and other gear. You could cut a window in the top of the case and put it outside so the sun will illuminate its dark recesses.

Or, better still, you could add case lighting.

You can get motherboards that have neon-colored plastic that seems to glow under ultraviolet light, and some IDE cables do the same thing. Your case is begging to be lit.

There are lots of ways you can light your case. In this day of plug-and-play modding, different kinds of lights are readily available in kits with adhesive and preinstalled wiring and Molex connectors for power from your PC's power supply. Lit fans are available, as are light-up power supplies.

In the early days of case modding, soldering was required to install lighting. Some modders want to go farther than just lighting their cases; they also want control over the lights, to be able to switch them on and off at their whim. That required installing a switch — say, from Radio Shack — and creating the light's own little circuit.

Things have gotten much easier. There are lights with external control pods, one of which I demonstrate in this chapter. Don't worry if you've never soldered a thing or if you don't even have a soldering iron — you can light your case the easy way.

If you really are interested in soldering and installing your own switches, there are numerous tutorials on the Web. Check out this one at Gideon Tech.com: www.gideontech.com/content/articles/192/1.

Understanding Lighting Technologies

When you're shopping for a lighting kit, you'll encounter three major lighting techniques: neon tubes, cold cathode fluorescent lamps, and LEDs. To clarify, I'm not talking about the little LEDs like the ones in the front of the case and in the DVD drive; I mean light bars consisting of many LEDs for illuminating the interior of the PC case.

Each of these lights is based on a different technology, although neon and cold cathodes are very similar. All are available in easy-to-use kits.

Neon lighting

Modding purists like to buy automotive neon lights that come with 12V cigarette lighter adapters, cut off the adapters, solder the wires to wires from a Molex connector, and circuit in a switch. Nowadays, that just isn't necessary. You can buy neon light kits from sites like Directron.com for $10 to $20.

Neon lights work in a similar way to fluorescent lights. Fluorescent lights contain mercury and an inert gas. Each side of the fluorescent light tube is fitted with an electrode. When the electrodes are charged, they cause the mercury to vaporize (turn into a gas) and electrons flow through it. This excites the mercury atoms, which causes them to give off light.

The light that mercury sheds is in the ultraviolet spectrum, which human eyes can't see. That's why the glass tube is lined with a substance called phosphor. The ultraviolet light inside the tube causes the phosphor to glow in a visible wavelength.

Neon tubes are also filled with gas and contain electrodes at either end. When the electrodes are charged, electrons flow through the gas, exciting the atoms in the gas and causing them to give off light. However, the gas in neon tubes, which is typically neon, argon, or something else, glows in the visible spectrum, eliminating the need for a phosphor coating. Different gasses glow in different colors, allowing the makers of neon tubes to create lights of all different colors.

Neon tubes come in various lengths. Typically, you'll mount them with Velcro or adhesive strips that come with the kit. They're normally straight and they're not flexible, so do some measuring before you order to be sure that the product will fit in your case. They generally draw a very small amount of power from the 12V rail, around 3W to 5W, and they generate very little heat. Most neon lights are rated to last around 15,000 to 20,000 hours.

Cold cathode lighting

Cold cathode fluorescent lights (CCFLs; shown in Figure 18-1), simply referred to as cold cathodes in the modding community, are very similar to fluorescent lights. The key difference is that they generate less heat than a fluorescent tube, making them ideal to light a PC case (and explaining why fluorescent lighting isn't an option for case illumination). Cold cathodes are often brighter than similar neon lights.

Figure 18-1:
A cold cathode tube.

Inside a cold cathode tube, mercury vapor and other gases are energized and throw off UV light. The tube is coated with various phosphors, which the UV light causes to glow; different phosphor combinations result in different color lighting.

Cold cathode tubes come with inverters that transform the DC current supplied by the system's power supply into AC current, which cold cathodes require to function. The inverter will look like a little, sealed box that you can place anywhere in the case, provided there's enough wire to reach. Typically, CCFLs demand less than 5W on the 12V line. Like neon tubes, CCFLs come in various lengths. Cold cathode lights should last around 30,000 hours.

LED lighting

LEDs are lights of various sizes that are used in all kinds of applications: digital watches, status lights in your computer, traffic signals, flat-panel television screens, structural illumination, automotive blinkers and brake lights, and, of course case lighting.

An LED is made of semiconductor material. Unlike incandescent lights, LEDs don't have hot filaments and generate very little heat. When the semiconductor material that comprises an LED is charged, it glows. Single-colored LEDs have two power legs (a positive lead and a negative lead). Multicolored LEDs have more positive power leads (for example, bicolored LEDs have two positive power leads). The color changes depending on which positive leg is charged.

For case lighting kits, LEDs are typically combined to form a long tube, or they're available in little units that you can position in tight areas of the case. The lights can be installed anywhere inside the case where they'll fit, and they're powered by the 12V line. LED lighting consumes very little wattage; a 4-LED strip I'm using for my case lighting project demands 2.4W. LED lights last a ridiculously long time, upwards of 50,000 hours.

Other Light Sources

Case lighting strips aren't the only lighting accessories to be purchased in easy-to-install kits. Lighting has become ridiculously popular in the modding world, and companies that make other components are cashing in on the phenomenon. There are flexible light tubes, glowing fans for various processors, and more. For my project, I used two light sources other than my LED tube.

Lit fans

Many companies make fans that glow when the system is powered up. Considering how many cases have numerous fan mounts, you can even use fans exclusively to light your case if you install enough of them. Think about installing lit fans in any blowholes you create and in other fan mount locations.

Like ordinary case fans, lit fans come with three-prong connectors for drawing power from the motherboard or Molex connectors, or both. They're typically lit with cold cathodes or with LEDs, and they demand a negligible amount of power more than that of ordinary fans.

Lit fans can come with one uniform color throughout their housings or with multiple colors. Multicolored fan lights can add pizzazz to a case, but you have to determine your own lighting strategy: You may want all blue lights, or a UV-lit case. I'm a sucker for variety, so I like multicolored fans. Check one out in Figure 18-2.

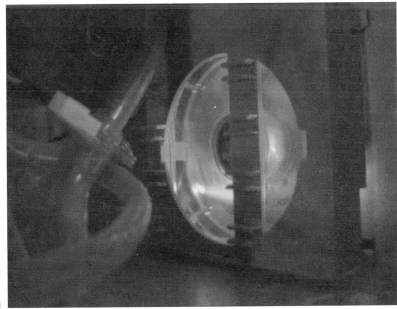

Figure 18-2:
This fan glows in three different colors.

Lit power supplies

Modding power supplies is a popular pastime, so of course PSU companies have begun to offer pre-modded models.

The power supply sits above the motherboard, putting it in a great position to provide illumination in the case. The internal fan sits directly above the CPU and its cooler, and most illuminated power supplies shed their glow through the internal fan hole — so a lit PSU is a great tool for lighting up the processor cooler (see Figure 18-3).

Figure 18-3:
Cool blue light comes from the interior fan hole of this power supply.

Be wary of buying power supplies from little-known brands. I've seen some really cool off-brand PSUs with clear housings and bright lights, but I prefer to buy PSUs from a manufacturer I trust. Look for reviews online and in PC tech mags that incorporate not only how cool a PSU looks, but also how well it works and how steady and accurate its power output is.

An Easy and Cool Lighting Project

I went Antec-crazy with my lighting equipment. I love Antec gear — I've always found it easy to use and reliable. You can go with whatever brand suits your fancy. This is an example of a simple case lighting project with some good variety, ideal for first-time modders.

When you install your various lighting accessories, make sure the computer is off and that the power cable is disconnected from the rear of the PC. Don't ever work on your computer with it plugged in.

My case contains a really cool DFI LANParty motherboard. The various plastic slots, sockets, and motherboard mounts are neon-colored, in yellow and orange, and are supposed to glow under UV light. The board also came with orange, rounded IDE and floppy cables that are also UV reactive.

For that reason, I chose a UV LED light strip to mount in the back of the case above the motherboard called the Antec illuminateUV Internal UV LED Light Tube (see Figure 18-4). As a cool bonus, it features an external control pod that I can use to set various options, including one to allow the LED strip to flash in reaction to sounds. When I blast MP3 files or gaming sounds through my speaker system, it flickers to the ebb and flow of the audio. If that's annoying, I can choose to keep the light illuminated all the time or to turn it off.

Figure 18-4:
Antec's
illuminateUV
LED Tube
kit.

The parts include the UV LED tube, adhesive strips to mount it, a little gate assembly that mounts in an expansion slot behind a PCI slot, an external control pod that plugs into the gate, and a Molex pass-through cable for power (see Figure 18-5). The UV strip and the Molex power cable both plug into the internal portion of the gate.

The control pod lets you adjust the unit's sensitivity to audio, to control how loud a sound has to be to trigger the light to flash.

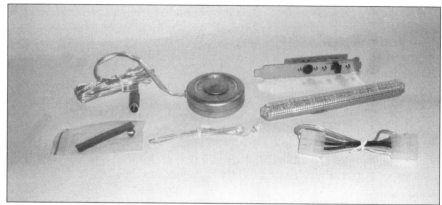

Figure 18-5:
The parts
of the
illuminateUV
LED Tube
kit.

If you don't want to mount the LED tube permanently, you can find a handy place in the case where you can use cable ties to fasten it into place. I used the adhesive to mount it along the expansion bus next to the PCI slots (see Figures 18-6 and 18-7). I realize that that's going to make it a pain in the keister to loosen and tighten the screws to get expansion cards in and out of the case, but I can live with that.

Figure 18-6:
Mounting
the UV tube.

Next, I got a multicolored 80mm fan with red, green, and blue LEDs. My case has a fan mount in the front at the bottom. The Antec TriLight LED fan comes with a Molex connector for power and a three-pin motherboard connector for monitoring the RPM rate (see Figure 18-8).

Figure 18-7:
The LED
tube lit up.

Figure 18-8:
Installing
the fan. This
case has a
plastic fan
bracket so I
don't have
to screw the
fan into
place.

Last, I secured an Antec TrueBlue illuminated 480W power supply. It casts a blue light through its internal fan hole. 480W is plenty of power for my Pentium 4 Extreme Edition 3.2-GHz-based system, even with the extra lighting.

With everything installed, I sealed up the case, plugged it in and powered it on. The cables glow nicely in the UV light of the LED tube, and the eerie blue from the power supply is nifty (see Figure 18-9 for a black-and-white version). I love the color splash from the LED fan in the front of the case. My lighting technique is rather chaotic, but I enjoy the effects.

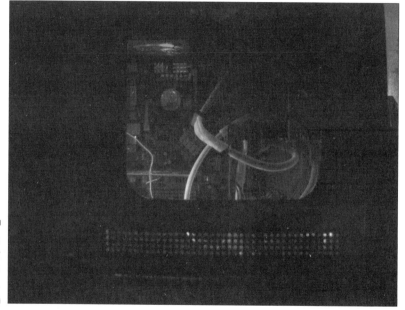

Figure 18-9:
The interior
of my case
all lit up.

Replacing LEDs

I know I said that I wouldn't be doing any soldering in this chapter. I guess you could say I lied. This is strictly optional; you don't have to replace any of the LED lights in your system, but it's about as simple a soldering procedure as there is and it can add a nifty, unique look to your mod.

Assembling the tools you'll need

Have your tools at the ready before you start your LED replacement project. You'll need:

  ✔ A screwdriver for disassembling the computer case

  ✔ Wire cutters

  ✔ Wire strippers, if you can't strip wires with the cutters

  ✔ A soldering iron

  ✔ Solder

  ✔ Electrical tape

Replacing the front panel LEDs

The easiest LEDs to swap out are the boring green or yellow or red lights in the front panel. Most cases have a green light that indicates whether the system is powered on, and a red LED that flashes during hard-drive access.

LEDs come in 3mm and 5mm sizes. Before you buy new LEDs for your PC's front panel, you should measure the width of the existing LEDs to ensure you get the right size. You'll have to take off the front panel and locate the LEDs — they're usually located right in the front panel, but sometimes they may be in the case chassis. You can usually easily remove the LEDs from the holes in which they're mounted by simply pressing or pulling on them. You'll need easy access to the LEDs and the wires to which they're connected (see Figure 18-10).

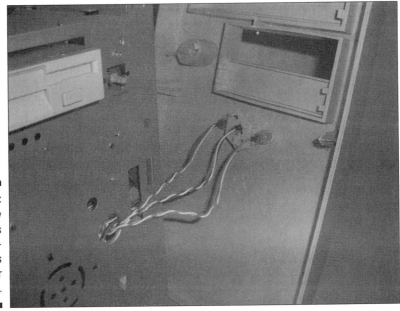

Figure 18-10:
Find a way to access the front-panel LEDs of your case.

After you've gotten your LEDs away from the front panel, measure them. Get new LEDs of the appropriate size from any case-modding retailer, and in the color you want. Modders seem to love blue LEDs. Be sure to get some extras if this is your first LED project, because you can easily make mistakes that compromise the LED.

Look at the LEDs: They have two legs. The longer one is the positive leg (called the *anode*), and the shorter one is the negative leg (the *cathode*). The leads are long, so you'll want to cut them down a little before you solder them to the wiring. Replace the LEDs by following these steps:

1. **Cut the old LEDs off the wiring with wire cutters, paying attention to which is positive and which is negative.**

2. **Strip the wires you just snipped.**

3. **Solder the bare leads of the new LEDs to the appropriate wires.**

4. **Wrap the solder joints in a layer of electrical tape to insulate them.**

5. **Insert the newly attached LEDs into the front panel or chassis the same way the old LEDs were seated.**

6. **Put the case back together and fire it up!**

   If the LEDs don't glow, either your case wiring to the motherboard's front panel connector is off, or you soldered the new LEDs on with the poles reversed. Don't worry, that won't cause any damage; simply replace the incorrectly placed LED with one of your extras with the poles correctly oriented.

Chapter 19

Adding Color: Painting the Case

· ·

In This Chapter

▶ Getting ready to paint

▶ Buying the paint you need

▶ Being safe when you're painting

▶ Sanding, sanding, and more sanding

▶ Applying primer

▶ Spraying on your color

▶ Adding a glossy finish

· ·

*T*hat boring, bland beige look of the stock case has to go. Even if your PC doesn't have the infuriating beige pall that appears on so many stock cases, you may not necessarily like its color. We're going to get rid of the old paint job and spray on a new one, one that's of a color of your choosing.

This walk-through assumes you're working with a steel case. Aluminum cases aren't always painted; the aluminum itself may have been electronically fixed with a permanent color that you won't be able to sand off. You can try to apply this procedure to an aluminum case, but it may not work.

A good paint job requires numerous steps. The thing you'll be doing the most of is sanding. Any paint job — from redoing a room in your house to slapping a new coat of paint on your computer equipment — involves a *lot* of sanding.

As with any project, prepping and planning pay off. You'll need to decide what color you'd like your newly painted case to be, where you're going to do the painting, where you'll set the case to let the paint cure, and other important factors.

Don't worry if you've never spray-painted before. It's not too difficult — you'll only need a few minutes to get the hang of it.

If you somehow screw up or don't like the way the paint job turns out, you can always let it dry, sand the case, and spray on a new coat. The only limitation is how many cans of paint you have on hand, and you can always go buy more if you run out.

Preparing for the Paint Job

As with our other projects, you should make ample preparations before you start painting. Gather your tools and materials, create a work area, and know exactly what you're going to do before you start.

I'll confide in you: I hate to paint. I hate sanding, I hate trying to get an even coat on my target, I hate sanding, I hate the smell that lingers in my workshop for days, I hate sanding, and I generally just hate the whole process. However, I love the way a newly painted case looks. It always ends up being worth the trouble when I do the job right.

Choosing a color

Spray paint comes in a huge variety of colors, from regular matte and glossy shades like red, gray, blue, green, and so on, to Day-Glo fluorescent colors, paint with metallic sheens, and other varieties. I'm a gunmetal gray kind of guy. I like drab blues, shades of gray, black, muted green, and other subdued colors. I've never used neon colors — I hate them. Also, they're extremely eye-catching; if you're going to have your case on your desk or table next to your monitor, a safety orange finish will constantly draw your attention from the corner of your eye.

Go to the hardware or paint store and look at the available colors of all-purpose paint, like Rust-Oleum or Krylon brands. The cap of the paint cans shows the color of the paint within. Imagine your computer case the same color as the color on the cap. That should help you decide what color you want to paint your case.

Consider a two-tone paint job. Maybe you'd like to paint the side panels one color and the front panel and drive bezels another, or paint the case one color and the drive bezels another. If so, you should pick colors that sit well together.

Deciding where to paint

Spray-painting blows fumes all around the area in which you're working. The fumes can be dangerous if they become concentrated in the air around you. So, be sure to do your painting either outdoors or in a large and well-ventilated room.

Never paint in a small, cramped area. If you do, you'll probably notice that you gradually become dizzy. You don't want this to happen: Trust me, I know. I made the mistake of spray-painting in an unventilated room without wearing a face mask. I was sick to my stomach and had a blinding headache for the rest of the day. Don't make the same mistake I did.

If you want to paint outside, you have to deal with the elements. Obviously, you can't paint on a rainy day. If you live in a dusty desert state, you should paint on a really calm day; if there's a breeze, the dust will stick to the wet paint, ruining your paint job. Painting on a windy day is impossible, because the wind carries the paint all over creation.

If you're painting indoors, you need to take precautions so you don't end up painting everything around your case panels. Spread lots of newspaper on the bench or floor where you plan to set the panels to avoid painting things you didn't intend to paint.

You'll need an out-of-the-way place to set your case parts after painting to let the paint cure. It shouldn't be humid; paint takes forever to dry in high humidity. I run a dehumidifier in my basement where my shop is because, without one, it gets really humid down there. The dehumidifier both protects my PC equipment and allows painting projects to dry quickly.

Gathering your tools and materials

When you've decided on a color and a place to paint, make a list and gather everything you need before you begin your painting project. Keep your tools organized so that when you need something, you know right where it is.

Here's everything you'll need for painting your PC's case:

✔ **Paint:** You'll want to spray on at least a couple coats of your color, so buy two cans — three if you've never spray-painted before and expect this to be a learning experience. I like to use quick-drying, all-purpose paint. America's Finest by Rust-Oleum sets in about an hour.

✔ **Primer:** Get one can of primer. Using primer is essential, because it prepares the surface for a nice, even paint job.

✔ **Clear enamel (optional):** If you want a nice glossy finish, and you want a bit of protection on your newly painted case, be prepared to add a coat of clear enamel, also called "clearcoat."

✔ **Screwdriver:** Use this to disassemble your case.

✔ **Lots of newspaper:** You'll spread this around your painting area to prevent painting things you don't mean to paint.

✔ **All-purpose surface cleaner:** Get something like Fantastik or Formula 409 to clean all the surfaces you plan to paint.

✔ **Rags:** You'll need these for surface cleaning and for wiping away the dust you generate while sanding.

✔ **Sandpaper:** Get a fine- and an ultrafine-grit sandpaper, perhaps 320 and 600 grit. (The lower the grit number, the coarser the paper.)

✔ **Sanding block:** Using a block is many orders of magnitude easier and more pleasant than sanding with the bare paper. Invest in a sanding block. You may have to cut the sandpaper into strips of the proper length and width for your block.

✔ **Scissors:** Use these to cut the sandpaper, if necessary.

✔ **Power sander and power sandpaper (optional):** If you have a power sander, you're better off than I am. Use it with the same grit sandpaper I recommend earlier.

✔ **Safety equipment:** Get a face mask to prevent accidentally inhaling paint, and goggles to keep errant paint and sanding dust out of your eyes.

Painting the Case Panels

Your first step in painting the case is taking it apart. Unplug the case and, using your screwdriver, remove each panel, including the front panel. Don't paint near your PC's chassis, or anything else you don't want to get paint on.

Remove any fan grills, case fans, windows, and other things attached to the case that you don't want to paint and set them aside. If you attached your window with some sort of permanent fasteners like rivets, you should cover the window with paper taped down securely.

Take the panels to your painting area, whether it's indoors or outdoors. If you're painting outdoors on the ground, place the panels on a hard surface, such as a slab of plywood or thick cardboard. Spread newspaper over the bench, floor, or anything you don't want painted.

Sanding, part 1 of 100

The first thing you need to do before you dare paint your case is clean it with clean rags and all-purpose cleaner. Dry it thoroughly.

Then it's time to sand. You can use wet/dry sandpaper or just sand the panels dry. You're not necessarily trying to sand all the old paint off the metal; your goal is to sand until you have a nice, smooth surface on which to spray the primer. Typical beige stock cases have a terrible paint job; if you run your hand over it, you can feel little bumps and impurities. You have to get rid of them. Smite them with your sandpaper.

Now is the time to put on your face mask and your safety glasses. You don't want to inhale the dust you sand off of your case, and you don't want it in your eyes.

Attach the coarser of the two sandpapers you purchased to your sanding block, cutting it with the scissors if needed. If you have a power sander, affix the coarser sandpaper to it. If you're using wet/dry sandpaper, sprinkle a little water on the panel before you start sanding. The panel only needs to be damp, not soaking wet.

Sand the panel with firm pressure. Go over each area several times. When you think you've sufficiently sanded an area, wipe it with a damp cloth to get rid of the grit and run your hand over it. It should feel very smooth. If it doesn't, sand it some more.

Sand the metal panels until they're all very smooth. When you're done, wipe them down with a damp rag until all the grit is gone. Make sure there's no dust on the surface at all.

For the front panel, which is probably made of plastic, sand it gently with the finer sandpaper. A few strokes will do — you're just trying to rough it up to give the paint a better surface to which to stick.

You don't have to sand to the bare metal, although if you're using a power sander you probably will see a lot of shiny steel when you get done. Don't worry if you do; that's not a bad thing — it's just unnecessary. Save yourself some work and sand only until the surface is smooth.

Spraying on the primer

Make sure the metal panels are clean and completely dry. Spraying a damp surface will dilute the primer and cause it to take an extremely long time to dry. You should plan to spray on at least two coats of primer.

Wearing your face mask and safety glasses, hold the can about 12 inches from the surface you're going to prime. Spray the primer on with an easy, back-and-forth motion. You're looking for an even coat, not a thick coat. Avoid moving the can too slowly or you can cause drips.

If you do end up with a puddle of primer instead of a nice, even coat, don't worry. You haven't ruined your project, you've only instigated an extra step. You'll have to let the primer cure completely, which takes several hours for fast-drying primer and a day or two for ordinary primer. Then you can sand the drips or puddles off of the surface and prime it again.

As you spray, moving the can back and forth, gradually move it vertically between each pass. Overlap each stroke. Spray until the entire surface is coated with as even a coat of primer as you can manage.

There's no need to prime a plastic front panel. Paint sticks to plastic with ease; the roll of primer on metal is to help adhere the paint to the panels.

When you're done with your first coat of primer, let it cure. Give fast-drying primer about 4 hours, even if the can says it dries in 20 minutes. Ordinary primer takes a minimum of 24 hours to completely cure.

If you painted outdoors, move the panels indoors to dry. Otherwise, you can end up with dust, cotton fuzzies, bugs, leaves, pine needles, cats, and other stray elements stuck to your paint job.

The next step, after the primer has cured, is to sand it. Use the fine sandpaper and sand the primer coat gently. You don't want to sand the primer off the case, you just want to get rid of any dust that may have settled on the surface. After sanding, clean the panels' surfaces thoroughly with a clean, moist rag. Dry them with another clean rag, and let them air-dry for a few minutes.

Apply another coat of primer the same way you did the first one, and let it cure. Sand the panels gently with fine sandpaper, clean them, and you're ready to add your color.

TIP

Alternative painting techniques

If you're new to case painting, I suggest you follow the procedure I outline in this chapter for your first mod. However, you can certainly feel free to experiment.

Consider creating a design on the case by using two different colors of paint. When you're done painting the entire case one color, mask off cool racing stripes or a design with masking tape, and apply a second color. When you remove the masking tape, you'll have a nifty pattern on your case.

Create a marbled look by priming and painting the case with spray paint, and then adding a latex-based paint by dabbing it on with a coarse sponge. Pick high-contrast colors for this technique, such as a blue background and black marbling. Finish the look with a few layers of clearcoat.

Share stories and get ideas from the modding community at large. Hit the forums at Gideon Tech.com and HardOCP's HardForum.com, as well as any of dozens of other modders forums. Be creative, experiment, and see what you can come up with.

Spraying on your color

Finally, you get to see what your case will eventually look like. Use the same method of applying the paint that you did with the primer. You're looking for a smooth, even coat. You don't want it too thin, which will make the surface look uneven with dull spots. Similarly, if you spray the paint on too thickly, you'll cause drips and you'll have to let it cure and sand them out.

Don't worry if your first coat isn't perfectly even. You're going to add more. Apply at least three coats of your color. This time around, include the front panel of your case. Remove the bezel covers and paint them too, but only give them two coats at maximum; if you paint them too much, they may not fit back in the case.

Let the paint cure and sand it gently between each coat. As you apply each coat, you'll notice that the paint job looks more and more even and uniform. When you're satisfied with the way the paint job looks, having added at least three coats (two to the bezel covers), you're done painting.

Adding clear enamel

By now you've probably grown tired of spraying and sanding, spraying and sanding. You don't *have* to do this next step — the paint job will hold up on its own — but unless you got some type of high-gloss or metallic color, the paint will be matte and, dare I say, dull. Consider applying a clearcoat. This will have the added benefit of protecting your paint job.

You use the exact same back-and-forth method for applying the clearcoat that you used for the priming and painting. You should apply the clearcoat layers rather thin, because it tends to drip easily. Dripping is especially a problem if your case has one large cover instead of individual panels; you can't lay the panels flat and horizontal. Let it cure completely and sand it with fine sandpaper in between each coat.

How many layers of clearcoat you choose to apply is up to you. If you want to keep the matte finish, only apply one or two layers. For a high-gloss look, apply at least three. Again, don't overcoat the front bezel covers or they may not fit back in the case.

When you've finally sprayed on your last coat of clear enamel, you're done with the painting and sanding — almost. There's one more optional step to consider (see the following section).

Painting the drive bezels

Your floppy drive (if you have one) and your optical drive are probably colored the same vapid beige that the cased was cursed with. You should strongly consider painting them the same color you painted the front panel; otherwise, they'll stand out as a constant reminder of how boring your case used to be before you modded it.

First, you'll have to remove the bezels from the drives. To do that, you'll have to remove the drives from the computer. Before you do, you may want to pop open the optical-drive tray so that you can get the little front plate off of it; it's much easier to let the PC do that for you than it is to do it manually.

Remove the bezels from the drives. They're usually clipped on in several places (see Figure 19-1). You may need a small flathead screwdriver to disengage the clips. Remove the front plate from the optical-drive tray. It may slide off easily, or it may be clipped on. Figure 19-2 shows all the drive bezel pieces disengaged.

Move the plastic bezel pieces to your painting area. Rough them up a little bit with a few strokes of fine-grit sandpaper, and clean them thoroughly. Then, using the painting technique that you've no doubt mastered by now, spray-paint them evenly.

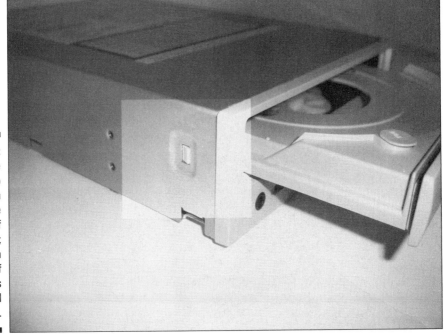

Figure 19-1:
Notice the clip mechanism in the middle of this image; this is an example of the drive's bezel fasteners.

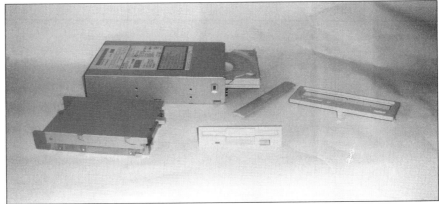

Figure 19-2:
Both drives with their bezels removed.

You don't need to use primer on plastic.

Add a couple coats of paint, followed by a couple coats of clear enamel, curing and sanding in between each application. Let them dry completely for

24 hours or so and snap them back into place on the drives. Finally, you can install the drives in the PC case, connect the cables, and sit back and admire your hard work (see Figure 19-3).

Figure 19-3:
A
completed
project.

Part V
The Part of Tens

The 5th Wave   By Rich Tennant

"Apparently most studies indicate that what people really want isn't more power or increased applications, but just really neat tail fins."

In this part . . .

*H*ere I provide you with a few little extras to take with
you before you go. I show you some really cool
peripherals that will offset your modded PC or that are
just nice to have. I suggest a bunch of more-advanced
mods that you can try when you're feeling more confident. And I show you some really cool Web sites to visit to
embrace the modding community and make informed
decisions when purchasing parts for projects.

Chapter 20

Ten Terrific Web Sites for Building and Modding

1 cover a lot of ground in this book, but, really, I only etch a tiny mark in the Plexiglas surface of extreme computing. Cranking up your PC's power, overclocking, super-cooling, cutting, lighting, painting have all been taken to amazing lengths. If a PC part exists, it's been modded. Modders go so far as to build their own astonishing cases in all shapes, sizes, and dimensions.

More than a few times in the pages of this book, I recommend that you go online for more information, modding ideas, modding guides, or reviews of hardware to buy for your PC. In this chapter, I share with you some spectacular sites to visit for such things. I'm not saying these are the best or most popular sites on the Web (some of them are); instead, they're the sites I go to when I want to see what's happening in the hardware realm. I've even contributed to some of them.

So set your browser for *stun* and aim it at these sites. If, when you get through scoping them out, you're still itching for more, hit the forums on these sites and ask the regulars what their favorite Internet destinations are. The modding and PC enthusiast communities are very accepting of new and curious users; as long as you're courteous and use good etiquette, you'll make a bunch of new friends.

ExtremeTech

www.extremetech.com

This Ziff-Davis powerhouse is a megasite that features cutting edge technology news, some of the best and most thorough reviews to be found on the Internet, a burgeoning community, and a laundry list of writers whose names are well known in the tech world: Loyd Case, Dave Salvator, and Jason Cross are just a few of the geniuses who bring you reviews, news, and hands-on looks at the newest and hottest gear in the tech universe.

The site features a strong front page with links to recent news, reviews, articles, and columns. Its content is then divided into several sections: "Core PC Tech," which deals with CPUs and key components; "3D Graphics, Audio, and Video," which features all manner of multimedia content; "Build It," which features hands-on do-it-yourself projects; a terrific discussion board; a shopping subsite with price comparisons and online store ratings, and more.

For a long time, the best sites on the Net for hard-hitting reviews and late-breaking news were little, independent sites run by hobbyists whose passion for technology outstripped their drive to milk the Internet for big money. Although that's still largely true, ExtremeTech represents an enthusiast site by a major company done right.

The [H]ard\OCP

www.hardocp.com

The site's curator, Kyle Bennett, freely admits that he has no idea what *[H]ard\OCP* means. A legendary figure in the PC enthusiast community, Bennett is known as much for his spirited nature as he is for his awesome, incredibly insightful reviews.

The [H]ard\OCP thrives on its widely linked reviews, but equally as compelling is the discussion area, the [H]ard\Forum. Frequented by some of the most colorful hard-core PC enthusiasts on the Web, the forum is entertaining just from the point of view of a lurker. It includes sections for discussion of all manner of hardware, cooling, overclocking, modding (Bennett indicates that it was the first modding forum on the Net), gaming, and much more. The [H]ard\OCP is one of the first destinations I hit each day.

AnandTech

www.anandtech.com

If you're looking to make an informed purchasing decision on virtually any PC part, you've got to stop by AnandTech. Anand Shimpi and his crack team of editors have achieved a startling level of respectability — fans of AnandTech are passionate about their devotion to the site. That devotion is well earned; few sites look as deeply into the products they review and the news they analyze, delving beyond the obvious and exploring every angle of each story.

One of the coolest features of AnandTech is the ever-updated price guides. Click on the Guides tab to see the selection of alarmingly frequent price guides for CPUs, memory, graphics cards, storage, and more. When you're done there, hit the real-time pricing engine located at www.anandtech.com/guides/priceguide.aspx to find out exactly what you should expect to pay for any component. Spend a few minutes at AnandTech, and you'll see why PC enthusiasts swear by it.

Gamer's Depot

www.gamers-depot.com

Its staff is small, but made up of passionate industry insiders. The site may not be huge, it may not be the most popular destination, but its founder and managing editor Duane Pemberton has an amazing knack for somehow landing hardware and game exclusives with shocking regularity.

Need some examples? Check out the eye-opening peer at the underbelly of the ATI-versus-NVIDIA battle here at www.gamers-depot.com/hardware/video_cards/ati/x700/ati_x700memo/001.htm. Or how about some early Medal of Honor: Pacific Assault screens posted before the review embargo was lifted at www.gamers-depot.com/sshots/mohpa/001.htm? Keep an eye on the Depot for scoops on the latest technology and games.

GideonTech

www.gideontech.com

I wrote a book on building and modding with GideonX, also known as the modding genius Ed Chen, and the response was mind blowing. One reader informed me that he was new to modding, but that the book's confident and reassuring tone brought it home that modding was well within his admittedly limited mechanical ability. Chen wrote the chapters he was referring to.

I continue to learn things from GideonTech, Chen's terrific site. It features a number of guides, from basic painting techniques to chopping a hard drive, from cutting blowholes to using vinyl dye to color plastic parts. The front page links to news and reviews from around the Web, focusing on the modding community.

Be sure to check out the popular forums. There are sections for discussing hardware, news, and all aspects of modding, including a place to post pics of your own projects. Let GidionX be your guide as you delve deeper into modding.

bit-tech.net

www.bit-tech.net

You don't have to live in the United Kingdom to get a kick out of what just may be the country's best modding site. It may be based on the Old World, but it features correspondents from the United States and Australia. The global team brings home reviews of all kinds of stuff of interest to modders, from cutting-edge gear like graphics cards and CPUs to modders' dream like cases and cooling gear.

The articles and features sections are rarely updated, but the content there is worth reading. You can find out all about water-cooling, find out about hardware like chipsets and graphics technology, and of course delve into extreme modding.

The strongest part of this strong site is the collection of forums. The highlights: the Modding and Project Logs discussions, in which modders share pictures and details of their projects and, often, the step-by-step procedure of how they actually go about creating their masterpieces.

PimpRig

www.pimprig.com

PimpRig has been growing constantly since its inception in June 2001, and possibly a major part of its appeal is the case gallery. Go to the site, click on the Gallery link at the top of the page, and prepare to take in what may be the largest collection of modding pictures on the Internet.

The most amazing thing about the PimpRig gallery is that not only are there a ton of mods (and wallpapers, and sig files, and other visuals), but a vast majority of those mods are pretty darn good. The best of the lot are in the

Pimpin Case Gallery; look at the paint job on The Deuce (`http://gallery.pimprig.com/showphoto.php?photo=4377&sort=1&cat=504&page=9`), or how about LegoLand (`http://gallery.pimprig.com/showphoto.php?photo=1024&sort=1&cat=504&page=23`), a case made out of your favorite plastic building blocks?

The Gallery isn't all there is to PimpRig. It features an excellent array of guides and how-tos, lots of reviews, a respectable forum community, and other nice tidbits. I love heading over to PimpRig when I need ideas for my next mod.

PC Modding Malaysia

`www.pcmoddingmy.com`

I'm based in the United States, and American readers may be thinking, "Why go all the way to Malaysia to find a modding site?" My answer: Because it's one of the best! With early reviews of the latest PC hardware, cooling, and modding products; up-to-the-minute news; useful articles on everything from wiring LEDs to overclocking the Pentium 4, there's something here for every modder.

Want to sleeve your own PSU cables? Check out the picture-filled guide at `www.pcmoddingmy.com/content.php?article.32`. Want to overclock your P4-based computer's RAM? Point your browser to `www.pcmoddingmy.com/content.php?article.57`. Discuss those articles and much more in the forums with modders from around the world.

I love the Chatbox. That's a little interface on the left side of the site in which you can simply type a quick message, and it's instantly posted. It's a great way to keep up with fellow modders.

Overclockers Australia

`www.overclockers.com.au`

This community-driven site bills itself as "Australia's Busiest PC Hardware Community," and I believe it. Although there's plenty of news, updated daily, and the review database is impressive, the best parts of OCAU are the forums and the PC Database. The latter is a showcase for community members' computer cases, and as I write this it contains 6,785 entries.

The forum, which requires registration even to browse, contains the usual discussion sections — modding, cooling, overclocking, troubleshooting, and so on — all of which are heavily populated with lots of friendly enthusiasts. It goes beyond that, though, with sections for sports and fitness, toys, vehicles, multiprocessing — there's even a flame-free forum for newbies!

As much fun as I have in the forums, my favorite part of the site is the PC Database. I love perusing the colorful cases, and there's page after page of projects. Overclockers Australia is the best reason for modding enthusiasts to visit the Land Down Under.

CaseModGod.com

www.casemodgod.com

Whether this site is truly divine may be a matter for debate, but one thing's for sure: If you want guides to dozens of creative modding projects, this is your site. Point your browser to www.casemodgod.com/howto.htm and discover how to build an LED "flame fan"; how to bend acrylic to make a window for your mouse; how to color a keyboard; and much, much more.

When you're done there, hit the forums, where you can discuss modding projects with the community at large and scope out mods by other modders, including an astonishing PC built inside a toaster.

Chapter 21

Ten Mods to Try for Your Next Modding Project

- -

- -

*I*f you work through all the chapters in this book, you'll do some serious work. You build a PC and performance-tune it to run lickety-split. You delve into the black art of overclocking; you install wicked cooling systems; you chop holes in it for fans; you cut a window into it; you light it up; you paint the case to transform it from dull beige to an awesome color of your choice — and you're not done yet.

Modding isn't about following convention. Because this book is for the beginning modder, I went with a pretty standard set of modding guidelines. However, there's much more to modding. Modding is a creative outlet — you can do anything you can come up with if you have the drive and the ingenuity.

In this chapter, I suggest ten mods you can do on your own. It's beyond the scope of this chapter to get into step-by-step how-to guides for every project I suggest. For that, you'll need to do some research on the Web, or forge your own path and come up with your own way of tackling these tasks. I do, however, offer hints based on how I've seen some similar mods done.

Just because you didn't read about it in this book doesn't mean a mod you may have thought of is impossible. I urge you to mod anything and everything you can get your hands on. See if you can get an inexpensive graphics card to perform like a cutting-edge model through overclocking and cooling.

Replace your motherboard, add RAM, upgrade your processor, and do whatever it takes to make your system faster. Add lights to everything. Cut windows in every part. If you can think of it, you can do it.

Modding Your Hard Drive

The first time you try this, you should do it on an old hard drive that you don't care much about. Hard drives are very precise, and they're extremely sensitive to dust. Companies that work on hard drives do so in clean rooms, and the employees wear special suits to prevent contaminants from entering the atmosphere.

With that in mind, you can open your hard drive, cut a hole into the top panel, and seal the drive back up. You'll need the proper tool to remove the hard drive screws (usually a Torx screwdriver), clear plastic to form the window, your trusty rotary tool, and a few other odds and ends.

You'll have to pull the drive apart, which will entail removing the cover from a rubber gasket. You should throw something over the open drive to prevent dust from entering the enclosure; I lay a slab of spare clear plastic on it. Then you'll cut the top of the drive, cut and attach clear plastic to the outside of the drive (there's no room on the inside), and seal the unit back up.

If you feel really daring, you can install an LED. You'll need to some electrical calculations: The LED will require a proper resistor. You can get power from the power leads of the female Molex connector on the back of the drive.

Controlling Your Fans

Back in the early days of modding, if you wanted to control the RPM speed of your case fans, you had to do some fancy wiring. You had to create your own circuits, install your own knobs, and if you didn't know quite a bit about DC circuitry, you were pretty much out of luck.

A lot has changed. Now you can go somewhere like FrozenCPU.com and buy fan control units like the Enermax Aluminum Multifunction Panel, a 5-inch drive-bay-mounted panel with temperature sensors and knobs to control up to four fans. It's a plug-and-play operation, with the electrical connections being a simple matter. The trickiest part of the installation will be placing the temperature sensors, particularly around the CPU.

Similar products make fan control a simple matter. Or, if you're adventurous and you know a bit about DC circuitry, come up with your own fan control system.

Replacing All Your PC's LEDs

In Chapter 18, I talk about replacing the LEDs in the front panel of the computer. Those green, red, and amber lights are so dull, and cool blue LEDs really bring the mod home.

With a little soldering knack, you can replace LEDs in all the components in the front of your system, including the floppy drive and the optical drives.

You'll have to remove the drives from the system, take off their front bezels, and probably remove part of their casing to get at the wiring you need to access. Solder and fit the new LED in place as best you can; you may have to do some shaving of the bezel openings or other wrangling to get the new LEDs in place.

I've replaced floppy and optical LEDs with blue and red lights. Nothing surprises people like seeing an ominous red light on the front of an unassuming floppy drive, whose light is normally green. A cool blue sheen to the DVD-+RW drive is a nifty effect, too.

Getting Fancy with Cutting

I cut a pretty basic window into a spare case for this book: a rectangle with rounded corners. That's a great shape to start with, especially if you've never cut metal before. Getting the hang of a rotary tool or a jigsaw on steel takes a fair bit of practice, and the beauty of using a simple shape is that, if you screw up the cut, you can cut a larger hole to mask your mistake.

But eventually, squares and rectangles will become boring. Why not try to cut something truly challenging into your next mod? Make a big letter X, or something with lots of rounded edges. If you're really up for a tough round of rotary-tool madness, stencil some lettering onto the case and cut out a message. Name your PC.

Surf the modding sites noted in Chapter 20 for ideas. There are some truly amazing windows that dedicated modders have cut out of their cases. I've seen mods in which, rather than use a stenciling technique, they've cut full-on designs into the metal that required some of the cutout pieces to be glued into place on the window. If you can draw it, with practice, you can cut it.

Decorating Your Window

Why have a plain window when you can enhance it with a startling, amazing design?

Using a grinding wheel on a rotary tool, or a sandblaster (which you can rent at most hardware stores), you can etch the clear plastic with a design of your liking.

You'll need to remove the window from your case and clamp it to a workbench, or take it outside for sandblasting. It's best if you have a pattern traced out before you begin; you can find cool designs online which you can resize and print out, or you can draw your own. Tape or clamp the paper with the pattern securely to your window. Then, preferably with a tapered grinding wheel, etch the pattern right through the paper.

With a sandblaster, you should use a new window with the protective plastic still on and a hobby knife to cut out the pattern. Alternately, you can cut the pattern out of thick paper and tape it securely to an existing window. Then blast the pattern onto the window.

If you don't feel like making permanent marks on your window, you can get your hands on a startling number of decals. There are brand-name patterns (like the ATI and AMD logos), familiar cartoon characters, and much more. They're easy to apply and make for really cool conversation pieces at LAN parties.

Cutting a Blowhole into a Window

Just because you put a window over your graphics card doesn't mean you don't have to cool it. Rather than purchase an expensive aftermarket graphics cooler, why not add a cheap 80mm fan to the side of your case that blows right onto the graphics card? You can cut a blowhole into a window without much difficulty.

The best way to do it is with a rotary tool fitted with a cutoff blade. Remove the window from your case and clamp it to a workbench. Then trace the pattern onto the window and cut the hole carefully.

Clear plastic cuts a lot faster than metal. If you've never cut clear plastic before, make a few precise cuts in a spare piece before you move on to the actual modding project. Get a feel for the tool before you make permanent changes to your good window.

Measure the screw holes carefully, squaring them up with the case. Then use a drill to make the holes. Add the fan and a cool fan grill and you're all set!

Adding a Lit Fan to Your Power Supply

You can cut your power supply open, or you can jazz it up by lighting one of its fans. For the coolest effect, replace the internal fan with a lit fan of the same size. Simply remove the old fan, clip the wires, clip the power connector off the new fan, solder the appropriate wires together, and install the new fan. Make sure you get the airflow direction correct.

Unplug your power supply and give it a few hours for its capacitors to bleed off their charges before you take it apart and work inside it. The components within a power supply can hold a charge for a long time — enough of a charge to remind you why you should never play with electricity.

Building a Clear Computer Case

This popular pastime has burgeoned into its own cottage industry: You can buy kits and even completely assembled computer cases comprised entirely of clear plastic. If you're up for a major challenge, however, you may try building your own clear computer.

This will take a world of planning and measuring. You'll need to consider a vast number of factors: how to mount the motherboard (you might install a motherboard mounting panel from an existing case — but then it wouldn't be clear!), how to mount and secure expansion cards, how to mount the power supply, how to mount the various drives, how to cool it, and more. Then there's the problem of how to connect the panels to each other and still be able to get inside the computer as needed (that rules out glue).

To fire up your creative synapses, you can access a clear case guide at Overclockers.com that may give you a few ideas. Just go to `www.over clockers.com/tips847/`.

Building a Mini-Computer for LAN Parties

It's no fun to lug that gigantic mid-tower case halfway across town to attend a LAN party. It's especially bad if you can't afford an LCD monitor with a fast enough pixel refresh rate to satisfy your need for perfect imagery; those CRT monitors are heavy.

Why not build a tiny computer? You can start with a small form factor computer or design your own small rig. You might start with a thin, rack mount server box (sometimes called a "pizza box" by IT nerds), or a mini-ITX box. You'll need to figure out a way to get a decent graphics subsystem into the box, to fit in a speedy CPU *with* cooling, to outfit the PC with audio passable for headphone use (this might be the one situation in which onboard sound is acceptable), and you'll need room to cram in a CD-ROM drive and a hard drive. Plus, you'll need to make sure the entire rig stays cool enough to run games without the processor erupting in flames.

There are countless guides on the Web about building a LAN party box. I've seen them built out of wood. In fact, you could build a computer case completely out of wood. You'll have the same considerations as those of building a clear computer, but a totally different surface on which to work your magic.

Back to the small form factor computer: To get you started, browse this guide at ExtremeTech.com: www.extremetech.com/article2/0,1558,1566253, 00.asp. Then take off on your own. Come up with something ingenious that will totally jazz your LAN-party buddies.

Building a Computer . . . Sans Case!

My last challenge to you is to do away with the case altogether. This is entirely possible, and it makes cooling the computer amazingly simple: All you need is active coolers on the CPU and the graphics card! No case fans are necessary!

Browse the Web and you'll encounter working computers built of components mounted to the wall, hanging from coat hangers, and spread across tabletops. You'll have to make sure you don't mount the gear to — or lay it upon — anything that's conductive. All the connections will have to remain intact on their own, so you'll need *some* sort of structural support. You'll want to be able to turn the PC on and off and reset it as needed, so you should find a way to work in power and reset buttons (which you can swipe from any case). Note that some motherboards come with little power and reset switches mounted right to the board, but they're a rarity..

Challenge yourself: Can you find a way to make a caseless PC portable? Can you do something cool with lighting — even without a window?

Chapter 22

Ten Awesome Accessories For Your Modded PC

*I*f you're a gadget-head like me, you dig not only the satisfaction you can get from a great mod, but all of computing in general. One of my favorite things about the PC marketplace is that there's a wealth of utterly cool gadgets to connect to a computer and enhance the experience.

I love electronic toys. I think things that make computers look cool are groovy to the highest order. I can't get enough of gaming gadgets. I could hook up different mice to my computers all day, just to try out all the buttons and ergonomic configurations. Give me something that lights up, or that puts vast amounts of music in my pocket, or that I can use to burn DVDs of my cheesy home videos, and I'll be thrilled.

This chapter has ten such devices highlighted for your consumption. In an industry filled with literally thousands of PC peripherals available to enhance the PC experience, I've tried, reviewed, rounded up, and generally enjoyed hundreds . . . and whittling down that number to ten was one of the most difficult things I had to do in the production of this book.

In the spirit of fun, I went for the coolness over practicality. I chose some of my favorite gadgets, some interesting new things, and some gear that I considered purely enjoyable — stuff you'd want to give as gifts to people who would then consider you one of the hippest folks around. Here's my list.

Razer Diamondback Gaming Mouse

Gamers think of their mice with similar regard to how soldiers consider their weapons. The mouse is the gamer's right hand. Being a gamer, I'd rather go mouse shopping than, say, eat.

Razer was the first company to take the idea of a dedicated gaming mouse seriously. With precision in mind, the company has designed ambidextrous mice with big buttons. The Diamondback (see Figure 22-1), Razer's latest masterpiece at the time of this writing, is a high-resolution optical mouse with terrific accuracy and a great, responsive feel. It takes 6,400 frames per second at 1,600 dots per inch, which, in optical mouse terms, means it's extremely accurate — it picks up even the slightest movement, making it perfect for high-octane first-person shooters. Check out `www.razerzone.com/diamondback.html` for more information.

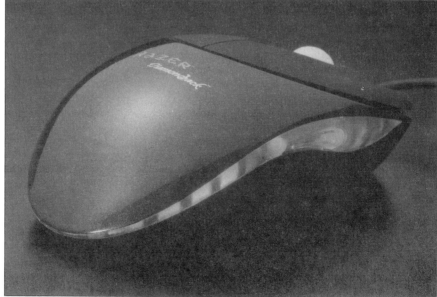

Figure 22-1:
The Razer Diamond-back is a prime cut gamer's mouse.

Robert Krakoff

Saitek Gaming Keyboard

Just as the gaming world has embraced mice over dedicated gaming devices like joysticks and driving wheels, so has it come to rely on keyboards. The standard first-person shooter controls call for a keyboard and mouse — the former used to move, jump, and interact with the environment. I've even seen T-shirts with the classic W-S-A-D key combo on them.

Saitek has taken the gaming keyboard to the next level (see Figure 22-2). It sports a futuristic, industrial look right out of a Quake title, and it's backlit with an eerie blue glow. The full-stroke keys are responsive and offer a terrific level of tactile feedback — exactly what a gamer looks for in a keyboard. As an added bonus, the keyboard comes with a separate 9-button programmable command pad with 2 shift buttons, allowing for a total of 27 commands. Check out www.saitekusa.com/usa/prod/gamerskey.htm for more information.

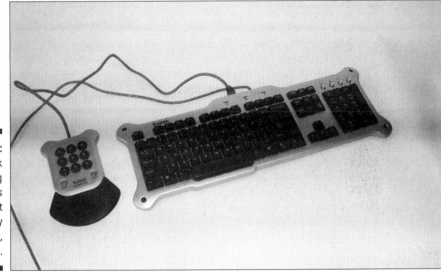

Figure 22-2:
The Saitek Gaming Keyboard is a great accessory to a lit, modded PC.

Apple iPod from HP

HP and Apple put their heads together, and the result is more than a bizarre two-headed beast: it's the Apple iPod from HP, a natural extension of the venerable iPod line and the first name in digital music (see Figure 22-3).

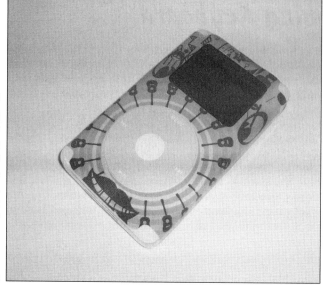

Figure 22-3:
The tiny
iPod weighs
only 5.6
ounces (the
20GB model,
that is) but
holds far
more than
its weight in
music.

This latest incarnation of the iPod comes in 20GB and 40GB capacities, which is enough room to hold 5,000 or 10,000 songs, respectively. That'll get you through the 12-hour plane flight to Tokyo, and so will the built-in lithium-ion battery, which lasts up to, well, 12 hours. The 2-inch LCD display comes with an LED backlight.

If you're an iTunes user, the iPod will automatically sync with it when you connect it to your PC with the speedy USB 2.0 interface. It supports play lists and sounds terrific, and there's more: It also has a calendar, a note reader, a music shuffle feature, and more. Portable digital music starts with iPod. Check out `http://h10049.www1.hp.com/music/us/en/ipod_flash.html` for more information.

Thrustmaster 2-in-1 Dual Trigger

Every gamer needs a gamepad. You absolutely need one for sports games, the rare PC fighting game, and driving games (if you don't have the room, or the inclination, for a driving wheel). Thrustmaster's 2-in-1 Dual Trigger gamepad (see Figure 22-4) has an added bonus: You can use it on both the PC and the Playstation 2.

Figure 22-4:
The 2-in-1
Dual Trigger
is ready for
PC and
Playstation 2
gaming.

With clickable dual analog mini-sticks, a digital/analog mode selector switch, and a d-pad, the Dual Trigger is ready for anything. Its standout feature, though, is the pair of programmable, progressive triggers, which can be instructed to mimic one or two axes and behave differently for different situations. Most important, the Dual Trigger is wonderfully comfortable with grips that will make your hands purr. Go to www.thrustmaster.com for more information.

MonsterGecko PistolMouse FPS

This'll turn heads. Your friends will wonder why in Heaven's name you bought a light gun for your PC when Duck Hunt is only for Nintendo. You'll respond triumphantly, "It's a mouse!" In fact, it's a mouse that *looks* like a gun (see Figure 22-5). You hold it like a pistol, while the optical sensor is in a base below your hand, which you keep pressed on a mouse pad. Its 800 dpi sensor is built for precision, and the grip, with a trigger for the left mouse button and a big thumb-operated scroll wheel, is built for fun.

It may seem unconventional, but using the PistolMouse for a while will convince you that this device is more than a gimmick. It's swift and accurate, responding to your slightest wrist motion. Sure, it takes a while to get used to it, but after you do, you may never go back to a regular mouse. The PistolMouse is that rare gadget that's both a great conversation piece and a useful gaming device. Go to `www.monstergecko.com/products.html` for more information.

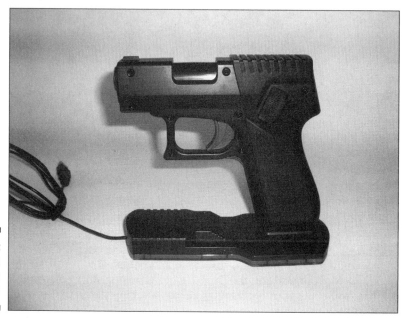

Figure 22-5:
It's not a
Glock, it's a
mouse!

Ray, by Everglide

Sometimes, you need something cool just for the sake of coolness. It's simple, elegant, and more than pure decoration: Ray, by Everglide, is a light-up mouse pad, and a nice mouse pad at that (see Figure 22-6). Powered by a USB port, it features bright blue LEDs that radiate out from the center. Beyond looking good, it's a low-friction mousing surface perfect for twitch gaming. Bring it to your next LAN party and tell 'em to dim the lights. Check out `www.everglide.com/ray.htm` for more information.

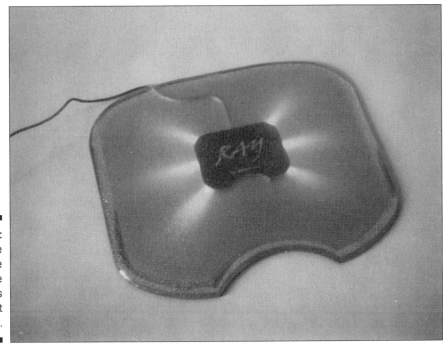

Figure 22-6:
The Everglide Ray mouse pad feels as good as it looks.

Logitech X-5500

You never know when you'll need 500 watts of sound. For instance, what do you do when you want to blow out all the windows in your house at the same time? Crank up the THX-certified 5.1 speaker X-5500 from Logitech (see Figure 22-7). It supports Dolby Digital, Dolby Pro Logic II, and DTS 96/24, as well as direct analog 6-channel sound, so you're ready for virtually any audio source, from DVDs and Playstation 2 and Xbox games to PC titles featuring EAX Advanced HD 4.0.

The 188W, 10-inch long-throw subwoofer blasts out the cleanest bass I've ever heard from a dedicated multimedia speaker system, and the satellites (62W each for the corners, and 68W front center) are stunningly precise. This speaker system sounds as good as living room systems that cost three times its price. Go to www.logitech.com/index.cfm/products/details/US/EN,CRID=2,CONTENTID=9486 for more information.

Figure 22-7:
Put your ear
to this page
to enjoy the
clarity of the
Z-5500.

Creative Zen Touch

To meet the deadlines for this book, I've worked around the clock on more than one occasion. Thankfully, I had a Creative Zen Touch portable music player (see Figure 22-8), whose battery allowed it to keep soothing me with sleep music for 24 hours straight. The songs never repeated, either, because the hard drive holds a whopping 10,000 WMA or 5,000 MP3 tunes.

Figure 22-8:
The Zen
Touch
breathes
new life into
the portable
digital-
music
industry.

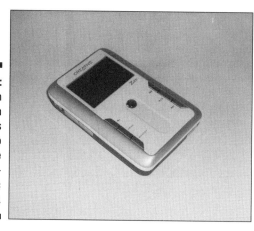

With the Zen Touch, you can create play lists on the go, with its cool blue backlit LCD screen. The USB 2.0 interface, along with AudioSync software, syncs up with your PC at blazing speeds. And its 20GB hard drive isn't just for music; the Zen Touch can store data files through a simple drag-and-drop interface to easily transfer them between computers. Turn to `http://creative.com/products/product.asp?category=213&subcategory=214&product=10274` for more information.

LG Super Multi DVD Drive GSA-4120B

It's not an external peripheral, but it's one device that I swear by. Instead of worrying about which DVD writing format, I got a drive that supports them all. The LG Super Multi (see Figure 22-9) was one of the first *dual-layer writers,* meaning it stores almost twice as much data as standard DVD-+RW drives: On dual-layer media, it can write 8.5GB of data. That's enough to back up most of my stuff before I do something foolish like reformat a hard drive. At the time of this writing, dual-layer drives and media were considerably more expensive than standard DVD gear, but I like to be on the cutting edge. Check out `www.lge.com`, then click on "Products" and then "Computer Product" to track it down.

Figure 22-9: With dual-layer capability and compatibility with every DVD writing standard, the LG GSA-4120B takes the guesswork out of DVD writing.

Logitech MX510 Optical Mouse

Logitech has always made excellent mice, but the company really turned my head when it unveiled the MX510, a true gamer's pointing device (see Figure 22-10). The 800 dpi sensor takes 5.8 megapixels worth of positional tracking pictures every second, making it incredibly accurate. The satiny look is cool, and the mouse itself is an ergonomic masterpiece with lots of programmable buttons.

Besides the standard left and right mouse buttons and the clickable scroll wheel, it includes "cruise" buttons above and below the scroll wheel for extended scrolling, and side buttons that can be used as Internet forward/back buttons. Its only downside is that it segregates out 10 percent of the population, because it's right-handed only. Sorry, southpaws! Check out http://www.logitech.com and search for "MX510" for more information.

Figure 22-10:
Logitech's
MX510 is a
gamer's
dream
mouse.

Index

• *B* •

• E •

• *N* •

• *O* •

• P •

Notes

Notes

Notes

Notes

Notes

BUSINESS, CAREERS & PERSONAL FINANCE

0-7645-5307-0

0-7645-5331-3 *†

Also available:
- Accounting For Dummies †
  0-7645-5314-3
- Business Plans Kit For Dummies †
  0-7645-5365-8
- Cover Letters For Dummies
  0-7645-5224-4
- Frugal Living For Dummies
  0-7645-5403-4
- Leadership For Dummies
  0-7645-5176-0
- Managing For Dummies
  0-7645-1771-6

- Marketing For Dummies
  0-7645-5600-2
- Personal Finance For Dummies *
  0-7645-2590-5
- Project Management For Dummies
  0-7645-5283-X
- Resumes For Dummies †
  0-7645-5471-9
- Selling For Dummies
  0-7645-5363-1
- Small Business Kit For Dummies *†
  0-7645-5093-4

HOME & BUSINESS COMPUTER BASICS

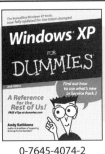

0-7645-4074-2

0-7645-3758-X

Also available:
- ACT! 6 For Dummies
  0-7645-2645-6
- iLife '04 All-in-One Desk Reference
  For Dummies
  0-7645-7347-0
- iPAQ For Dummies
  0-7645-6769-1
- Mac OS X Panther Timesaving
  Techniques For Dummies
  0-7645-5812-9
- Macs For Dummies
  0-7645-5656-8

- Microsoft Money 2004 For Dummies
  0-7645-4195-1
- Office 2003 All-in-One Desk Reference
  For Dummies
  0-7645-3883-7
- Outlook 2003 For Dummies
  0-7645-3759-8
- PCs For Dummies
  0-7645-4074-2
- TiVo For Dummies
  0-7645-6923-6
- Upgrading and Fixing PCs For Dummies
  0-7645-1665-5
- Windows XP Timesaving Techniques
  For Dummies
  0-7645-3748-2

FOOD, HOME, GARDEN, HOBBIES, MUSIC & PETS

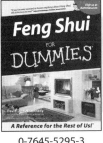

0-7645-5295-3

0-7645-5232-5

Also available:
- Bass Guitar For Dummies
  0-7645-2487-9
- Diabetes Cookbook For Dummies
  0-7645-5230-9
- Gardening For Dummies *
  0-7645-5130-2
- Guitar For Dummies
  0-7645-5106-X
- Holiday Decorating For Dummies
  0-7645-2570-0
- Home Improvement All-in-One
  For Dummies
  0-7645-5680-0

- Knitting For Dummies
  0-7645-5395-X
- Piano For Dummies
  0-7645-5105-1
- Puppies For Dummies
  0-7645-5255-4
- Scrapbooking For Dummies
  0-7645-7208-3
- Senior Dogs For Dummies
  0-7645-5818-8
- Singing For Dummies
  0-7645-2475-5
- 30-Minute Meals For Dummies
  0-7645-2589-1

INTERNET & DIGITAL MEDIA

0-7645-1664-7

0-7645-6924-4

Also available:
- 2005 Online Shopping Directory
  For Dummies
  0-7645-7495-7
- CD & DVD Recording For Dummies
  0-7645-5956-7
- eBay For Dummies
  0-7645-5654-1
- Fighting Spam For Dummies
  0-7645-5965-6
- Genealogy Online For Dummies
  0-7645-5964-8
- Google For Dummies
  0-7645-4420-9

- Home Recording For Musicians
  For Dummies
  0-7645-1634-5
- The Internet For Dummies
  0-7645-4173-0
- iPod & iTunes For Dummies
  0-7645-7772-7
- Preventing Identity Theft For Dummies
  0-7645-7336-5
- Pro Tools All-in-One Desk Reference
  For Dummies
  0-7645-5714-9
- Roxio Easy Media Creator For Dummies
  0-7645-7131-1

* Separate Canadian edition also available
† Separate U.K. edition also available

Available wherever books are sold. For more information or to order direct: U.S. customers visit www.dummies.com or call 1-877-762-2974.
U.K. customers visit www.wileyeurope.com or call 0800 243407. Canadian customers visit www.wiley.ca or call 1-800-567-4797.

WILEY

SPORTS, FITNESS, PARENTING, RELIGION & SPIRITUALITY

0-7645-5146-9

0-7645-5418-2

Also available:
- Adoption For Dummies
  0-7645-5488-3
- Basketball For Dummies
  0-7645-5248-1
- The Bible For Dummies
  0-7645-5296-1
- Buddhism For Dummies
  0-7645-5359-3
- Catholicism For Dummies
  0-7645-5391-7
- Hockey For Dummies
  0-7645-5228-7

- Judaism For Dummies
  0-7645-5299-6
- Martial Arts For Dummies
  0-7645-5358-5
- Pilates For Dummies
  0-7645-5397-6
- Religion For Dummies
  0-7645-5264-3
- Teaching Kids to Read For Dummies
  0-7645-4043-2
- Weight Training For Dummies
  0-7645-5168-X
- Yoga For Dummies
  0-7645-5117-5

TRAVEL

0-7645-5438-7

0-7645-5453-0

Also available:
- Alaska For Dummies
  0-7645-1761-9
- Arizona For Dummies
  0-7645-6938-4
- Cancún and the Yucatán For Dummies
  0-7645-2437-2
- Cruise Vacations For Dummies
  0-7645-6941-4
- Europe For Dummies
  0-7645-5456-5
- Ireland For Dummies
  0-7645-5455-7

- Las Vegas For Dummies
  0-7645-5448-4
- London For Dummies
  0-7645-4277-X
- New York City For Dummies
  0-7645-6945-7
- Paris For Dummies
  0-7645-5494-8
- RV Vacations For Dummies
  0-7645-5443-3
- Walt Disney World & Orlando For Dummies
  0-7645-6943-0

GRAPHICS, DESIGN & WEB DEVELOPMENT

0-7645-4345-8

0-7645-5589-8

Also available:
- Adobe Acrobat 6 PDF For Dummies
  0-7645-3760-1
- Building a Web Site For Dummies
  0-7645-7144-3
- Dreamweaver MX 2004 For Dummies
  0-7645-4342-3
- FrontPage 2003 For Dummies
  0-7645-3882-9
- HTML 4 For Dummies
  0-7645-1995-6
- Illustrator CS For Dummies
  0-7645-4084-X

- Macromedia Flash MX 2004 For Dummies
  0-7645-4358-X
- Photoshop 7 All-in-One Desk
  Reference For Dummies
  0-7645-1667-1
- Photoshop CS Timesaving Techniques
  For Dummies
  0-7645-6782-9
- PHP 5 For Dummies
  0-7645-4166-8
- PowerPoint 2003 For Dummies
  0-7645-3908-6
- QuarkXPress 6 For Dummies
  0-7645-2593-X

NETWORKING, SECURITY, PROGRAMMING & DATABASES

0-7645-6852-3

0-7645-5784-X

Also available:
- A+ Certification For Dummies
  0-7645-4187-0
- Access 2003 All-in-One Desk
  Reference For Dummies
  0-7645-3988-4
- Beginning Programming For Dummies
  0-7645-4997-9
- C For Dummies
  0-7645-7068-4
- Firewalls For Dummies
  0-7645-4048-3
- Home Networking For Dummies
  0-7645-42796

- Network Security For Dummies
  0-7645-1679-5
- Networking For Dummies
  0-7645-1677-9
- TCP/IP For Dummies
  0-7645-1760-0
- VBA For Dummies
  0-7645-3989-2
- Wireless All In-One Desk Reference
  For Dummies
  0-7645-7496-5
- Wireless Home Networking For Dummies
  0-7645-3910-8

HEALTH & SELF-HELP

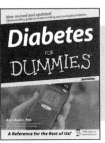

0-7645-6820-5 *†

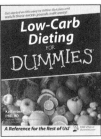

0-7645-2566-2

Also available:

- Alzheimer's For Dummies
  0-7645-3899-3
- Asthma For Dummies
  0-7645-4233-8
- Controlling Cholesterol For Dummies
  0-7645-5440-9
- Depression For Dummies
  0-7645-3900-0
- Dieting For Dummies
  0-7645-4149-8
- Fertility For Dummies
  0-7645-2549-2

- Fibromyalgia For Dummies
  0-7645-5441-7
- Improving Your Memory For Dummies
  0-7645-5435-2
- Pregnancy For Dummies †
  0-7645-4483-7
- Quitting Smoking For Dummies
  0-7645-2629-4
- Relationships For Dummies
  0-7645-5384-4
- Thyroid For Dummies
  0-7645-5385-2

EDUCATION, HISTORY, REFERENCE & TEST PREPARATION

0-7645-5194-9

0-7645-4186-2

Also available:

- Algebra For Dummies
  0-7645-5325-9
- British History For Dummies
  0-7645-7021-8
- Calculus For Dummies
  0-7645-2498-4
- English Grammar For Dummies
  0-7645-5322-4
- Forensics For Dummies
  0-7645-5580-4
- The GMAT For Dummies
  0-7645-5251-1
- Inglés Para Dummies
  0-7645-5427-1

- Italian For Dummies
  0-7645-5196-5
- Latin For Dummies
  0-7645-5431-X
- Lewis & Clark For Dummies
  0-7645-2545-X
- Research Papers For Dummies
  0-7645-5426-3
- The SAT I For Dummies
  0-7645-7193-1
- Science Fair Projects For Dummies
  0-7645-5460-3
- U.S. History For Dummies
  0-7645-5249-X

Get smart @ dummies.com®

- **Find a full list of Dummies titles**
- **Look into loads of FREE on-site articles**
- **Sign up for FREE eTips e-mailed to you weekly**
- **See what other products carry the Dummies name**
- **Shop directly from the Dummies bookstore**
- **Enter to win new prizes every month!**

Separate Canadian edition also available
Separate U.K. edition also available

Available wherever books are sold. For more information or to order direct: U.S. customers visit www.dummies.com or call 1-877-762-2974.
U.K. customers visit www.wileyeurope.com or call 0800 243407. Canadian customers visit www.wiley.ca or call 1-800-567-4797.

Do More with Dummies
Products for the Rest of Us!

From hobbies to health, discover a wide variety of fun products

DVDs/Videos • Music CDs • Games
Consumer Electronics • Software
Craft Kits • Culinary Kits • and More!

Check out the Dummies Specialty Shop at www.dummies.com for more information!